DEMOCRATIZATION AND THE MEDIA

Of Related Interest

FACTIONAL POLITICS AND DEMOCRATIZATION
edited by Richard Gillespie, Michael Waller and Lourdes López Nieto

DEMOCRACY AND NORTH AMERICA
edited by Alan Ware

CIVIL SOCIETY
Democratic Perspectives
edited by Robert Fine and Shirin Rai

SOCIAL DEMOCRACY IN A POST-COMMUNIST EUROPE
edited by Michael Waller, Bruno Coppieters and Kris Deschouwer

POST-COMMUNISM AND THE MEDIA IN EASTERN EUROPE
edited by Patrick H. O'Neil

ECOLOGY AND DEMOCRACY
edited by Freya Mathews

THE STATE IN WESTERN EUROPE
Retreat or Redefinition?
edited by Wolfgang C. Müller and Vincent Wright

THE POLITICAL ECONOMY OF REGIONALISM
edited by Michael Keating and John Loughlin

THE DEMOGRAPHIC STRUGGLE FOR POWER
The Political Economy of Demographic Engineering in the Modern World
by Milica Zarkovic Bookman

Democratization and the Media

edited by
VICKY RANDALL

FRANK CASS
LONDON • PORTLAND, OR

First published in 1998 in Great Britain by
FRANK CASS PUBLISHERS
Newbury House, 900 Eastern Avenue,
London, IG2 7HH, England

and in the United States of America by
FRANK CASS PUBLISHERS
c/o ISBS
5804 N.E. Hassalo Street
Portland, Oregon 97213-3644

Website: http://www.frankcass.com

British Library Cataloguing in Publication Data

Democratization and the media
 1. Mass media – Political aspects 2. Mass media – Influence
 3. Press and politics. 4. Democracy – Social aspects
 I. Randall, Vicky
 321.8

ISBN 0 7146 4894 9 (cloth)
ISBN 0 7146 4446 X (paper)

Library of Congress Cataloging in Publication Data

Democratization and the media / edited by Vicky Randall.
    p. cm.
    Originally appeared as a special issue of Democratization, summer
1998.
    Includes bibliographical references and index.
    ISBN 0-7146-4894-9. – ISBN 0-7146-4446-3 (pbk.)
    1. Mass media–Political aspects. 2. Democracy. I. Randall,
Vicky. II. Democratization.
P95.8.D427 1998
321.8'09'045–dc21   98-6865
                                                             CIP

This group of studies first appeared in a Special Issue on
'Democratization and the Media' of *Democratization* (ISSN 1351-0347)
5/2 (Summer 1998) published by Frank Cass.

Printed in Great Britain by
Antony Rowe Ltd., Chippenham, Wilts.

Contents

Introduction

VICKY RANDALL

This collection examines the relationship between democracy, democratization and the mass communications media. Most of all its focus is on the contributions, both positive and negative, of the media to the process of democratization and to the functioning of democracy. But to the extent that this is a separable question, it is also interested in the implications of democratization and democracy for the institutions of the mass media.

These are matters of critical importance for the understanding of continuity and change in contemporary political systems. And indeed the significance of the media's political role is increasingly recognised in studies of the more established democracies, especially the United States. On the other hand the relationship between the media and the process of democratization has been relatively neglected by political scientists until very recently.[1]

The topic is of course vast, and no claim is made here to cover it comprehensively. None the less, through a happy combination of editorial design and individual contributors' preferences, the ensemble of studies both reflects diversity and provides scope for comparison on a number of dimensions. Most obviously, the context of analysis ranges not only in terms of geographical location but also in terms of regime type, from established democracies – the United States, Britain and France – to countries in the later stages of democratic transformation in the former Soviet bloc (Poland) and in East Asia (Taiwan); to Mali in West Africa where democratization is much less secure; to the Middle East, China and by contrast affluent Singapore where it remains largely an aspiration.

One of the difficulties in the way of generalizing about the media is their heterogeneity. Just for example and sticking with the most obvious, newspapers rely upon the written word; they can, potentially, communicate a great deal of information, but at the same time low levels of literacy can restrict their reach. By contrast, television communication depends on images, whose emotional impact can be intense but whose informational content is often unclear. In this volume, different examinations focus on different aspects of the media. Some concentrate on the press (Cloonan; Rodan), Mary Myers' focus in Mali is on radio, Annabelle Sreberny-

Mohammadi concentrates on the impact of television in the Middle East, while Mark Wheeler examines the implications of the new Information Communication Technologies (ICTs).

But a further potentially fruitful variation amongst the analysts concerns the way that central issues are conceptualized, which in turn can have some bearing on the way in which they are investigated or elaborated. As readers of *Democratization* will need no reminding, conceptions of democracy differ and there is still less agreement around its defining criteria or prerequisites. Most of the studies here tend to work with fairly conventional understandings of democracy in terms of the functioning of central political institutions and processes, but in their discussions of media issues in Mali and the Middle East, Myers and Sreberny-Mohammadi concentrate on more 'cultural' aspects, understanding these to include power relations, including gender relations, at the local or familial level. Wheeler introduces a further concern with 'economic democracy' or democratic relationships within the economic sphere. Martin Cloonan, writing about the British press, and Richard Cullen and Hua Ling Fu, looking at possible harbingers of democratization in China, hone in on particular aspects of democracy, in the former case the relationship between democracy and privacy, in the latter the relationship between democracy and rights.

The topic, then, is vast but the range of material goes some way to meet its dimensions of variability. In some ways a more intractable and fundamental problem in examining the relationship between the media and democracy is the extent to which, in practice, they are interdependent. By definition, the media mediate; they do not stand independent of a given social system but instead provide channels of communication between elements within it. To varying degrees this has meant that they are instrumental to dominant institutions and interests within the society. Yet having said that, even in the sphere of politics there may be important ways in which the media themselves contribute to the content of their messages, and especially to its form. But the embeddedness of the media within the wider society also makes it almost impossible to establish what direct *effects* the media are having which cannot be attributed to other social processes, or how media messages are actually received. From early assumptions – either that they were absorbed uncritically (the hypodermic syringe analogy of the Frankfurt school) or, at the other extreme, that they were absorbed selectively to reinforce pre-existing beliefs and values – understanding has progressed.[2] Within the confines of political science, individual studies still seek to measure the impact of specific media-relayed messages, most notably during election campaigns, on audience attitudes. But there is also growing recognition that the media's direct message may be less important than the effects both on the process and on the agenda of politics.

Notwithstanding these analytical difficulties, we can none the less ask, in what ways has it been suggested that the media *could* contribute to democracy and democratization? In fact there is general consensus that the media play a vital role. Many would argue that, in modern societies and outside of the most local arenas, media of mass communication that are to a significant extent 'free' are essential to democracy. First, it is suggested, information is power. As David Mervin emphasizes in his analysis of the media's place in American politics, the media should act as conduits of vital political information, which may also mean providing guidance as to the interpretation of that information, so as to enable citizens to participate meaningfully in public political life. This function is especially important during elections. Second the media should constitute a means of expression for the full range of political interests and viewpoints and a forum for public debate. This is similar to Habermas's notion of the media as a 'public sphere', discussed in the contribution by Raymond Kuhn: Kuhn defines the public sphere as 'an institutional framework and set of practices which encourage wide and inclusive public debate about issues of social and political importance'. A further role, suggested elsewhere by Michael Gurevitch and Jay Blumler,[3] is to provide incentives to citizens to become more informed and involved; this comes closer to a mobilizing function. Last but by no means least, the media must act as watch-dogs guarding against abuse of power by the public authorities. That is the role sometimes encapsulated in the term 'Fourth Estate', coined by Lord Macaulay as early as 1832, to describe the emergence of the press to rival the power of the other three great estates, that is the Lords, both temporal and spiritual, and the Commons.[4]

As already noted, less has been written, explicitly, about the media's role in democratization. Under repressive regimes it is in any case by definition extremely difficult for the media within a country to live up to these ideals. Even so, elements of the media, and especially what can be termed the 'alternative' media, can help to maintain a tradition of independent criticism and to undermine regime legitimacy.[5] Still more subversive, in many cases, have been the international media, whose messages it has proved increasingly difficult and expensive to keep out. It is Samuel Huntington who first pointed out the importance of the part they have played in what he calls the current 'third wave' of democratization, through their contribution to the 'demonstration effect'. Largely as a result of the dramatic expansion in global communications in the post-war era and in particular 'the blanketing of the world by TV and communications satellites in the 1970s', he argues that this effect ensured that 'by the mid-80s the image of a "worldwide democratic revolution" undoubtedly had become a reality in the minds of political and intellectual leaders in most countries of the world'.[6]

As the process of democratization gathers pace, the national media can play a vital role in mobilization, urging the people to defy the old order and participate in the shaping of the new.[7] In any ensuing elections their contribution in providing information and elucidating choice is particularly important. What Sanford Ungar has written specifically of press freedom applies to freedom of the media in general: 'Once in place, it is an extraordinarily powerful catalyst for other democratic reforms'.[8]

What on the other hand are the implications of democracy for the media? What media policies do democratically-formed governments pursue and what policies should they pursue? As stated above, for many, a defining feature of a democracy is that its media are 'free'. Without such freedom it is argued the the media cannot properly perform their informational and watch-dog functions. But this raises questions about the meaning, or content, of freedom in this context. To the extent that not only government control but also government support is withdrawn, the media will not be autonomous so much as exposed to the pressures of market forces. Do these not also constitute a major set of constraints? Moreover how is this freedom to be reconciled with another kind of argument, that which emphasises the need for pluralism within the media? In other words, in order for the media to play their proper part in maintaining democracy, must they too be democratized? To quote James Curran, the media system:

> should be organized in a way that enables diverse social groups and organizations to express alternative viewpoints ... It should assist collective organizations to mobilize support; help them to operate as representative vehicles for the views of their supporters; and aid them to register effective protests and develop and promulgate alternatives.[9]

Considerations such as these point to the need for some regulation of the privately run media, but what form should this take? They may also seem to indicate the need for some public subsidy to newspapers and for public service broadcasting, but these issues are by no means cut and dried. Such dilemmas pose themselves most urgently for newly democratizing societies: as Frances Millard explains graphically while musing on the case of Poland, there is simply no universal template of press and broadcasting freedom that can be stencilled mechanically on to different political-cultural configurations.

The issues raised in these introductory remarks will be resumed in the Conclusion but they of course scarcely do justice to the rich detail and subtle analysis of the individual contributions. I do not intend to provide summaries of the essays that follow. Reading the editor's comments should be no substitute for engaging with the essays themselves.

NOTES

1. As discussed in Vicky Randall, 'The Media and Democratisation in the Third World', *Third World Quarterly*, Vol.14, No.3 (1993), pp.625–46. For a recent exception, however, see Thomas E. Skidmore (ed.), *Television, Politics and the Transition to Democracy in Latin America* (Baltimore, MD: Johns Hopkins University Press, 1993).

2. This is discussed for instance by Denis McQuail in *Mass Communications Media* (London: Sage, 1991).

3. See Michael Gurevitch and Jay G. Blumler, 'Political Communication Systems and Democratic Values', in Judith Lichtenberg (ed.), *Democracy and the Mass Media* (Cambridge: Cambridge University Press, 1990), pp.269–89.

4. Cited in Douglas Kellner, *Television and the Crisis of Democracy* (Boulder, CO: Westview Press, 1990), p.12.

5. See, for example, the role of the press in Zambia under Kaunda, discussed in Gatian F. Lungu, 'The Church, Labour and the Press in Zambia; The Role of Critical Observers in a One-Party State', *African Affairs*, Vol.85, No.340 (1986), pp.385–410.

6. See S.P. Huntington, *The Third Wave: Democratization in the Late Twentieth Century* (Norman, OK and London: University of Oklahoma Press, 1991), pp.100–02.

7. A dramatic example was the 'catalytic' role of TVGlobo in the 1984 Presidential elections in Brazil, described in Cesar Guimaraes and Roberto Amaral, 'Brazilian Television: A Rapid Conversion to the New Order', in Elizabeth Fox (ed.), *Media and Politics in Latin America* (London: Sage, 1988) pp.125–37.

8. Sanford J Ungar, 'The Role of a Free Press in Strengthening Democracy', in Judith Lichtenberg (ed.), *Democracy and the Mass Media* (Cambridge: Cambridge University Press, 1990), pp.368–98, p.370.

9. James Curran, 'Mass Media and Democracy: A Reappraisal', in James Curran and Michael Gurevitch (eds.), *Mass Media and Society* (London : Edward Arnold, 1991), p.103.

The News Media and Democracy in the United States

DAVID MERVIN

A full understanding of any modern, democratic political system requires some grasp of the role of the media and nowhere do the media play a more significant part in politics than in the United States. The focus of this study is the media as a news source. Following an introduction, the discussion notes the emergence of television and its eventual supplanting of newspapers as the principal means whereby Americans obtain political news. Consideration is given to legal and judicial developments in the 1960s that have helped to make the media in the US the freest in the world with exceptional opportunities to scrutinise politics and politicians. Events in the 1970s such as Vietnam, Watergate and changes in Democratic Party rules, which together brought about a sea change in journalistic attitudes and greatly magnified the role of the media in the political process, are also given particular attention. Further discussion centres on some of the problems of governability and touches on the consequences for foreign and national security policy making that follow from the emergence of satellite technology. The conclusion refers to the consequences for democracy arising from the various changes that have occurred in the past three decades.

Introduction

It is remarkable that there are still introductory text books on the politics of the United States that routinely cover topics such as the Constitution, federalism, Congress, the presidency, parties, pressure groups, and the Supreme Court, but give little space, and in some cases none at all, to that awesome contemporary force in American politics, the media. It is manifestly the case that the media, both print and electronic, fulfil vital functions in any democratic political system. Above all else the media, in their various guises, provide channels of information and means by which that information can be interpreted and placed in context. If the people are to govern themselves in any meaningful sense, they must be reasonably well-informed. They need help in identifying problems, in agenda setting and in weighing policy alternatives. They require guidance and assistance in the evaluation of programmes and in assessing the credentials of candidates for office. The media moreover, perform an essential role in a democratic polity in ensuring that public officials are held to account for their actions. Citizens, in other words, look to the media to assist them in the processes of 'public deliberation'.

A vigorous democracy cannot settle for a passive citizenry that merely chooses leaders and then forgets entirely about politics. Such a citizenry would not know what it wanted its public officials to do or what they were actually doing. An ignorant public would have no way to hold its officials to account. There would be a very attenuated sort of democracy, if any sort at all. In order that the public can actively control what the government does, the public, collectively, must be well informed. Some kind of effective public deliberation is required that involves the citizenry as a whole.[1]

If the media have an important role in any democratic polity then its significance is infinitely greater in the United States than anywhere else. In part, this is attributable to the intensely decentralized nature of the American political system. The centrifugal distribution of political power in that country, not only between the branches of government, but also within those branches, provides for multiple points of access and works against the instinctive inclination of political leaders to monopolize information. There is consequently far greater scope for the press to scrutinize politics and politicians than is the case in more centralized systems.

The notorious weakness of American political parties also does much to explain the weight of the media in politics. It is a mark of that weakness that parties lack the means to control the electoral process in the manner of European parties, creating a vacuum that the media are only too willing to fill. Elsewhere, candidates for public office are selected by party elites whereas the extensive use of intra-party, primary contests for such purposes in America facilitates a leading, if not dominant, role for the media in the selection process. The fragility of party then further reveals itself at inter-party, general elections. Party programmes and the identification of voters with their party are far less meaningful than in other countries; voters are more vulnerable to the appeals of candidates as individuals and freely engage in ticket-splitting; all circumstances which provide greater opportunities for the media than are available elsewhere. As Thomas Patterson has said: 'Although national voting in all Western democracies is media-centred in the sense that candidates depend primarily on mass communication to reach the voters, no other democracy has a system in which the press fills the role traditionally played by the political party.'[2]

The press in other countries is hampered by stringent libel laws and cultural norms that allow politicians to enjoy freedom from media scrutiny and make it possible for them to cloak their activities in secrecy. American politicians share the same inclination to conceal their activities from the public, but are obliged to operate in a quite different political culture – one where the public's right to know what is being done in their name is accorded far greater respect. These cultural differences provide for less inhibited media, protected by the First Amendment and benefiting from remarkably anaemic libel laws which have become even weaker in recent decades.

The focus of this study is the media as a news source. The discussion begins by noting the emergence of television and its eventual supplanting of newspapers as the principal means whereby Americans obtain political news. Consideration is then given to legal and judicial developments in the 1960s that have helped to make the media in the US the freest in the world with exceptional opportunities to scrutinize politics and politicians. Events in the 1970s such as Vietnam, Watergate and changes in Democratic Party rules, which together brought about a sea change in journalistic attitudes and greatly magnified the role of the media in the political process, are also given particular attention. Further discussion centres on some of the problems of governability detailed in the previous section and touches on the consequences for foreign and national security policy-making that follow from the emergence of satellite technology. The concluding section summarizes what has gone before and refers to the consequences for democracy arising from the various changes that have occurred in the past three decades.

The Rise of Television News Coverage

The 1960s were crucial in the history of the United States. This was the era of the Vietnam war, of the Kennedy assassination, the Great Society and extensive civil rights protest, but most importantly, for the purposes of this study, it marks the beginning of the substantial intervention of television into American politics. At the outset of the previous decade, less than ten per cent of households possessed television sets, whereas, by 1960 they were to be found in nearly nine out of ten households. In those early years, average television viewing was around five hours per day, a figure that has increased to a remarkable average figure of seven hours per day since the early 1980s.[3]

In the early years of television most stations were affiliates of one or other of the major networks – CBS (Columbia Broadcasting System), ABC (American Broadcasting Corporation) or NBC (National Broadcasting Corporation), but the rapid growth of cable television in the last 20 years has eroded network dominance. Thus, in 1977 less than 17 per cent of households with television sets were linked to cable outlets, whereas, in 1995, this was true of 65 per cent of such households. The weakening of the position of the networks is also reflected in viewing figures with the networks seeing their 70 per cent of audience share in the early 1980s reduced to 52 per cent by 1993/1994.[4]

It is apparent that since the 1960s, television has supplanted newspapers as the principal source of political news. As television has grown so newspaper circulation figures and the importance of newspapers as purveyors of political news have declined. In 1960, newspaper circulation as a percentage of the population was, at 32.6 per cent, not far below the peak year of 1947 when it had been 37 per cent, whereas by 1991 the figure had declined to 23.9 per cent.[5] When Americans were asked in 1961 where they obtained most of their news, with more than one answer permitted, 52 per cent indicated television, 57 per cent newspapers and 34 per cent radio, figures which 30 years later, had changed to 81 per cent television, 35 per cent newspapers and 14 per cent radio.[6] Also in 1961, in answering a question designed to establish which medium respondents found most believable, 39 per cent specified television, 24 per cent newspapers and 12 per cent radio; in 1991 answers to the same question broke down as 58 per cent television, 20 per cent newspapers and six per cent radio.[7] Another poll, in 1992, provided further evidence of the large shift to television as the predominant source of political news. When asked how far they paid attention to newspaper articles about the presidential campaign nine per cent of respondents indicated 'a great deal', 15 per cent 'quite a bit', 20 per cent 'some', six per cent 'very little' and 50 per cent 'none'. Responses for the same question with regard to television news were 20 per cent 'a great deal', 29 per cent 'quite a lot', 28 per cent 'some', 11 per cent 'very little', and 13 per cent 'none'.[8]

It is evident that most Americans now depend on television for news; it is the source they most often draw upon and that which they generally regard as the most reliable. But just how satisfactory is television as a news source? In a number of respects it would seem to be a less adequate vehicle for the transmission of news than newspapers. As Neil Postman has argued coming to grips with political news presented in print requires a far greater degree of intellectual effort than watching television:

> To engage the written word means to follow a line of thought, which requires considerable powers of classifying, inference-making and reasoning. It means to uncover lies, confusions and over-generalizations, to detect abuses of logic and of common sense. It also means to weigh ideas, to compare and contrast assertions, to connect one generalization to another ... In a culture dominated by print, public discourse tends to be characterized by a coherent orderly arrangement of facts and ideas.[9]

The primary purpose of television, by contrast, is to amuse rather than to edify the viewers; it is 'a medium which presents information in a form that renders it simplistic, nonsubstantive, nonhistorical and noncontextual; that is to say information packaged as entertainment'.[10]

Watching television newscasts clearly does not engage the mind in the same way as reading columns of newsprint. Television is, first and foremost, an entertainment medium; the time available for news broadcasts on commercial channels is moreover, very limited. The principal news programmes put out by the major networks, the half hour, nightly news casts, provide only 22 minutes of air time, excluding commercials. Inevitably, the coverage of political news is brief and superficial; complexities have to be skimmed over and there is no opportunity to debate controversial matters in the sort of depth that informed decision-making requires and that newspapers, theoretically at least, can provide. In short, television news broadcasts do not replicate what newspapers can contribute to the processes of public deliberation as Walter Cronkite, formerly of CBS, and the doyen of American television newscasters confirms:

> The major problem is simply that television news is an inadequate substitute for a good newspaper. It is not too far a stretch to say that the public's dependence on television for the bulk of its news endangers our democratic system ... The sheer volume of television news is ridiculously small. The number of words spoken in a half hour broadcast barely equals the number of words on two thirds of a standard newspaper page. That is not enough to cover the day's major events at home and overseas. Hypercompression of facts, foreshortened arguments, the elimination of extenuating explanation – all are dictated by television's restrictive time frame and all distort to some degree the news available on television.[11]

Cronkite's eventual successor as CBS anchor, Dan Rather, made the same point when he reflected on the shortcomings of television coverage of the presidency. '[T]here is no way, that I, or any other White House correspondent ... can come out there in a minute and 15 seconds and give the viewer even the essence, never mind the details or the substance [of a president's policies] ... One of the great difficulties of television is that it has a great deal of trouble dealing with any subject in depth.'[12]

Television news suffers not only from the limited time available, but also from the never ending quest for good visuals. News editors are naturally anxious to avoid, as far as possible, items that are visually uninteresting. BOGSAT – bunch of guys sitting around talking – for example, is to be avoided.[13] Earnest discussions of policy do not make for good television; if the fickle viewer's attention is to be drawn and held, eye-catching pictures, involving action, if possible, are needed.[14] As Roger Ailes, a well-known Republican media consultant, put it 'If you have two guys on a stage and one guy says "I have a solution to the Middle East problem" and the other guy falls into the orchestra pit, who do you think is going to be on the evening news?'[15] TV coverage of such an event would be dominated by lingering shots of the unfortunate accident, whereas a newspaper report, while mentioning the incident, would be less likely to give it prominence to the exclusion of serious consideration of what had been discussed.

Pictures, rather than illuminating complex situations, often distort the reality – oversimplifying and exaggerating, emphasizing the ephemeral and the trivial at the expense of the truly consequential. Rex Granum, a producer for ABC News, who also served as a deputy press secretary in the Carter White House, usefully compares television and newspaper coverage. He suggests that the emphasis on pictures in television leads to exaggeration; thus the shots of Carter and Begin and Sadat embracing at Camp David after the signing of the peace agreement in 1979, provided some 'just wonderful visuals' and presented the illusion of complete success. A newspaper reporter by contrast could be expected to offer a more balanced picture, emphasizing the importance of the achievement, but also, providing essential background, drawing attention to the long and difficult history of the Middle East problem and perhaps, noting that appearances could be deceptive. On the other hand, an unduly negative impression would be left by television coverage of a presidential speech where heckling took place and tomatoes were thrown afterwards. A television newscast would deal with the incident in a one minute spot and '[t]he visuals of the tomatoes splattering on the secret service agent would be the lasting impression that you would come away with ... [whereas a print reporter] would talk about what was said in the speech and so forth, that he was heckled throughout, and then three tomatoes were thrown'.[16] The picture conveyed by a newspaper reporter would be more complicated and closer to the reality than the clear, but ultimately simplistic impression conveyed by the television camera.

Television news editors, with their constant preoccupation with visual imagery, have also helped to bring about distortions in public understanding of how the American political system actually works. That system involves an extraordinarily complex and subtle distribution of power that television news is unable to come to terms with. Those who work in the medium have a compulsive desire to personify complexity and, in covering national politics, this leads to an obsessive interest in the activities of the president. Quite contrary to the intentions of those who drew up the Constitution, the chief executive is constantly presented to the public as the embodiment of the American government; success or failure in policy-making is perceived as turning on the behaviour of the man in the White House. In fact, the president is a Gulliver figure, tied down by a myriad of restraints, rather than the Leviathan so often conveyed by television presentations. Unlike the prime minister in a parliamentary system, and in contrast to the images provided by TV, the president does not sit at the hub of a centripetal distribution of political power. The reality is that he is hedged in and restrained on all sides and obliged to share power with other institutions, most notably a formidable legislative branch.[17]

Congress however gets short shrift from those responsible for television news and it receives far less attention from the media than the president. Committee meetings, the principal means whereby Congress conducts its business, make for wall-to-wall BOGSAT and it is very difficult to make legislative proceedings comprehensible to viewers:

> The way Congress works makes it difficult to cover. A bill is introduced, a subcommittee holds a hearing. The subcommittee considers it, holds a markup, and passes it to full committee. Full committee marks up and passes it to the floor, where it may or may not be changed again. If it passes, it then goes to the other body where it may go through the same process and pass in a different form. Then the two bodies hold a conference and come up with something else again. At what point in the action is it a story? How many stories have you read or seen about tax legislation, and what do you really know about where it stands or what's in it.[18]

Making such complexity intelligible to a mass audience is daunting enough for print reporters, but is especially difficult for those who work in television news programmes. If the matter is covered at all the complexities are likely to be overridden by personification, focusing on committee chairman and party leaders, despite the fact that power in Congress is widely diffused in what is a, largely leaderless, labyrinthine institution.

The Legal and Judicial Context of News Coverage

It has been argued here that the 1960s were notable in the history of the media in politics in the US for the displacement of newspapers by TV as the principal source of political news. Other developments in the same era helped to give substance to the claim that the media in the US, both print and broadcast, are probably the freest in the world.[19] Journalists and news executives elsewhere do not enjoy the same advantages. In the United Kingdom for instance, reporters have to operate in a culture marked by restrictive libel laws and a willingness to tolerate secrecy in government. In the US, by contrast, the Supreme Court has made it virtually impossible for public officials successfully to sue critics of their official conduct even where the criticisms are demonstrably false. In Britain, newspapers making allegations against public officials need to be completely confident of the truth of their charges if they are to avoid costly libel suits, whereas the context in the United States is quite different, as the Supreme Court made clear more than 30 years ago in their judgement in a famous case. The case was concerned with a libel action brought by L.B. Sullivan, the Commissioner for Public Affairs for the city of Montgomery in Alabama. He claimed that he had been libelled in a full page advertisement, written by civil rights activists, and published in the *New York Times*. The Supreme Court, while recognising that a number of the allegations made in the advertisement were not true, went on to say:

> A rule compelling the critic of official conduct to guarantee the truth of all his factual assertions – and to do so on the pain of libel judgments virtually unlimited in amount – leads to a comparable 'self-censorship' ... Under such a rule, would-be critics of official conduct may be deterred from voicing their criticism, even though it is believed to be true and even though it is, in fact true, because of doubt whether it can be proved in court or fear of the expense of having to do so. They tend to make only statements which 'steer far wider of the unlawful zone'. The rule thus dampens the vigor and limits the variety of public debate. It is inconsistent with the First and Fourteenth Amendments.[20]

This extraordinarily liberal view was only slightly modified by the Court conceding that a public official ought to be able to sue those who made false allegations about his or her official conduct if it could be proved that the statement in question was 'made with "actual malice" – that is, with knowledge that it was false or with reckless disregard of whether it was false or not'.[21] This qualification means little however, since, as Justice Hugo Black noted, malice is 'an elusive, abstract concept, hard to prove and hard to disprove'.[22] Black, in any case, in company with his colleagues Justices Douglas and Goldberg, had no time for the malice qualification; they insisted that the First and Fourth Amendments to the Constitution gave citizens and the press an absolute, unconditional right to criticise official conduct.

The American media also enjoy incomparable opportunities for gaining access to information. Again this contrasts sharply with the United Kingdom, a country with a culture that permits public officials to shroud their activities in secrecy and to maintain close control over the dissemination of information. According to one scholar, in Britain,

> Secrecy is the bonding material which holds the rambling structure of central government together. Secrecy is built into the calcium of a British policy-maker's bones ... It is the very essence of the Establishment view of good government as private government

carried on beyond the reach of the faction of political party, the tunnel vision of pressure group and the impertinent curiosity of the journalist … secrecy is as much a part of the English landscape as the Cotswolds. It goes with the grain of our society.[23]

The norm of secrecy in Britain is elaborately institutionalized in the Official Secrets Act which makes it a criminal offence for anyone who works in the civil service to pass information of any sort to unauthorized persons. This remarkably wide-sweeping legislation embraces everyone from cleaners and chauffeurs to permanent secretaries, applies in theory to all forms of information, whether secret or unclassified, and extends throughout the entire life of the employee concerned. Imposing restrictions more appropriate to a country behind the Iron Curtain of the past, the Official Secrets Act is just one of a number of devices employed in Britain that allow those in authority to manipulate and restrict news gathering by the media.[24]

Needless to say, public officials in the United States make use of secrecy where they can, but their scope is far more limited. Populism and a degree of openness, rather than hierarchy and secrecy, prevail in the American political culture. There is a widespread belief that the people have a right to know what is being done in their name. The Freedom of Information Act (1964) and the Supreme Court decision in the Pentagon Papers case are concrete manifestations of such sentiments.[25] The Freedom of Information statute requires federal officials to provide citizens with access to public records on request and, while some exemptions are permitted on national security and other grounds, in general, the legislation has made it possible for journalists and others to gain access to an enormous range of governmental information.

In the Pentagon Papers case, the federal government sought to prevent the publication of secret documents included in a history of American policy towards Vietnam that had been leaked to the press. The Supreme Court took the view that the First Amendment implied that any such prior restraint entailed a 'heavy presumption against its constitutional validity' and concluded that the government had not provided an adequate justification. By any standard this was a remarkable decision, testifying once again, to the great importance attached to the freedom of the press.

1970s Developments and the News Media

The Vietnam War which ended in 1975, and the Watergate scandal that came to a head in 1974, together mark a major turning point in the history of the media in politics in the United States. Since World War II, at least, the

American press had been rather naive and deferential, rarely challenging the official line, accepting at face value what politicians told them, and showing little inclination to pry into their private lives.[26] Vietnam and Watergate ended all this. Those in power were now shown to have lied to the American people on a grand scale and it was journalists who led the campaigns to bring this scandalous conduct to light. In particular, two junior *Washington Post* reporters, Bob Woodward and Carl Bernstein, took advantage of those weak libel laws and the implications of the Sullivan judgement discussed above, to write a series of incriminating stories – the Watergate stories – that played an important part in bringing about the forced resignation of President Nixon.[27] Those who work in the American media continue to feed off this famed triumph of investigative journalism. 'It remains the inspiration for a generation of reporters, a justification for journalistic intrusion and a paramount example of how the balance of power has shifted from the politicians to the news media.'[28]

In short, the Vietnam War and the Watergate affair brought about sea changes in the attitudes of American journalists. Henceforth, the assumption was that most public officials were dishonest and untrustworthy and little that they said could be accepted at its face value. The appropriate role for journalists in the circumstances, was to be latter-day Woodwards and Bernsteins, resolutely pursuing investigations and rooting out the endemic scandal and corruption in public life.

There were other significant changes in the early 1970s. In 1968, the Democratic Party suffered a particularly traumatic national convention. Largely because of the unpopularity of his Vietnam war policy, President Johnson withdrew from the race and the nomination eventually went to his Vice President, Hubert Humphrey, who defeated Eugene McCarthy in an acrimonious contest in Chicago, attended by violence on the streets outside the convention hall. McCarthy had run as an anti-war candidate in the primaries, in contrast to Humphrey who had not entered a single primary election and was effectively hand-picked by the party leadership. In reaction to these events, a reform movement emerged in the Democratic Party which set in train a series of rules changes, of which the most important were those that led to the proliferation of presidential primaries after 1972. In 1968, only 17 states had presidential primaries and less than half of the delegates to the Democratic convention were from 'primary' states, whereas in 1992, 40 states held some sort of presidential primary and nearly 90 per cent of Democratic delegates were from such states.[29] The effect of these and other rules changes designed to maximize popular participation has been to deprive American parties of control over the process whereby presidential candidates are selected and to create a void which the media has moved to fill.

The original purpose of those who devised presidential primaries early this century, was to weaken the power of the party bosses and machines and to place the vital function of candidate selection in the hands of the people. From the beginning, the reasoning behind this strategy was suspect, for the people, generally, have neither the capability nor the inclination to select candidates for public office without guidance. If the voters are to make sensible, well-informed choices they obviously need help in understanding policy questions and in making judgments about the leadership skills of alternative candidates. In other democracies the structures of party provide this essential assistance, but in the United States, primaries have now effectively removed party leaders from the presidential nomination process and left the voters to fend for themselves.[30]

In the circumstances, the role of the media has become decisive; it is to the press that the voters must turn for knowledge and guidance. Indeed, it is a remarkable and insufficiently recognized fact that in the selection of candidates for the most important political office in the world party leaders have been displaced by television journalists and news executives. Parties now do little more than provide an umbrella under which the nomination is contested; a competition mediated by the press with television in the leading role. The intra-party nature of presidential nominating contests has always allowed the press to play a part, but since the early 1970s and the proliferation of primaries, that role has become infinitely larger. As Thomas Patterson puts it: 'Once upon a time, the press occasionally played an important part in the nomination of presidential candidates. Now its function is always a key one. The news media do not entirely determine who will win the nomination, but no candidate can succeed without the press. The road to nomination now runs through the newsrooms.'[31] Similarly, Nelson Polsby and Aaron Wildavsky remark 'Were officials of political parties able to select their own candidates, the media would matter much less. But with primaries replacing caucuses and conventions it is fair to say that candidates have to care much more about how they do on television than about whether they please the leaders of their party.'[32]

As we have seen however, television is of questionable value as a source of political cues. Television news is inevitably brief, superficial and simplistic in its coverage of political affairs. It is unduly concerned with visual images and relentlessly personalistic in its approach; it is primarily concerned with amusing, or entertaining viewers, rather than enlightening them. This need to entertain leads those who work in television to focus much of their effort on the game rather than the substance of politics.[33] They have relatively little interest in issues, or policy alternatives, instead presenting politics as yet another form of sporting contest with individuals competing against one another for political advantage. Their coverage, in other words, regularly degenerates into 'horse race journalism', full of speculation as to who is ahead and who is behind, who are the front runners and who are the dark horses, all at the expense of more serious consideration of what is at stake. Such trivialisation of politics was evident in the presidential primaries in 1992 when, out of 1,039 news stories on television, 31 per cent dealt with horse race matters, 33 per cent were concerned with the character of the candidates and only 36 per cent were centred on policy issues.'[34]

Television and Governability

The 'televization' of American politics has undeniably had a number of detrimental consequences.[35] The treatment of politics as a form of entertainment, the 'surface-skimming' of television news and the obsession with good visuals, have all contributed to a debasement of the processes of public deliberation.[36] Furthermore, television has done much to bring about the chronic weakening of American parties as electoral mechanisms. Parties are indispensable to democratic politics, but, as E.E. Schattschneider made clear many years ago, parties unable to control the means whereby candidates obtain nominations are hardly parties at all.[37] When it comes to the vital matters of screening and selecting presidential candidates television has been allowed to elbow parties aside, turning the nomination process into a festival of triviality and entertainment, where TV pundits are the arbiters of choice and performance before the cameras is the pivotal determinant of success or failure.

Television has also exacerbated the inherent problems of governability in the US political system. It is a medium ill-suited to dealing with the complexities of an intensely diffused structure of power. It seeks to overcome these difficulties by personifying the subject matter, explaining and interpreting political events through leading individuals. The president accordingly receives a disproportionate share of attention from those responsible for TV news. As a result of television coverage he is perpetually in the public eye and the impression is created that he is the one player in the system in a position to make things happen. He is presented as the man able to bring about change, as the man who, if he had the ability and the motivation, could eliminate the budget deficit, or secure the passage of health reform. But these are, of course, illusions. The fact is that the president:

> operates in a system that affords him limited ability to meet these expectations single-handedly. The open, personalized, presidential view of the legislative process portrayed on television is at odds with

the complex, internal, bureaucratized, congressional mechanism that actually evaluates policy options and writes the law. Television may have opened the legislative process to millions of American homes, but it has not changed the institutional restrictions that make progress difficult and slow ... The president is still only one player, and contrary to what television suggests, he doesn't always hold the best cards.[38]

The conduct of foreign and national security policy has been made immeasurably more difficult by the onset of television. In the pre-television age, presidents and their officials pursued their foreign policy agendas without the close scrutiny and the concomitant pressures experienced by their more recent successors. Without television it is doubtful whether the Vietnam War would have ended when it did. The constant diet of war pictures relayed to the American people in their living rooms undoubtedly helped to swing public opinion against the war. And then President Johnson's acceptance that the war could not be won is reliably reported to have resulted from the intervention of a TV news anchorman. Walter Cronkite of CBS visited Vietnam and argued, on his return, that the war was unwinnable. On hearing this Johnson, who assumed that Cronkite was vastly influential with the American people, declared 'It's all over' and the reversal of American policy began.[39]

The role of television in shaping American foreign policy has been further advanced by the development of satellite technology. During the Vietnam War film had to be transported long distances before it could be shown on television, but now satellite television brings the horrors of war before the people with riveting immediacy and the possibility of policy consequences. Thus a few years ago, the withdrawal of US forces from Somalia occurred sooner than policy-makers planned, following public reaction to satellite pictures of the body of a dead American serviceman being dragged through the streets of Mogadishu.[40]

Similarly, as the Clinton Administration struggles to implement a coherent policy in Bosnia, it must constantly be aware of the ubiquitous cameras of satellite television. According to one account, Christiane Amanpour, a high profile reporter for CNN (Cable News Network) with a 'nose for death and destruction', is a particular concern of policy-makers. 'Imagine a situation in which the Bosnian Serbs start pitchforking babies and Christiane Amanpour shows up and shows it all on CNN' one Pentagon planner was quoted as saying with 'an almost audible shudder'. Another official meanwhile said that the same reporter had become a symbol of 'the evil press that undermines military policy and creates political pressures that can't be dealt with rationally... She is a particular obsession with the military. We routinely sit around and try to figure out how to react when she shows up at the scene of some tragedy.'[41] The capacity of television to limit the options of policy makers was evident enough during the Vietnam conflict, but that capability has become much greater since the inception of satellite technology.

Arising partly from an understandable desire to deny America's enemies operational advantages, the military have, in recent years, sought to curtail the activities of the media in war situations. This occurred in Grenada, Panama and Haiti and most notably during the Gulf War. Despite these constraints the latter conflict was the first in 'history in which live television cameras were able to capture some scenes or elements of the actual battle…' People all over the world were able to sit at home and watch bombs landing in Bagdad, scud missiles hitting in Israel and Saudi Arabia, Egyptian troops crossing into Kuwait on the first day of the ground war, and the liberation of Kuwait City as these events were actually happening.'[42]

From a 'democratic' point of view the possibility of scenes 'live from the battlefield' can be seen in a positive light. As the Republican Senator from Arizona, John McCain, has noted 'We are very selective in our morality because it is driven by the television cameras, and it it is not all bad by the way. I still believe that World War I wouldn't have lasted three months if people had known what was going on in that conflict.'[43] No doubt this is true. If the people in Britain had been in receipt of live pictures of the carnage then taking place in France, we can be reasonably sure that the war would have ended much sooner than it did, with countless lives saved.

To set against that scenario, what if television cameras had been on hand to record live (and allow the Germans to observe) the D-Day landings? Hitler believed the early landings were a feint and that the full invasion would come further East. Accordingly he refused to allow reserves to be moved West in time, a crucial error from which he would almost certainly have been saved if television via satellite had then existed.[44] In all probability the end of the war in Europe would have been delayed and many lives would have been lost. It is self-evident that there are hazards in freely revealing to the world the disposition of forces and other information that may give advantages to the enemy.

Conclusion

A full understanding of any modern, democratic political system requires some grasp of the role of the media and nowhere do the media play a more significant part in politics than in the United States. This can be attributed to an intensely decentralised constitutional framework, chronically weak political parties and liberal interpretations of the principle of press freedom.

Since the 1960s, television has superseded newspapers as the principal source of political news, a development which has, in a number of respects, diminished the quality of news coverage. Unlike print journalism, television is primarily an entertainment medium; its approach to political news is accordingly simplistic, insubstantial and personalistic, as well as being overly dependent on visual images.

Not all the effects of the 'televization' of American politics, however, have been negative. The amount of political news made available by the media these days is enormous. The cameras and microphones of C-Span allow those who so wish to follow debates in the US Congress and to witness other political events. Similarly, the Public Broadcasting System nightly news broadcasts offer regular doses of non-trivial, in-depth coverage of political matters. Even the commercial networks, from time to time, make sizeable contributions to the processes of public deliberation. Televised congressional hearings have periodically provided great national political seminars where the pros and cons of momentous issues such as McCarthyism, the Vietnam War, Watergate and the Iran-Contra affair, have been laid before the American people in detail. Hearings to consider presidential nominations to federal offices, while sometimes descending into unseemly farce, have often made important contributions to the political education of the citizenry.

It is nevertheless difficult to avoid somewhat negative conclusions about the role of the media as a purveyor of political news in the United States in the late twentieth century. The advent of television has added to the quantity of news available, but the imperatives of the industry have been detrimental to its quality. Furthermore, while the media in America have always been remarkably free, since the 1960s, this has been taken to new, some might say excessive, heights with journalists ruthlessly exploiting the developments discussed earlier – the liberality of Supreme Court judgments, the aftermath of the Vietnam and Watergate crises and changes in the rules of the Democratic Party.

Freedom carries with it responsibilities and several authorities have raised questions about how satisfactorily those who currently work in the media are meeting their obligations.[45]

Journalists and news executives today stand accused of abusing their privileged position and of instigating public cynicism towards the political process. The incessant trivialization, the superficiality, the horse-race journalism and the constant drum-beat of negative stories have all helped to undermine politics and politicians, and to erode public confidence in the way they are governed. This is the era of 'attack dog journalism' where reporters and editors are obsessively concerned with exposing scandalous conduct and politicians are obliged to bear an unprecedented intensity of scrutiny.

There is however some evidence to suggest that the American public has become increasingly disillusioned with the news coverage of the media. At present, President Clinton's standing in the public opinion polls remains high despite wave upon wave of negative stories about his private life. Other polls meanwhile show that increasing numbers of Americans have less confidence in the news media now than was the case only a few years ago.[46] Other evidence shows that fewer people than ever before are watching network news and newspaper readership is in steady decline. For some time there has been a well-documented decline of confidence in government in the US and the news media contributed much to that decline, but now the media itself is suffering from a serious crisis of confidence.

NOTES

1. Benjamin Page, *Who Deliberates? Mass Media in Modern Democracy* (Chicago, IL: University of Chicago Press, 1996), p.5.
2. Thomas Patterson, *Out of Order* (New York: Vintage Books, 1994), p.37.
3. Figures from Harold Stanley and Richard Niemi, *Vital Statistics on American Politics* (Washington, DC: Congressional Quarterly Press, 1994), Table 2-1, p. 53. *Note*: While the figures may not be directly comparable, one source calculates average daily viewing figures in the UK in 1990 as 3 hours and 24 minutes, that is less than half the US figure. See *The World Alamanac and Book of Facts* (UK Edition) (London: Pan Books, 1992), p.294.
4. Neilson Media Research figures, *The World Almanac and Book of Facts 1996* (Mahwah, NJ: Funk and Wagnalls, 1995), p.259 and 261.
5. Stanley and Niemi, op. cit., Table 2–3, p.56.
6. Ibid., Table 2–12, p.74.
7. Ibid.
8. Ibid., Table 2–11, pp.72–3.
9. *Amusing Ourselves to Death: Public Discourse in the Age of Show Business* (New York: Penguin Books, 1985), p.51.
10. Ibid., p.141.
11. Walter Cronkite, *A Reporter's Life* (New York: Alfred Knopf, 1996), p.375.
12. As quoted in Fred Smoller, 'The Six O'Clock Presidency: Patterns of Network News Coverage of the President', *Presidential Studies Quarterly*, Vol.XVI, No.1 (1986), pp.31–49.
13. See Larry Warren, 'The Other Side of the Camera: A TV Reporter's Stint as a Congressional Aide', *PS*, Vol.XX, No.2 (1987).
14. For discussion of the structural bias in television news see Austin Ranney, *Channels of Power* (New York: Basic Books, 1983), Ch.2.
15. Cited in Patterson, op. cit., p.152.
16. Smoller, op. cit., p.36.
17. For further discussion see Matthew Kerbel, *Remote and Controlled: Media Politics in a Cynical Age* (Boulder, CO: Westview Press, 1995), pp.110–14. *Note* This is not to ignore the fact that, in the right hands, television can considerably enhance the power of a president. See, for example, Thomas Cronin, *The State of the Presidency* (Boston, MA: Little, Brown & Co., 1980) Ch.3, 'The Textbook and Prime-Time Presidency'.
18. Warren, op. cit.
19. See, for example, Robert Lineberry, *Government in America* (Glenview, IL: Scott, Foresman & Co., 1989), p.361.
20. *New York Times Co v Sullivan* 376 US 254 (1964), p.279. *Note*: The recent experiences of the *Guardian* newspaper in pursuing allegations of malfeasance against Members of Parliament demonstrates the much more restrictive circumstances for journalists in the UK.

The editor of *The Guardian*, Alan Rusbridger, in writing about the case involving a libel suit brought by Jonathan Aitken MP against the newspaper said:

> In America and many other countries the Aitken case would probably never have come to court, because their laws are framed to encourage, rather than discourage, newspapers in the exercise of fair scrutiny of people who choose to go into public life, with all its privileges and responsibilities. Under these laws, Aitken would have had to prove malice or recklessness before being able to launch an action.

'Burdened with Proof', *The Guardian* (26 June 1997), p.23.
21. Ibid.
22. Ibid., p.293.
23. Peter Hennessy, *Whitehall* (London: Fontana Press, 1989), pp.346–7.
24. For others such as the lobby system and D notices see Clive Ponting, *Whitehall: Tragedy and Farce* (London: Sphere Books, 1986), Ch.5.
25. *New York Times Co. v United States* 403 US 713 (1971).
26. This era has been dubbed one of 'lap dog journalism'. See Larry Sabato, *Feeding Frenzy: How Attack Journalism Has Transformed American Politics* (New York: The Free Press, 1991), p.25.
27. The success of Woodward and Bernstein was, of course, subsequently immortalized in a well-known film, *All the President's Men*, with Robert Redford and Dustin Hoffman playing the two intrepid reporters.
28. Ellen Hume, 'The Weight of Watergate', *Media Studies Journal*, Vol.11, No.2 (1997) (Internet).
29. Stanley and Niemi, op. cit., Table 4–9, p.148.
30. See Thomas Patterson, *The Mass Media Election:How Americans Choose Their President* (New York: Praeger, 1980), Ch.14, 'The Importance of Political Institutions'.
31. Patterson, *Out of Order*, op. cit., p.33.
32. *Presidential Elections*, 8th edition, p.120.
33. See Patterson, *Out of Order*, op. cit., pp.57–65.
34. Stanley and Niemi, op. cit., Table 2–6, p.63.
35. The expression in quotation marks is Austin Ranney's. See *Channels of Power*, op. cit., p.108.
36. 'Surface-skimming' is from David Paletz and Robert Entman, *Media Power Politics* (New York: Free Press, 1981), p.21.
37. *Party Government* (New York: Farrar & Rinehart, 1942), pp.101–2.
38. Kerbel, op. cit., p.102.
39. Ranney, op. cit., pp.4–5.
40. Barrie Dunsmore, 'Live from the Battlefield', in Pippa Norris (ed.), *Politics and the Press* (Boulder, CO: Lynne Rienner, 1997), pp.259–60.
41. Michael Dobbs 'Foreign Policy by CNN', *Washington Post National Weekly Edition* (31 July–6 Aug., 1995), p.24.
42. Dunsmore, op. cit., pp.242–3.
43. Ibid., p.259.
44. Ibid., p.244.
45. See Patterson, *Out of Order*, op. cit., Sabato, op. cit. and James Fallows, *Breaking the News: How the Media Undermine American Democracy* (New York: Pantheon Books, 1996).
46. A recent Pew Research Center survey found, for instance, that only 26 per cent admitted to enjoying network news 'a great deal' compared to 42 per cent who felt the same way in 1985. Similarly 27 per cent now say that they look forward to reading a daily newspaper compared to 42 per cent who said the same in 1985. Jack Nelson, 'Major News Trusted Less, Poll Says', *Los Angeles Times*, 21 March 1997 (Internet).

The Media and the Public Sphere in Fifth Republic France

RAYMOND KUHN

This study examines the public sphere credentials of the media (press, radio, television and new communication technologies) in Fifth Republic France. Commercial ownership and control of much of the contemporary media, image-based electoral competition and a legacy of state interference in news management have severely undermined the capacity of the French media to function effectively as a public sphere. State financial support and regulation to promote pluralism and diversity have met with mixed success, as the larger domestic media companies seek to pursue commercially-driven corporate strategies in transnational European markets. Finally, the potentially democratizing impact of the introduction of new communication technologies still remains largely a matter of speculation. In general, the French experience during the Fifth Republic demonstrates the difficulties rather than the possibilities of creating and maintaining a mediatized public sphere which avoids the pitfalls of state control and market domination.

In a recent book entitled *Médias et Démocratie: La Dérive* the political scientist Roland Cayrol presents a largely negative picture of the relationship between politicians, the media and the audience in contemporary France.[1] Cayrol argues that while the media are an indispensable part of contemporary democratic politics, French citizens are being short-changed in terms of the quality of information which they need in order to understand the workings of the political system and make an informed choice at elections. Television in particular has fundamentally altered the process of political communication in the Fifth Republic – personalizing politics, reducing political discourse to 'sound bite' exchanges and turning debate into an entertainment-driven spectacle. The French voter is now open to seduction by politicians who have been taught by their communication advisers how to manipulate the media for their own partisan objectives. Meanwhile journalists have neither the capacity, the willingness, nor the time to act as a reflective filter for public opinion. Cayrol contends that political reform, audience education, better training for media personnel and stronger journalistic codes of practice are all required if the French media are to play a full part in the democratic process.

Though he does not use the term, Cayrol's critique suggests that the media in France fall far short of functioning as a 'public sphere', that is an institutional framework and set of practices which encourage wide and inclusive public debate about issues of social and political importance. Applied to the media, this concept derives from the work of Jürgen Habermas, in particular his study *The Structural Transformation of the Public Sphere.*[2] Though the historical accuracy of this analysis has been questioned,[3] the concept has been taken up by various academic commentators as a useful normative device for framing discussion of an ideal-type relationship between the media and politics in advanced societies.[4] In particular, the idea of the media as public sphere has been contrasted with two undesirable but historically prevalent conditions of market domination and state control.

This study examines the public sphere credentials of the media in Fifth Republic France (1958–). It argues that commercial ownership and control of much of the contemporary media, image-based electoral competition and a legacy of state interference in news management have severely undermined the capacity of the French media to function effectively as a public sphere. State financial support and regulation to promote pluralism and diversity have met with mixed success as the larger domestic media companies seek to pursue commercially-driven corporate strategies in transnational European markets. Finally, the potentially democratizing impact of the introduction of new communication technologies still remains largely a matter of speculation.

Commercialization of Broadcasting

One of the major developments in the media system of the Fifth Republic has been the economic liberalization and subsequent expansion of the broadcasting sector since the early 1980s. As new radio stations and television channels have come on stream, so audience usage of these media has grown, with the result that France is now a highly mediatized society. Yet many broadcast media outlets operate as simple commercial entities. Much of their output is entertainment-oriented, with several of the most successful initiatives in broadcasting, such as the pay-television (tv) channel Canal Plus and the radio network NRJ, largely eschewing a political information function.

Television

Up until the start of the Mitterrand presidency in 1981 television was managed as a state monopoly. Originally established by the wartime Vichy regime for radio, this legal framework was extended to include television and was maintained by all governments of Fourth and Fifth Republics prior to Mitterrand's advent to power. During the 1980s, however, the French television system underwent extensive and radical change. The Socialists'

1982 legislation on audio-visual communication (*la loi Fillioud*) abolished the state monopoly, opening up the medium to commercial players in an unprecedented economic liberalization of the sector. Europe's first terrestrial pay-tv channel, Canal Plus, began transmissions in 1984, while two new commercial channels started broadcasting in 1986.[5]

The first right-wing 'cohabitation' government under the premiership of Jacques Chirac (1986–88) quickly introduced its own legislation in the audio-visual field (*la loi Léotard*). This accentuated the commercialization of the system by privatizing the main national public sector channel, TF1, whose franchise was awarded to a consortium dominated by the Bouygues construction company. This privatization destabilized the whole television sector, compelling the two remaining public sector channels to compete with their commercial rivals on the latter's terms. Competition for viewers and advertising revenue intensified, with an emphasis on entertainment programming to attract mass audiences. The rapid liberalization of the sector proved unsustainable and in 1992 one of the recently established commercial channels, La 5, went into liquidation in the face of mounting debts.

While the expansion in the supply of television programming has generated increased audience usage of the medium, it has had mixed consequences for political communication. On the one hand, television is the French public's single most important source of political information, especially for national and international news. It is also the political medium in which the public have expressed most confidence, ahead of radio, daily newspapers and weekly magazines.[6] On the other hand, commercialization of the medium has resulted in the marginalization of old-style political debates in schedules and a tendency for politicians to seek exposure to a larger audience in non-political talk shows. Moreover, viewers now have greater flexibility in avoiding politics on television by switching channels and concentrating on a diet of entertainment.

Radio

Following the abolition of the state monopoly, radio also expanded during the early years of the Mitterrand presidency, with private interests taking a dominant stake in this sector. In the early 1980s the floodgates were opened to an apparently infinite number and astonishing variety of small, privately run, local stations, catering for a wide range of social, cultural and community groups nationwide.[7] While some individual radio stations were associated with clearly defined socio-political organizations, the waveband as a whole exhibited a high degree of pluralism from which no major legitimate tendency of opinion in French society was excluded. Even groups marginalized or shunned by the traditional public sector broadcasting organizations, such as ethnic minorities and gays, found a place on the radio frequency spectrum.[8] As a result, the FM waveband came to constitute a mediatized public sphere. This open and diverse system did not survive for very long. It was prey to financial problems and in a struggle for market domination (and in some cases mere survival) networks were formed, with the result that the system became dominated by a few big players. The era of the small artisanal station of the early 1980s gave way to a system dominated by highly professional commercial companies, seeking to maximize their audience share by targeting listeners on the basis of sophisticated market research. Of the approximately 1,800 radio stations broadcasting in France, small scale community outlets are now in a distinct minority, even though an attempt has been made through regulation to protect community radio stations from being totally squeezed out of the sector.

With oligopolization has come a certain sameness in output. The dominant format is a combination of music and news, as stations compete to deliver a particular type of audience to advertisers. There is an evident lack of choice in much of the programming across different stations, many of which for reasons of cost leave little space for local expression either in terms of news coverage or programme production.[9] In short, the system has moved from state monopoly to unparalleled diversity to a commercial oligopoly in the space of a few years, with the result that 'the fundamental objectives of the radical media legislation of 1982 such as radio pluralism, the creation of numerous independent stations or journalistic diversity (at the local level) have not been achieved'.[10]

Decline of the Press

Since 1958 sales of general information daily newspapers have continued their postwar decline. This has particularly affected national dailies, whose dropping circulation figures have been only partly offset by the growing popularity of weekly news magazines. Though sales of provincial dailies have held up reasonably well, the cost has been a considerable depoliticization in the content of many of them as they seek to maximize their local and regional readerships.

In general, therefore, the French press is in a poor condition to contribute to the media's role as a public sphere. Both the number of individual newspaper titles and overall circulation figures have plummeted since the boom years immediately following the Liberation during which circulation figures for daily newspapers reached an all-time high. The French now lag behind most of their west European neighbours in terms of newspaper readership, despite a large increase in population and the spread of formal education since 1945.[11] Well under half the adult population read a newspaper every day and circulation figures are particularly low among young people. While the high cost of newspapers and weaknesses in the distribution network have contributed to this situation, many newspapers have also failed to adapt their coverage to attract new readers. In addition, there is evidence of a declining trust on the part of readers in newspaper content and less willingness than before to believe in the independence of journalists.[12]

National newspapers produced in Paris have fared particularly badly during the Fifth Republic and the lack of a mass market national newspaper is especially evident to British observers. In contrast, weekly news magazines such as *L'Express*, *Le Nouvel Observateur*, *Le Point* and *L'Événement du Jeudi* have successfully penetrated the French market. These magazines have grown in popularity, in part because their political partisanship is more muted than in the case of most Paris dailies such as *Le Figaro* (conservative) and *Libération* (centre-left). The notable exception to the partisanship of the Paris newspaper press is *Le Monde*, which acts as a forum for political debate, aspires to comprehensive, multi-faceted coverage of national and international politics and allows different interests to be represented in its columns. Its serious and highly analytic approach is exemplified by the dense nature of its layout and lack of photos. The weekly news magazines and *Le Monde* thus make an important contribution to the functioning of the press as a public sphere. However, because of the social composition of their readerships, their impact is largely confined to the well-educated and politically interested sections of French society.

Provincial newspapers have fared better than their national counterparts, with several major titles, such as *Ouest France*, enjoying a dominant position in their respective regional markets and benefiting from relatively healthy circulation figures.[13] Several big provincial dailies have built up important regional press groups, centring on the major title and including other smaller titles in the region. However, the comparative success of the provincial press has been achieved at the cost of downgrading their political information function in favour of local news, sport, leisure and human interest stories.[14] As a result, for readers of provincial newspapers the press is a poor source of information on national and international politics.

Mediatization of Electoral Competition

The commercialization of a large share of radio and television and the parlous state of much of the newspaper press represent important elements in the structure and functioning of the French media which need to be taken into account in any evaluation of their capacity to function as a public sphere. Another aspect of such an evaluation is the use of the media by political elites, notably but not exclusively during election campaigns, to win public support. The mediatization of electoral competition during the Fifth Republic has involved the use of political marketing techniques by candidates and an emphasis on image projection in campaigns, with television in particular largely replacing traditional intermediaries such as political parties in the process of electoral mobilization.

The role of television is central to the mediatization of political discourse in France. Television began to acquire the status of a mass medium at the same time as the establishment of the new political system of the Fifth Republic. The medium was implanted and its social usage routinized during the de Gaulle presidency (1958–69) when sales of television sets rocketed and television viewing became a prime leisure activity. The 1965 presidential contest is generally regarded as the first television election in France and the first campaign in which political marketing was employed.[15] Since then, politicians have learned to adapt to the needs of television and the terms in which political messages are framed have considerably altered.

As a medium of political communication, television is better suited to the conveying of feeling and emotion than the exposition of rational analysis. Voters have become accustomed to seeing their politicians on screen and, whatever the artificiality of the mediatized product, the feeling of direct contact in comparison with the print medium cannot be denied. This has encouraged politicians' concern with image projection. A weak or confused image is deemed to be an electoral liability, as Raymond Barre and Edouard Balladur discovered to their cost in the 1988 and 1995 presidential campaigns respectively. In the run-up to the 1995 presidential elections Chirac consciously sought to improve his popular image as an over-excited and impetuous politician – an image reinforced by the puppet character in the highly popular *Bébête Show* – by adopting a more relaxed and self-controlled posture on television.[16]

French politicians now pay at least as much attention to the packaging of their messages as to their content, in the belief that favourable television coverage is essential for electoral success. Opinion polls provide information about the values and attitudes of the electorate, allowing candidates to adapt their electoral image accordingly. The resultant packaging of politics has given rise to a new set of political actors – communications consultants – whose prime function is media promotion. Jacques Séguéla, for example, was instrumental in the successful promotion of Mitterrand as presidential candidate in 1981 and in particular for the slogan of 'la force tranquille', which effectively combined the image of strength of purpose with calm determination for the Socialist candidate. In the 1988 contest Séguéla was again a key figure in Mitterrand's election campaign. This time the sitting President successfully projected a Gaullian image of a unifying statesman, standing above the turmoil of party politics.[17] Image projection is seen as increasingly important in election campaigns because traditional electoral cleavages such as class, religion or regional differences are being replaced by more pragmatic and volatile voting behaviour. Voter identification with parties and political sub-cultures has declined during the Fifth Republic as many French citizens have come to adopt a more consumerist attitude to electoral choice. The causes of this partisan dealignment are many and varied: the weakening of traditional societal divisions; a decline in religious practice; urbanization; the perceived failure of successive governments of Left and Right since 1981 to resolve France's socio-economic problems, particularly unemployment; and the increased salience of political issues, such as Europe, which do not fit neatly into a traditional Left-Right polarization. As traditional sociological determinants of voting behaviour lose their grip on the electorate, so the mediatization of a candidate has become more important for electoral success and a coherent ideologically-based programme less significant.

News Management

In addition to paying growing attention to their mediatized electoral image, political elites invest substantial resources in competing to structure the media's news agenda. The executive has always played an important role in respect of news management activities. In the case of the press the practice has strong historical roots,[18] while in the Fifth Republic executive intervention was extended to include the broadcast media. In the early years of the regime, for example, as de Gaulle sought to implant the political system and build up a popular consensus underpinning the new constitutional framework, the executive's control of television's news output was particularly severe. Sympathetic appointments to key decision-making posts within the state broadcasting organization were supplemented with official directives and censorship of news content by the Ministry of Information.[19] At times such control could be crude, with opposition politicians kept off the screen and the Gaullist viewpoint pushed mercilessly in television news bulletins. This systematic intervention in news management on the part of the executive even led one commentator to describe the regime as a 'telecracy' – government by television.[20]

The limitations of the Gaullist approach to agenda setting did not long survive de Gaulle's resignation from the presidency in 1969. The backlash came in 1968 when students and workers protested against the paternalistic nature of Gaullism, including the appropriation of the state broadcasting service, the ORTF, for government propaganda.[21] Under de Gaulle's two conservative successors at the Elysée, censorship and crude news management fell out of favour, while the executive took steps to be seen as distancing itself from control of political content on television. The Ministry of Information, authoritarian symbol of Gaullist control of state television news, was abolished in 1969.

However, while some steps were taken after 1968 to reduce the capacity of the state to intervene directly in news output, a clean break with the culture of interventionism proved impossible. Under Presidents Pompidou (1969–74) and Giscard d'Estaing (1974–81) the tendency for the executive to regard broadcasting as a part of the state apparatus remained apparent. Emphasis was placed by the Élysée on the appointment of political sympathizers to key managerial and editorial posts. Pompidou called the state broadcasting organization 'the voice of France', while Giscard d'Estaing's attempts to give greater independence to broadcasters were undermined by the unfavourable political situation throughout much of his presidency, the interventionist tendencies of some of his most powerful ministers and his own unwillingness fully to embrace the logic of his reformist measures.

Following Mitterrand's accession to the presidency, the establishment of regulatory authorities in the broadcasting sector was designed in part to create a buffer between political elites on the one hand and journalists and news editors on the other. As in the case of the press, the executive's attempts at news management in the broadcasting sector are now based more on its status as a primary definer rather than a monopoly controller.[22] The President and his advisers ('the Élysée'), the Prime Minister and his staff (the 'Matignon') and other government ministries are key primary definers for the contemporary French media. On major domestic and foreign policy issues their input helps to helps to structure the terms of the debate and the parameters of issue coverage. For example, the executive stages special events for the media, including presidential press conferences, interviews with journalists and television appearances by the President and his ministers. As a result, the executive's perspective on events usually has little difficulty in finding a channel in most of the media.

This is not to say that during the Fifth Republic the executive branch has always been successful in imposing its version of events on a compliant media and a credulous audience. In fact, attempts by the executive to control the news agenda have come up against several constraints. First, as sender of the message the executive has often been internally divided, with disagreement on policy issues frequently being reflected in media coverage. Sometimes the disagreements have been based on party political divisions within the governing coalition, for example in the late 1970s between

Gaullists and Giscardians and in the early 1980s between Socialists and Communists. Since 1986 three experiences of cohabitation (1986–88, 1993–95 and 1997–) have institutionalized division at the very heart of the executive, pitting a President of one political grouping against a Prime Minister and parliamentary majority of another. Currently the Gaullist President Chirac and the Socialist Prime Minister Jospin are engaged in competition to impose their respective 'spin' on media coverage of issues such as immigration, Europe and unemployment.

Secondly, the executive's version of events may be challenged by a variety of other political actors who gain media coverage for their views. The views of the National Front on immigration, for example, challenged the official orthodoxy of the Socialist government in the early 1980s. Jean-Marie Le Pen's television appearances later bolstered support for his party's racist platform, helping not just to push the issue of immigration up the political agenda but also to impose a dominant framework for media coverage of this issue which placed governments of both left and right on the defensive.

Thirdly, the media themselves may challenge the official perspective. This aspect of independent media activity should not be overemphasized in the French case. Compared with the American and British experiences, the practice of investigative journalism is poorly implanted in French journalistic culture, with the notable exception of the satirical weekly Le Canard enchaîné. In addition, French media are constrained by strong privacy legislation. None the less, during the Fifth Republic some media have performed the function of watch-dog on elite behaviour, bringing issues into the public domain and embarrassing leading government figures. Examples include the Bokassa diamonds affair during the Giscard d'Estaing presidency and the sinking of the Greenpeace boat, the Rainbow Warrior, under Mitterrand.

Finally, contemporary audience reception theory demonstrates that different audiences 'read' the same media message in a variety of ways. Among other variables, class, gender, age, political affiliation and personal experience influence the decoding of a message by readers, listeners and viewers. Messages are not imposed in a top-down fashion, but rather audiences may accept the preferred encoded reading, negotiate with it or reject it. During the 1968 events, for example, significant sections of the French population rejected the pro-governmental message that was being put across by the state monopoly broadcasting organization. In part this was because contradictory messages more sympathetic to the protest were being disseminated by other media. However, audience response was also influenced by their perception of the legitimacy of the primary sender (in this case the Gaullist executive), the institutional credibility of the medium (the state broadcasting corporation) and the professional reputation of media professionals (the ORTF journalists).

State Support and Regulation

The executive's attempts to set the news agenda, particularly the crude interventionist practices of the de Gaulle era, have certainly militated against the emergence of a mediatized public sphere in the Fifth Republic. It would be misleading, however, to portray the relationship between the state and the media during the regime in a wholly negative light. The state has also played a positive role to promote diverse and pluralistic media through financial support and regulation. The state's roles as enabler and regulator have to be weighed in the balance with those of censor and primary definer.

However, it is also fair to say that neither financial support nor regulation has effectively compensated for the increasingly commercial functioning of much of the media. In part this is because of self-imposed limits on the scope of support and regulation, in part because regulations have not been fully implemented and in part because the regulatory authorities have not always been free from charges of political partisanship.

The Enabler State

A system of state financial assistance to newspapers has existed during the Fifth Republic under governments of both Right and Left. This is one legacy of a wide-ranging programme of state support to the press which was established after the Liberation when post-war governments sought to establish a press system sheltered from what were perceived to be the undesirable consequences of the operation of the free market in the newspaper industry.

State aid to the press has taken the form of both direct financial support and indirect subsidies, with the latter much the more important of the two. Indirect support has embraced tax concessions on profits for investment purposes (for example the purchase of new equipment), a reduced Value Added Tax (VAT) rate on sales, various tax allowances and exemptions, and reductions in certain state tariffs (post, telegraph and telephone). Direct financial assistance has included a support fund for daily newspapers with low levels of advertising revenue. Since within the European Union the French system of state support has been among the most generous, it is reasonable to ask how effectively the system has functioned.

Critics of state aid have focused both on the principle and the practicalities of its operation. The objection on principle is that such aid has unjustifiably distorted the mechanisms of the free market, making newspapers less likely to take risks and to be dynamic and entrepreneurial, or to respond to changing social and economic circumstances. The practical criticism is that because it has been insufficiently targeted, state aid has done little to help newspapers with a weak financial base and a significant information function. At the same time, the system has been limited in scope. For example, there has been no state aid, either in the form of subsidy or preferential loans, to help in the foundation of new newspapers. Overall, therefore, the system has tended to favour the *status quo* rather than encouraging new initiatives.

Public sector radio and television have also received financial support from the state through the licence fee, the level of which is set by the government and approved by Parliament on an annual basis. Though the licence fee system is not technically a state grant to the broadcasting media, the principle of licence fee funding could be viewed as an attempt to shelter a part (and before the abolition of the state monopoly all) of the broadcasting sector from commercial pressures. However, against this one has to note that since the introduction of advertising on the ORTF channels in 1968, licence fee funding has not been the sole means of financing public sector television. Particularly since the break-up of the ORTF in 1974, the increased role of advertising in the funding of the public sector companies has severely limited the effectiveness of this method of finance in helping to promote a public sphere in television.

The Regulatory State

In addition to financial support for sections of the media, the state has been active in regulating the media during the Fifth Republic, especially the broadcasting sector. The two main areas of regulatory intervention by the state have concerned ownership and content.

For the first 25 years of the Fifth Republic the issue of ownership was scarcely a priority on the media policy agenda. It is true that immediately following the Liberation the state had introduced anti-trust legislation in the press sector. However, these rules were more honoured in the breach than in the observance as commercial concerns quickly came to outweigh regulatory proprieties in a declining newspaper market. For 40 years the anti-trust provisions remained largely unused by Fourth and Fifth Republic governments.

It was only during the Mitterrand presidency that the question of media ownership became a matter of salience on the policy agenda. This was for two main reasons. First, in the press sector the Hersant group had over the previous few years acquired a significant share of the newspaper market, largely through the acquisition of existing titles such as *Le Figaro*. The right-wing political sympathies of the Hersant newspapers were anathema to the Socialists and the government decided to act to curb the group's growing media power. A new press act was introduced by the Socialists in 1984 to limit concentration in the newspaper industry by setting permitted thresholds in both national and provincial markets. This created huge media and political controversy, with opponents arguing that the legislation was an illegitimate interference in the economic freedom of the press and a vindictive measure aimed specifically at Hersant. More importantly, the Constitutional Council ruled certain of its key provisions unconstitutional and non-retrospective in their application. The 1984 press act was revoked by the incoming right-wing government in 1986 and replaced with more liberal legislation on permitted shares of the market which any single group could own.

Second, economic liberalization of broadcasting following the abolition of the state monopoly had opened up market entry in this sector to press groups among others. The continuing decline of the newspaper industry had encouraged various press groups to expand out of their core activity and diversify into the growing sectors of private local radio and commercial television. Meanwhile commercial and industrial companies had also moved into the domestic audio-visual media sector, building up important stakes in terrestrial and cable television. These new players in the market diversified from their original spheres of non-media activity (for example, construction in the case of Bouygues) and used their power base in these economic areas as a launch pad into the burgeoning audio-visual media. With the potential for a few companies to establish dominant market positions across different media sectors, the state authorities acted to establish a framework for the regulation of ownership both within and across these sectors.

Complex rules based on market share and potential audience size were introduced in 1986 to govern mono-media and cross-media ownership, with the Constitutional Council playing a key role in the formulation of the legislation. The effect was the establishment of an elaborate anti-trust regime governing the whole communications sector (press, radio, terrestrial television and the new media of cable and satellite) and imposing limits on the development of multimedia groups. However, while these provisions may well have been precise from a purely statistical perspective, they were also extremely liberal and allowed significant mono-media holdings and cross-media diversification so as to promote the interests of French media companies in European and global markets.[23] Legislation introduced in 1994 further relaxed the ceilings on the maximum market share a company could possess.

The view that ownership of the media has to be regulated if they are to be pluralistic still retains a hold in French public policy, as can be seen from the stance adopted by the Constitutional Council and the legislative measures introduced by government. However, it is also clear that, more than half a century after the introduction of anti-trust legislation for the press, the media policy environment in France has changed beyond recognition. The decline of newspapers, expansion of the broadcasting media and advent of cable and satellite have shifted the balance away from the print media and towards their audio-visual counterparts. Public policy decisions have opened up the audio-visual sectors (new and old) to private players. Technological change and the corporate strategies of large companies have introduced a supranational dimension to policy making as media companies move across previously well-defended national boundaries, following corporate strategies based on the vertical integration and internationalization of their media interests.

In particular, recent French governments have been conscious that their domestic media companies are not particularly large by international standards. The argument in favour of allowing a high degree of concentration of media ownership and control (and minimizing foreign participation) has been justified on the grounds that this would allow French companies to compete on a more level playing field with other European, Japanese and American groups. The dilemma for French policy makers is that the national market is not large enough both to sustain a wide range of domestic media players and at the same time provide France with companies which can compete with the global giants on equal terms. Nor is the European Francophone market of much help in this respect. Much of the state's regulatory effort is now dominated by economic concerns: the need to promote French media companies in international markets. The result is a set of regulations which prioritize economic and industrial objectives at the expense of public sphere concerns with pluralism in ownership and control.

In addition to ownership regulations the state continues to impose rules on media content. These have been applied more to broadcasting than the press because of frequency scarcity and the impracticality for most of broadcasting's history of a free market in radio and television provision. As part of its public service remit, state monopoly television was supposed to be impartial in its political coverage. However, compliance with this obligation of impartiality clashed with the executive's willingness and power to intervene in news management. As long as broadcasting was regarded by ministers as part of the state apparatus, impartiality in political coverage remained in practice an elusive goal.

The creation of regulatory authorities for broadcasting following the 1982 legislation improved the situation, albeit gradually and unevenly.[24] One objective in creating a regulatory authority was to help protect broadcasting professionals such as journalists from illegitimate political pressures. By monitoring political output and publishing their findings, the regulatory authorities could seek to ensure that the media complied with their obligation to be impartial. Crucially, this depended on the regulatory authorities being regarded as independent and legitimate across the spectrum of political elites. Unfortunately, but perhaps predictably, this legitimization process proved highly problematic.

Between 1982 and 1989 no fewer than three different regulatory authorities succeeded each other: the High Authority (1982–86), the National Commission for Communication and Liberties (1986–89) and the Higher Audio-visual Council (1989–).[25] This turnover reflected the failure of the first two regulatory bodies to be regarded as independent of the governments which created them. The High Authority, for instance, was perceived by many on the right to be a tool of the Socialist government, while the National Commission for Communication and Liberties was reviled by the left for its alleged pro-right sympathies and publicly denounced by President Mitterrand in 1987.[26] Its successor, the Higher Audio-visual Council, has had a longer shelf life than its two predecessors combined and the fact that it was not replaced by Chirac on his accession to the presidency perhaps indicates an emerging elite consensus on the Higher Audio-visual Council's performance of its duties in the area of political information.

Greater balance in broadcast media coverage of mainstream political parties is certainly a welcome advance on the blatantly partisan coverage of the early years of the Fifth Republic. Against this, however, has to be weighed the reduced obligations in terms of political information across the broadcasting sector as a whole. While the heavily regulated public sector channels may be playing a more satisfactory public sphere role than in the past, many more lightly regulated services make little or no public sphere contribution. Moreover, much of the state's regulatory thrust in matters of content has been dominated by cultural rather than information concerns, in particular the desire to protect French culture from Anglo-American media product.

New Technology

Can new communication technologies assist in the creation of a mediatized public sphere in France, empowering users by giving them access to information previously restricted to elites? Early experience from other advanced societies, notably the United States, has suggested that technological developments like the Internet can lead to the emergence of new fora of political communication alongside the established mass media of press, radio and television. Such technologies allow a more direct form of communication both between political elites and voters and among voters themselves, bypassing the intermediary filters of media professionals such as journalists.

There is no doubt that technological developments have in the past had important consequences for the process of political communication in France. Major technical advances in the publishing industry and transportation infrastructure, for example, lay at the heart of the flourishing of the newspaper press in the late nineteenth century and the introduction into the market of what were to become mass circulation popular newspapers. The arrival of radio in the first half of the twentieth century and, even more so, the spread of television since the 1950s have radically altered the way in which political information has been disseminated and received.

The impact of more recent technological developments in the media is harder to assess. For example, while the introduction of new technology in the newspaper industry in the 1970s and 1980s had huge consequences for employment practices by revolutionizing publishing methods, it did not have a major influence in reducing the costs of entry into the newspaper market. New technology did not reverse the decline in circulations of daily newspapers, did not produce greater diversity of titles and tended to reinforce pre-existing patterns of press ownership and control.

In the audio-visual media, the desire to exploit new communications technology for economic and industrial purposes underpinned state-backed projects in cable and satellite in the first half of the 1980s. For example, the huge potential of fibre optic and switched star networks for the provision of a wide range of interactive services persuaded the French government to invest in an ambitious state-led national cable project between 1982 and 1986, which involved the participation of local authorities and private utility companies. Simultaneously, the state provided public resources for the construction and launch of a direct broadcasting satellite, TDF1, to ensure that France would not be left out of what was hoped would be a lucrative hi-tech market for satellite hardware.

None the less, cable and direct-to-home satellite are still not major players in television distribution in France. Despite heavy state-backing in the early 1980s and since then a more market-led approach, cable has so far made little impression. By the mid-1990s cable was available to about a quarter of French households, of which about a quarter actually subscribed to the service. This gave a national hook-up rate of well under ten per cent. Direct-to-home satellite broadcasting has had even less success. The reach of the new media remains constrained partly because of supply factors (for example, the high infrastructural investment costs for cable which means that it is still unavailable in many parts of the country) and partly because of lack of consumer demand. As a result of the low market penetration of cable and satellite, rolling news channels such as LCI and Euronews have had only a minor impact on the French audience.

The principal contemporary technological development in French television is digitalization. Digitalization allows for more information (for example, television channels) to be transmitted by cable, satellite and terrestrial transmission than current analogue forms of distribution. Digital technology not only improves quality of sound and picture, but also facilitates inter-activity between user and service provider. Various French media companies, including TF1 and Canal Plus, have invested heavily in digital technology in the 1990s in a bid not only to dominate what they hope will be a strong domestic market, but also to position themselves as important transnational players at the pan-European level. It is impossible to predict the impact of digitalization on the audio-visual media's political information function. More dedicated news channels are an obvious future development. It is noticeable, however, that much of the debate so far has concerned programme rights in areas such as sport and films. Commercial considerations are driving the transition to digital television in France, as evidenced by a discourse which emphasizes consumer choice rather than citizen empowerment.

The other major awaited technological development in the late twentieth century French media system are the information superhighways. It is widely believed that these will revolutionize the way in which information is transmitted by providing users with on-line access to a huge array of information services and opening up new lines of interactive communication. In contrast to previous high-tech developments in the communications area, the French government has not embraced a state-backed grand action plan for the construction of the information superhighways. The failure of the cable plan in the early 1980s, a more cautious approach generally to state *dirigisme* and the lack of public funds have all contributed to a more modest and flexible approach on the part of the government. However, one important similarity with previous high-tech developments is present. According to one commentator, 'French policy for Information Superhighways is ... driven by economic and industrial considerations. ... the main issue is not what people need and want, and what is the social utility of new infrastructures, but the place of French industry on the world market.'[27]

Apart from the now outdated Minitel, the current impact of on-line information services in France is not very great. The reach of the Internet, for example, is still extremely limited, with the technology largely being accessed by academics and researchers. By late 1996 there were only

230,000 machines connected to the Internet and barely one per cent of the population over 15 years old accessed Internet websites.[28] Indeed only 16 per cent of French households had access to a personal computer. Of course, low audience take-up is normal in the early stages of a technology's market entry. The established print and audiovisual media all took time to implant themselves as mass means of communication. Television, for example, began transmission in 1936 but did not fully achieve the status of a mass medium until more than a quarter of a century later. Moreover, it is likely that young people socialized in the computer era will increasingly use the Internet and other on-screen information services for political information purposes.

Low audience demand has not prevented political actors from participating as service providers on the new technology. Government ministries, Parliament and political parties among others have created web sites for the dissemination of information about their activities. The National Front, for instance, was 'ahead of other French parties in establishing a substantial site on the Internet'.[29] Yet for the moment the arrival of mainstream French political actors on the Internet seems more an act of symbolic representation – a desire to be seen to be in the vanguard of technological modernization – rather than a substantive contribution to the political communication process. In particular, it remains to be seen whether minority political groups marginalized by the traditional mass media will find the Internet a more democratic technology.

What is clear is that the traditional mass media of press, radio and television, with their journalistic intermediaries and filtering processes between politicians and audiences, will remain important actors in the political communication process for some considerable time to come. In fact, just as the arrival of television did not kill off radio or the press, it is unlikely that new information technologies will ever wholly supplant the established print and audio-visual media. In addition, several publishing groups, national and regional newspapers, radio stations and television companies have established their own web-sites, some using sound and video as well as text, in an attempt to benefit commercially from the provision of new on-line services and not to be displaced as purveyors of information as a result of a technological shift. The unanswered, and as yet unanswerable, question is what impact new information technology will have in reshaping the mediatized public sphere in France.

Conclusion

In several key respects the structures and functioning of the French media system have changed beyond recognition since the establishment of the

Fifth Republic in 1958. After a hesitant start in the 1950s, television implanted itself as a mass medium during the de Gaulle presidency. The incremental expansion of television supply during the 1960s and 1970s (one new channel in each decade) was followed by a blossoming of additional channels during the Mitterrand presidency as an era of scarcity gave way to an age of comparative abundance. New means of signal delivery such as cable and satellite broke the technical straitjacket of television's formative years, while digitalization will further increase the amount of television programming which can be distributed. Radio provision has also grown during the 40-year life-span of the regime, flourishing particularly in the early 1980s. In contrast, newspaper circulations, especially of those papers produced in Paris, have declined, though perhaps not as dramatically as one might have anticipated in the light of the audio-visual media's growing market penetration.

In terms of the role of the media as a public sphere, some developments have been positive. These have included a reduction in state control of television's news agenda, the creation of a regulatory authority for the broadcasting sector and a greater emphasis on the need for political impartiality in broadcast news output. In the light of the history of partisan political control of television and the previous unwillingness of the government to establish a 'hands off' relationship with broadcasting management, the abolition of the monopoly in 1982 represented an important symbolic and substantive step away from state ownership and control. Other developments appear negative. These include the reduced importance of public service values in television and politicians' emphasis on image and packaging in political communication.

At the beginning of the regime the main impediment to a mediatized public sphere was political control of broadcasting by the state. Now the problem lies more with the commodification of much media product in an increasingly commercialized sector of economic activity. Positive aspects of state activity through the performance of its enabling and regulatory roles have mitigated but not prevented this commercializing trend. The economic well-being of French media companies in transnational and international markets has tended to prevail as a policy objective over the importance of pluralism and diversity within the domestic market. In short, the French experience during the Fifth Republic demonstrates the difficulties rather than the possibilities of creating and maintaining a mediatized public sphere which avoids the pitfalls of state control and market domination.

NOTES

1. Roland Cayrol, *Médias et Démocratie: La Dérive* (Paris: Presses de Sciences Po, 1997).
2. Jürgen Habermas, *The Structural Transformation of the Public Sphere* (Cambridge: Polity Press, 1989). The work was first published in Germany in 1962.
3. Nicholas Garnham, 'The Media and the Public Sphere', in Craig Calhoun (ed.), *Habermas and the Public Sphere* (Cambridge, MA and London: The MIT Press, 1992).
4. Oliver Boyd-Barrett and Chris Newbold (eds.), *Approaches to Media* (London: Arnold, 1995), pp.229–68; James Curran, 'Mass Media and Democracy Revisited', in James Curran and Michael Gurevitch (eds.), *Mass Media and Society* (Second Edition) (London: Arnold, 1996).
5. Raymond Kuhn, *The Media in France* (London: Routledge, 1995), pp.165–84.
6. Jacques Gerstlé, *La communication politique* (Paris: Presses Universitaires de France, 1993), p.108.
7. Annick Cojean and Frank Eskenazi, *La folle histoire des radios libres* (Paris: Grasset, 1986).
8. On ethnic minority radio see Richard L. Derderian, 'Broadcasting from the Margins: Minority Ethnic Radio in Contemporary France', in Alec G. Hargreaves and Mark McKinney (eds.), *Post-Colonial Cultures in France* (London: Routledge, 1997).
9. Geoff Hare, 'The Law of the Jingle, or a Decade of Change in French Radio', in R. Chapman and N. Hewitt (eds.), *Popular Culture and Mass Communication in Twentieth Century France* (Lampeter: The Edwin Mellen Press, 1992).
10. Marcel Machill, 'Le paysage radiophonique français', *Médiaspouvoirs*, Vols.43–44 (1996), pp.161–75. The quotation is from the article's conclusion on p.174.
11. Pierre Albert, *La presse française* (Paris: La documentation française, 1990).
12. Yves Guillauma, *La presse en France* (Paris: La Découverte: 1988), p.124.
13. Louis Guéry, *La Presse Régionale et Locale* (Paris: Centre de Formation et de Perfectionnement des Journalistes, 1992), p.89.
14. Jean-Marie Charon, 'Cinquante ans de presse française', *Médiaspouvoirs*, Vols.39–40, (1995), pp.53–61.
15. Noël Nel, *Mai 1981 Mitterrand président* (Paris: La documentation française, 1995), p.25.
16. Gérard Leblanc, 'La Décision des Indécis', *Médiaspouvoirs*, Vol.38 (1995), pp.23–9.
17. Susan Hayward, 'Television and the Presidential Elections April–May 1988', in John Gaffney (ed.), *The French Presidential Elections of 1988* (Aldershot: Gower, 1989).
18. Kuhn, pp.65–9.
19. Jérome Bourdon, *Histoire de la télévision sous de Gaulle* (Paris: Anthropos/INA,1990); Institut Charles de Gaulle, *De Gaulle et les médias* (Paris: Plon, 1994).
20. Claude Durieux, *La Télécratie* (Paris: Tema, 1976).
21. Comité d'Histoire de la Télévision, *Mai 68 à l'ORTF* (Paris: La documentation française, 1987).
22. On the concept of primary definition see Stuart Hall *et al.*, *Policing the Crisis* (London: Macmillan, 1978), pp.57–60.
23. Raymond Kuhn, 'France', in Vicki MacLeod (ed.), *Media Ownership and Control in the age of convergence* (London: International Institute of Communications, 1996), pp.49–63.
24. Richard Barbrook, *Media Freedom* (London: Pluto, 1995), pp.148-189.
25. Laurence Franceschini, *La régulation audiovisuelle en France* (Paris: Presses Universitaires de France, 1995).
26. On the work of the High Authority see Michèle Cotta, *Les miroirs de Jupiter* (Paris: Fayard, 1986).
27. Thierry Vedel, 'French Policy for Information Superhighways: The End of High-Tech Colbertism', unpublished paper, p.3.
28. Philippe Bailly, 'Le Web en quête d'organisation des contenus', *Médiaspouvoirs*, Vols.43–44, (1996), pp.53–9; Jean-Louis Constanza and Ignacio Garcia Alvez, 'L'évolution de l'Internet: mythes et réalités', *Médiaspouvoirs*, Vols.43–44, (1996), pp.35–46.
29. Christopher Flood, 'National Populism', in Christopher Flood and Laurence Bell (eds.), *Political Ideologies in Contemporary France* (London: Pinter, 1997), p.105.

The Media and Intra-Party Democracy: 'New' Labour and the Clause Four Debate in Britain

DOMINIC WRING

This study considers the role and increasing influence of the media in internal Labour Party affairs. Consideration is given to the activities of three 'auxiliary' institutions that became central actors within party debates during the leadership of Neil Kinnock. These are the external agenda-setting print media popular amongst party members; the opinion research based on questioning of the electorate or, more specifically, those seen as potential Labour supporters; and, managing both the media and research, the burgeoning cadre of specialist advisers and aides working for the leader. The latter part of the study examines the defining moment of Tony Blair's three-year period as Labour leader in opposition, that is, his successful attempt to re-write the party's statements of aims and values including the revered Clause Four. It will be shown how Blair used the reformed party structures bequeathed him by predecessor Kinnock to manage discussion and deliver a victory not certain at the outset of the debate. In winning the argument, the leadership demonstrated how its powerful position derives not just from its place in the party hierarchy but also from its ability to use the media to structure and control debate.

Introduction

On 29 April 1995 Labour held a special interim conference to conclude a discussion over the party constitution begun six months earlier by leader Tony Blair. In front of the assembled delegates was a single motion calling for the replacement of the 75-year-old clause that contains the organizational 'mission statement' of aims and values. The resolution, carried by a comfortable margin, succeeded in overturning a restatement of faith in the old constitution passed at the 1994 Annual Conference, paradoxically the event which had launched the debate. More remarkable than the special conference result was the symbolism of a major Labour meeting slow hand-clapping National Union of Mineworkers' leader Arthur Scargill for questioning the legitimacy of the proceedings. The treatment of Scargill, who ten years previously won Annual Conference support in spite of strong opposition from the Kinnock leadership, was indicative of a changed party culture. This perception was reinforced by the warm response given Blair and his supporters. The reasons for this transformation, and the contribution to it of political marketing, form the basis of discussion below.

The notion that there is an inherent tendency towards the centralization of power within a party was first popularized by Robert Michels. In his influential study of the German Social Democrats, Michels argued that organizational democracy was a practical impossibility due to the inherent tendency of the hierarchy or leadership to centralize power within itself. This, he argued was 'the iron law of oligarchy'.[1] Significantly Michels, in developing his thesis, noted the importance of the media: 'The press constitutes a potent instrument for the conquest, the preservation and the consolidation of power on the part of the leaders'.

Applied to Labour Michels' thesis appeared to have some validity, at least until the trauma of 1931 when the then leader and prime minister Ramsay MacDonald deserted his party to set up in coalition government with the Conservatives. Since then the internal politics of the organization have been characterized as a vibrant, sometimes unmanageable 'broad church' coalition of interests, though the varying success of leadership in maintaining control of the party has been discussed by McKenzie, and by Shaw.[2] This analysis is concerned with examining how and why the present 'New' Labour leadership have been able successfully to subjugate dissident factions in a way which would appear to give renewed relevance to Michels' thesis. Particular attention will be paid to the way certain agenda-setting media have been used by the main agents responsible for the party's transformation.

The initial part of the discussion will examine the organizational legacy Neil Kinnock bequeathed to his successors John Smith and Tony Blair. It will be shown how new structures consolidated during the marketing-driven Policy Review enabled the leadership to exert considerable control over a once notoriously fractious party, to the extent that Labour rather than the Conservatives now enjoys a reputation for being disciplined and centralized. The piece will conclude by examining the debate surrounding Tony Blair's successful attempt to re-write the aims of the party as set out in its constitution. It will be demonstrated how Blair was able to use the new institutional arrangements to win the case for a revision of the document and, in particular, its revered Clause Four. Arguably the defining moment in Blair's three years as Leader of the Opposition, the move proved critical to the relaunch of the party as 'New' Labour.

The Kinnock Legacy

The Policy Review of 1987–90 marked a watershed in modern Labour Party history. An exercise that repositioned the Party nearer what was perceived to be the electoral centreground, the Review served as an important strategic turning point. Labour embraced a more intensive, marketing-focused approach to campaigning. Consequently the use of professional research and consultancy, once limited to party publicity activities, began to inform policy formulation.[3] This change, made in the aftermath of a third consecutive election defeat, has proved to be of critical importance to the centralization and retention of power by each of the three successive leadership teams that have presided since 1987.

The function of 'agenda-setting' is central to understanding why the Policy Review and subsequent leadership exercises have played such an important role in restructuring the party. Cohen distinguished the core feature of this concept when he wrote: 'the press may not be successful much of the time in telling people what to think, but it is stunningly successful in telling its readers what to think about'.[4] Having been popularized in a celebrated study of election campaigning,[5] Steven Lukes adopted the phrase 'agenda-setting' to identify what he called one of the three 'faces' of power that determine outcomes within an organization.[6] Similarly, in their assessments of internal Labour Party bargaining procedures, both Minkin and Koelble point to the importance of agenda-setting in framing internal debate.[7] Both studies concentrate on analysing organizational decision-making during the 1970s and early 1980s, a period characterized by 'crisis management' and dominated by a concerted attempt to shift power away from the Labour leadership at Westminster. Those in the vanguard calling for reform, mainly left-wingers active in the trade unions and at grassroots' level, focused their efforts on setting the agenda of Labour's Annual Conference. As Henry Drucker noted, this supreme decision-making body, labelled the 'parliament of the movement' by former leader Clement Attlee, meant a delegatory form of self-governance embodying a commitment to internal democracy.[8]

When it was founded there was a degree of accountability within the Labour Party largely absent in the more hierarchical organizations of political opponents, some state institutions and commercial firms including those owning and running mass media interests. An organization whose political influence has grown with the progress of the twentieth century, the mass media have traditionally been viewed with hostility by many Labour partisans and trades unionists. Ironically the same external media now play an important role in the internal governance of the party, helping the leadership maintain control of the organization and dominate debate. This development has had important consequences for Labour's previously federal, participatory structures.

To better understand the changed nature of party organization the next sections will consider the increasingly central role played by three 'auxiliary' institutions in shaping and determining decision-making outcomes.[9] First, and most importantly, there has been the growth in size and importance of a leadership bureau of full-time staff and part-time advisers responsible for implementing and, increasingly, devising strategy. With the emergence of this elite there has been a parallel growth in the party's reliance on another auxiliary in the form of a select group of external media contacts. In return for privileged access, these media outlets have been responsible for the subtle conduit of pro-leadership viewpoints to the general and, more importantly, internal party publics. Finally, in terms of the input side to the debate, there has been increasing preoccupation on the part of the hierarchy and its bureaucracy with the attitudes of those deemed to be floating voters and thus essential to any electoral success. These opinions, as enunciated in polling research, have guided the thinking of the leadership, its agents and media outlets to the extent that the views of potential Labour supporters have manifested themselves as another highly influential auxiliary institution.

The New Party Machinery

The strategic changes forged during and after the Policy Review helped centralize power within the Labour leadership who, by skilful use of external media channels, were able to co-ordinate internal agenda-setting and continually outmanoeuvre rival factions and malcontents. The notion of increased professionalism aiding the emergence of elitist parties is not new. In the 1960s, political scientist Leon Epstein drew attention to this relationship when he used the term 'contagion from the right' to describe the possible emergence of American-style cadre parties in Europe.[10] More recently Panebianco has focused on the growing importance of the 'electoral professionals'.[11] Writing at the time of Labour's Policy Review, *Tribune* editor Phil Kelly forecast the potential beginnings of such a realignment of power in the party:

> If it becomes a mass party which takes its membership seriously, and involves them in policy-making and implementation, then it will need a system of internal management based on consensus. If it descends into a media-oriented marketing organization for top politicians, then it will need internal discipline which will make the fifties seem liberal by comparison.[12]

Prior to the late 1980s agenda-setting in the Labour Party was chiefly understood to mean the ability of leaders, groups and factions to influence policy and organizational decisions through the mobilization of internal opinion. The party's strategic development has intensified these actors' reliance on external mass media as a vehicle for political communication. This relationship has transformed the basis of internal agenda-setting and contributed to an erosion in the once strong horizontal decision-making structures, most obviously the Annual Conference and Constituency Labour Parties (CLPs).[13] Where opinion formers once strove to put their case across in labour movement papers like *Voice of the Unions* and *Tribune*, they now seek to use sympathetic external media such as *The Guardian*, *The Independent* and *Daily Mirror* to disseminate their viewpoint. Given its already privileged position, a leadership with coherent strategies has significant leverage over party rivals. This advantage has been enhanced by the growing role of the mass media, an aspect of contemporary politics recognized in two of the most thorough recent investigations into Labour Party structures. Observing the evolution of the party in the early 1990s, Lewis Minkin was swift to identify the growing presidentialization of the organization. Referring to its leader, he noted:

> His office now housed an unprecedented proliferation of aides, assistants and advisers, with an overview of, and involvement in, all aspects of Party activity and all dimensions of the links with the unions. In effect there was now an Executive Office of the Leader ... [providing] the basis of a centralized power structure unique in Labour Party history.'[14]

The 'Executive', that is, the Leader's Office at Westminster, derived its political authority from close working relationships with Kinnock. Senior Office aides, together with those in the party's Campaigns' Directorate and with senior marketing advisers, formed what Shaw calls the new 'strategic community'.[15] Together these overlapping bodies have helped centralize power within the party to an even greater extent than that managed by Harold Wilson and his famed kitchen cabinet.[16] The success of this strategy has been reflected in elections to the 29-member National Executive Committee (NEC), the institution at the apex of the extra-parliamentary party. The number of leadership critics has slowly eroded from a majority in the late 1970s to the point in 1993-94 when all dissident voices were temporarily voted off the body.

Another aspect to the centralization of power has been the increasing prominence of the political public relations expert or 'spin doctor' as epitomized by Peter Mandelson. First as Director of Labour Party Campaigns and Communications in the second half of the 1980s and subsequently as MP for Hartlepool, Minister without Portfolio and a confidant of Tony Blair, Mandelson's name has become synonymous with controversy.[17] It is difficult to think of any other Labour official since former General Secretary Morgan Philips who has been regarded with similar awe by both allies and opponents in the party. Most of this comment has focused on the supposed skill and deviousness of Mandelson as an adviser. But much of it fails to appreciate, or otherwise obscures the reality that his position of strength derives from a close working relationship with the leader, in an evolving political culture which increasingly affords the mass media a greater influence over party affairs. It is perhaps significant that Arthur Scargill, in drawing up his blueprint for his own rival Socialist Labour Party, acknowledged the power of New Labour 'spin doctors' as one of the reasons for breaking with his old colleagues.[18]

The Media of Agenda-Setting

In tandem with its growing influence within the party, the bureaucracy has attempted to mobilize opinion in favour of the leadership through the cultivation of external media contacts. This section discusses the way in which this activity has restructured debate and accountability within the party and further aided the centralization of power.

Before the Policy Review, agenda-setting within the Labour Party centred on influencing decisions made by Annual Conference and implemented in the interim by its NEC. Public debate centred around left journals *Tribune*, *New Statesman* and now defunct party titles like *Labour Weekly* and *New Socialist*. After 1987, as the strategic orientation of the party began to change, the potential influence of external media broadly favourable to Labour increased. Since then newspapers with an anti-Conservative bias like *The Guardian* and *Daily Mirror* have become important for the dissemination of new ideas and thinking throughout the party and especially within the elite at Westminster and CLP level. In addition such material often serves as a useful cue for broadcast media reports of internal Labour business.

The Guardian, collectively owned by the Scott Trust, regularly features writers sympathetic to the liberal left and the Blair leadership in particular. Recently these have included John Gray, Geoff Mulgan, Martin Kettle, and Chair of the Trust Hugo Young. Together with much of the newspaper's political coverage in the period 1992-95, these columnists have tended to exhibit a positive attitude towards the 'modernization' of Labour project. Admittedly there are contributors hostile to 'New' Labour such as Francis Wheen, Paul Foot and Steve Bell, but their opinions tend to diverge from the newspaper's editorials. When set against the overt partisanship of pro-Conservative qualities *The Times* and *Daily Telegraph* it is unsurprising that *The Guardian* fills a void in the market with its support for Labour and, on certain occasions, the Liberal Democrats. However, when considered in intra-party terms, this coverage has added significance because it invariably favours the Labour 'modernizer' position as opposed to what have been collectively labelled 'traditionalists'.[19]

The other major Labour-supporting newspaper, the *Daily Mirror*, has a long history of endorsing successive party leaderships. During the 1995

Annual Conference the title and its political editor John Williams were particularly strong in their advocacy of the leadership position following the education debate, the most controversial of the week.[20] The paper has also co-sponsored the official Labour Party 'Red Rose' tour designed to attract new members and, in theory at least, more readers. Despite occasional disagreements, such as the call by the *Daily Mirror* for the resignation of Harriet Harman following the MP's decision to send her son to a selective school, editorials have tended enthusiastically to endorse the positions of Tony Blair and his supporters.

Both *The Guardian* and *Daily Mirror* enjoy circulations well in excess of an individual Labour membership estimated to be in the region of 300,000 to 350,000. Predictably there is considerable shared allegiance to the party and those titles deemed most supportive of it. Seyd and Whiteley calculate 35 per cent of members read *The Guardian*, 27 per cent the *Daily Mirror/Record*, seven per cent *The Independent* and 15 per cent others. Only 13 per cent read no national newspaper.[21] The first two titles alone boast more members as readers than the combined sales of Labour-supporting publications like *Tribune, New Statesman, Labour Left Briefing, Chartist* and *Red Pepper*, all of which have run editorials critical of the leadership from a left perspective in the period between 1992 and 1995. Whilst these titles rely on small circulations of a few thousand, *The Guardian* alone sells between 400,000 and 500,000 copies per day and has an estimated readership of at least twice that. As the Labour Party metamorphoses from an organization based upon strong horizontal structures into a more top-down leadership driven vehicle, the potentially pivotal role of these national newspapers becomes more obvious. This is especially the case as the party moves towards embracing 'One Member, One Vote' for the selection of parliamentary candidates, leadership elections and referenda on constitutional and policy matters.

The growing links between Labour leaders and their supporters in the press provide them with an important source of practical as well as psychological support. Additionally the intensification in contacts between media and party has helped cement the relationship between journalists and the new core of political professionals, some of whom are one and the same. This has had a significant impact on the culture of the party, with the emergent 'strategic community' conveying a very different impression of Labour to that previously presented by the affiliates in the trade union movement. This increasing professionalization of politics, and the central importance it attaches to deliberations between middle-class graduates on the Labour frontbench and in the media, signals a change of emphasis in an organization whose proletarian heritage and image used to differentiate it from rival parties.[22]

The Importance of Marketing Research

Private polling, that is, opinion research commissioned by parties, is not new to British politics. Nevertheless the importance attached to this form of data as a source of electoral feedback has grown in recent years and is borne out by an increase in the amount as well as the type of polls being commissioned. Where parties once relied on quantitative opinion research methods such as the large-scale survey, they are now also funding ongoing qualitative studies of voter attitudes in the form of focus groups. Typically these focus groups consist of about six to ten people sharing a weak partisanship and/or similar socio-economic background. A trained moderator facilitates a recorded discussion which aims to explore voters' deeper seated value and attitude structures in order to put the answers given to quantitative surveys in perspective.

Parties have long used small group discussions in their electioneering work: the inter-war period saw the Conservatives holding cottage coffee mornings whilst Labour relied on impromptu back street meetings to target the electorally important group of women voters. Though both efforts were primarily propagandist in intent, they constituted a potentially instructive source of feedback. In the strict sense of the term, focus group research became a strategic reality for parties with the advent of more adventurous election advertising campaigns in the 1960s and 1970s.[23] Interest in these methods intensified during the 1980s when the Conservatives experimented with various qualitative tools and the Labour-run Greater London Council used similar methods to some effect in a memorable attempt to stave off its own abolition.[24]

During the Kinnock leadership, focus group research became an important means by which Labour monitored changing trends in popular opinion. From 1985 to the 1987 election qualitative studies of public attitudes were commissioned on an ad hoc basis. Later, during the Policy Review, focus group data relating the opinions of floating voters became integral to debate.[25] These results, together with quantitative survey data, helped to provide some of the momentum behind subsequent changes in policy and organization. It was a factor Kinnock acknowledged as crucial to the exercise because, as he saw it, the process was 'reinforced periodically by using the Shadow Communications Agency to give presentations which … assisted in the efforts to sustain the movement of the Review in the desired direction'.[26]

Similarly, in the aftermath of the 1992 election defeat, focus group findings once again became an important source of information for Labour leaders trying to make sense of the result. If anything the deep scepticism towards the accuracy of traditional polling evident following the 1992 campaign[27] has created a climate in which greater value is attached to the findings of qualitative based political research. This has had a significant impact on strategic debates inside the Labour Party.

The rest of this account turns to discuss more recent political developments, specifically the six month debate over the Labour Party constitution that took place between late 1994 and early 1995. For historian Brian Brivati the issues raised in this period underlined Labour's past organizational 'conservatism' and attachment to a set of institutional arrangements which, he argued, had been 'retained because of their historical importance rather than their contemporary relevance.'[28] Central to this discussion were disagreements over Clause Four. Despite being just a part of the constitution, the extract was the only section of the document subjected to real scrutiny and argument. Indeed in discussing the outcome of the debate, media commentators frequently spoke of Tony Blair's having been successful in re-writing Clause Four (part IV) rather than the whole statement of aims that defined the party.

Clause Four

Since the Labour Party constitution was formally drafted in 1918 its fourth clause has traditionally been regarded as the organizational mission statement. The importance attached to the declaration was underlined in the late 1950s when Clause Four (part IV) began to appear on each annual issue of party membership cards.[29] Heavily symbolic, these sentences provide the backdrop to one of the most contentious debates to take place in the history of the party.

The Controversy over Clause Four

The importance of Clause Four or, more specifically, part IV derives from its stated aim of achieving a more equitable society through the pursuit of public ownership programmes. Drawn up by leading Labour intellectual Sidney Webb in 1918, the statement reflected the party's aspiration to emancipate people via greater socialization of the economy. Following the end of the Attlee administration in 1951 it became clear not every Labour politician agreed with the aim of Clause Four, by now widely interpreted as a call for the extension of nationalization in light of the government programme implemented during the late 1940s. So-called 'revisionist' objections to the notion of realizing party goals through state ownership formed the basis of Anthony Crosland's influential book *The Future of Socialism* (1956).[30]

Following Labour's third successive election defeat in 1959, leader Hugh Gaitskell moved to try and change the wording of Clause Four in the belief that party policy on nationalization was electorally unsaleable at a time of perceived economic affluence and security. In his attempts to change the constitution, Gaitskell found himself blocked by a powerful coalition inside the party consisting of trades unionists and left-wingers. Though he ultimately failed in his bid to delete the wording, Gaitskell nevertheless succeeded in showcasing and making Clause Four central to the party's identity.

Though the party card continued to retain the Clause, few subsequent policy pronouncements made use of the wording. Following the Policy Review of the late 1980s public ownership as a strategy of economic management was abandoned as a priority for an incoming Labour government. After the 1992 general election indifference on the part of some towards Clause Four began to turn into outright hostility. Bill Jordan, President of the Amalgamated Engineering Union, was vocal in his call for the scrapping of the wording.[31] Soon after, Campaigns Co-ordinator Jack Cunningham also urged the abandonment of Clause Four.[32] The following year, in the middle of the so-called 'Clintonization' debate over whether Labour should move further into the political centreground, the idiosyncratic MP Frank Field declared his opposition to Clause Four,[33] a view echoed by an editorial in *The Times* a week later.[34]

Speculation over a possible re-write of the constitution increased with the publication of a pamphlet by leading modernizer Jack Straw questioning the party wisdom of relying on the by now 75-year-old Clause.[35] Influential support for Straw came from a Fabian Society inquiry into the party constitution presided over by Lord (Peter) Archer which pointedly refused to include the old wording in its proposed revised version of the document.[36] Those pressing for reform were joined by Roy Hattersley[37] and eventually, in a later but symbolically important intervention, former leader Neil Kinnock who concluded his BBC television documentary *Tomorrow's Socialism* by making reference to the issue.[38]

Despite the obvious enthusiasm of some in the party for changing the constitution, Clause Four was reaffirmed at the 1993 Annual Conference. Support for the old wording could even be found in the key modernizer journal *Renewal*.[39] For his part Labour leader John Smith who succeeded Kinnock was decidedly agnostic in public when asked about the matter.[40] His attitude appeared to dampen speculation about the possibility of reform up until his untimely death in 1994. When Tony Blair, the favoured candidate to succeed Smith to the Labour leadership, was asked by David Frost whether he would press for changes to the party constitution he replied: 'I don't think anyone actually wants the abolition of Clause Four to be the priority of the Labour Party at the moment. I don't think that anyone is saying now, in the run up to an election, that this is what we should focus on. The vast majority of the British people don't sit out there and debate the intricacies of the Labour Party constitution.'[41] Blair's sentiments appeared to reflect mainstream opinion within the party. As seasoned political commentator Paul Anderson pointed out during a leadership election campaign which itself had followed on from the momentous decision to adopt 'One Member, One Vote': '... no one is suggesting that further reforms of the Labour constitution are on the cards this side of an election'.[42]

Within three months of taking up the party leadership Blair changed his mind and, in his first Annual Conference address at the helm, publicly stated his intention to go for a re-write of Clause Four. Declaring 'Let us say what we mean and mean what we say', Blair never mentioned the Clause by name during the speech, choosing to rely on his press officers to point out the specifics to assembled broadcasters and journalists. If the declaration excited the media it did not move delegates in formal debate two days later. Proposed by Glasgow Maryhill CLP delegate Jim Mearns, a motion calling for the reaffirmation of Clause Four led to impassioned speeches from defenders including David Winnick MP and opponents, notably communication workers' union leader Alan Johnson and modernizing MP Denis MacShane. The motion was passed by a narrow margin, the front-page of *The Guardian* tersely reporting 'Vote for past defies leader'.[43] Inside the same edition, the setback was reported to have been 'airily dismissed' by the Blair camp. The next time the subject came to be debated by a national Labour conference the way in which the agenda was framed would be considerably more favourable to the leadership.

The Momentum behind Blair

In putting their case for reform of Clause Four, modernizers such as Blair argued Labour needed to update the party constitution to show it embodied 'a radical and realistic vision of democratic socialism for the next millennium'.[44] Adopting a similar tone Janet Anderson, Secretary of the Tribune Group of MPs, argued the need for an effective 'mission statement':

> At a recent meeting of the Tribune Group, the editor of *Tribune* Newspaper said he would be worried if the debate about Clause Four became simply one about 'marketing' the party. But that is precisely what we have to do. We have to persuade people to our point of view. Every time we campaign, we seek to market the Labour Party ... But, in order to do it, we need a clear message of what we stand for.[45]

In addition to the apparent electoral capital to be made out of the exercise, a successful rewrite would likely increase Blair's status both within the party and with the general public at large.

In their plans to reform Clause Four, the leadership had a considerable organizational advantage over their opponents not least because they were able to use party funds and guaranteed television airtime to support their campaigning. Two editions of the *Labour Party News (LPN)*, the regular publication mailed to all members, ran prominent features on the debate. Despite the absence of an officially sanctioned alternative to the existing Clause Four, the special issue distributed in January 1995 included contributions from nine leading party figures broadly favourable to change with only three against. The following edition of *LPN* in March reported on the soundings Tony Blair had been taking with regional meetings of Labour members. Mirroring the Clinton approach to campaigning, the Labour leadership also commissioned a video that was sent out to complement local branch discussions of a specially drawn up Clause Four consultation document. Despite the apparent openness of the process, sections of the party were concerned about the implications of the debate. One member, John Solomon, summed up this body of opinion when he noted:

> We were bombarded by propaganda from Walworth Road, including a special edition of *LP News*, the content of which was largely in favour of change and a glossy covered booklet. There was also a colourful video to help with the questions, even laying out the time which should be spent in replying to each section of the values. Peculiarly enough, during all this time there were no proposals of any actual change to be made to Clause Four; no real substance to consider, only a reiteration of values and three vague issues to which a response had to be made. So much for weeks of consultation; a very costly exercise, a softening up process, known in marketing terminology as 'demand plasticity'. (I)t was a marketing ploy. And this massive consultation (sic) programme was going to be processed by March 15th? Poor Walworth Road. How did they manage or did they? In fact, the new Clause IV was made public on March 13th. Many of us wish we could receive our renewed L(abour) P(arty) membership cards as quickly as that.[46]

Blair and the modernizing camp also benefited from something they could not have foreseen for certain: a divided opposition.

The surprise when the leader launched debate over Clause Four was visible later that evening on the *Midnight Special* programme.[47] Featuring two Labour MPs closely aligned on the centre-left, the discussion led them to differing interpretations of the day's event. For his part Peter Hain recognized that to mount a serious campaign against the leadership might undermine Blair's authority in the party and with the wider public. By contrast Jean Corston lamented the debate was taking place at all, primarily because it deflected attention away from what she perceived to be the issues and problems facing her constituents.

The cautious approach of Corston and Hain was mirrored by the newsletter of their parliamentary 'What's Left' caucus. This recognized the dilemma facing the Labour left: should they campaign to keep, reword or add to the existing Clause Four?[48] The latter positions, respectively championed by the joint *Tribune* and *New Statesman* editorial teams and London MEP (Member of the European Parliament) Stan Newens, helped complicate the debate. The other viewpoint was supported by the appropriately named 'Defend Clause Four' campaign which received backing from MPs and MEPs in the left-wing Socialist Campaign Group together with a few members of other factions, most notably right-winger Gwyneth Dunwoody and centrist Andrew MacKinlay.[49] Like the other left campaigns, publicity material from the Group stressed the need to maintain the party's stated belief in public ownership as a way 'to realize our commitment to equality, freedom and social justice'.[50]

Blair, then, enjoyed a significant advantage over his opponents given his organizational resources and the relative simplicity and unified theme of his case. In addition, the modernizers' position was once again augmented by use of media sources and opinion poll data.

The Use of Agenda-setting

The wisdom of Blair's decision to re-write Clause Four appeared to be challenged by Gallup opinion poll results published in the middle of the debate. These findings contrasted with earlier MORI data which had suggested floating voters would be more likely to support Labour if the Clause was changed.[51] Reported in the *Daily Telegraph*,[52] the Gallup findings indicated 37 per cent of the general public supported the original wording, 28 per cent did not with 35 per cent undecided. The results, whilst inconclusive, could have suggested public ownership might be a strong campaign theme for Labour. Ironically, writing on the same day in another newspaper not generally popular with party members, veteran columnist Keith Waterhouse developed this point when he commented:

> What privatization now means, in the public mind, is a licence to print money to pay the bonanza and other jackpot benefits of chief executives. Privatization is now private in the sense of hands off, keep out. And Tony Blair chooses this moment to tour the country persuading the brothers and sisters to ditch Clause 4. Some sense of timing.[53]

In marked contrast to the Gallup polling figures, a previous Fabian Society-sponsored research series of relevance to the Clause Four debate had received much greater attention in the anti-Conservative press. Commissioned during the Smith leadership, the pamphlets were written by modernizing MP Giles Radice and Fabian Director of Research Stephen Pollard. Each used focus groups to analyse the political attitudes of voters in marginal seats who had considered supporting Labour in 1992 but in the event stayed Conservative. The work made an impact by, as Tony Blair put it in opening his 1945 anniversary lecture, 'turning the attention of the party towards lost voters in the South'.[54] Reflecting their geographical bias the series was known as 'Southern Discomfort' and provided Labour modernizers with a supply of useful data. All three editions proved influential in focusing minds on their call for the symbolic dropping of Clause Four as a demonstration of the party's desire to change. Their importance in the subsequent debate was later acknowledged by the Society in its promotional literature:

> The Fabian Society paved the way for the introduction of 'One Member, One Vote' and the new statement of aims and values which replaced the old Clause Four. Our path-breaking series of pamphlets on the attitudes of swing voters in the south of England – the 'Southern Discomfort' series – prepared the ground for the modernization of Labour's Constitution and policies.'[55]

Whilst the official National Executive Committee report referred to the party's loss of electoral support amongst a multitude of demographic groups,[56] the pamphlets focused on people in social categories C1/C2, resident in target seats mainly in the south-east, aged 25–50 years old with children. Despite this narrow base and the problems associated with extrapolating too much from focus groups, the material appeared in several reports and features, creating the impression that it was a scientific type source of considerable authority. Quite apart from the choice of sample selection and dangers of undertaking qualitative research in isolation from traditional forms of polling, little was made of the potential psychological need of participants to justify their previous vote for the Conservatives with overly negative commentaries about Labour.

More relevant to the immediate debate over Clause Four were the research exercises commissioned by some of the trades unions. Like the *Southern Discomfort* work, the results appeared to reinforce the modernizer case. The first survey research, organized by the consultancy Union Communications, suggested as many as 72 per cent of members in affiliated unions wanted the constitutional changes to be made.[57] Another poll, conducted for the Amalgamated Engineering and Electrical Union (AEEU), resulted in a response of 91 per cent in favour of revising the Clause. Considered in relation to the conflicting Gallup data in the *Daily*

Telegraph,[58] the statistics support the notion that the question was a key factor in determining outcome, an issue of importance when it came to the decision by others to ballot their memberships. The move to hold what effectively amounted to a referendum on the party constitution was a significant step away from a representative to a more direct form of internal democracy. Like the switch to 'One Member, One Vote' for leadership and candidate elections, the move has implications for the future conduct and outcome of party debates.

The communications' workers union, the only union to go to ballot, won a significant vote of confidence for the modernizers' plans. Both *The Guardian* and *Daily Mirror* gave prominent coverage to the result.[59] By contrast other executives and local parties conducted their consultation exercises through the usual constitutional means of meetings and workplace liaison. By March 91 CLPs had declared their support for the maintenance of the existing Clause Four,[60] a factor which probably loomed large in the leadership's ad hoc decision to encourage constituency parties to ballot members in place of the previously binding local General Committee system of voting.[61] When two of the largest affiliates, the public sector workers union UNISON and the Transport and General Workers Union (TGWU) remained firm in their commitment to the Webb wording, an editorial in the *Daily Mirror* denounced them as 'undemocratic'.[62] Some party modernizers questioned the legitimacy of these affiliates' position in the party: 'It is the votes of ordinary members which have driven the Clause IV change, not the pronouncements of trade union executives'.[63] The same issue of the LCC newsletter went on to list results from the few hundred constituency parties who had voted for change as against the handful who did not.

The decision by the TGWU not to ballot members led to a rift between General Secretary Bill Morris and the Labour leadership.[64] More dramatically it also provided the impetus for a serious challenge by modernizer Jack Dromey for Morris's position later in the year.[65] Other acrimonious episodes during the debate formed the basis of press reports which tended to favour the leadership. In particular the near-half of Labour MEPs who publicly declared their allegiance to Clause Four with a front-page advertisement in *The Guardian* on the day Blair came to address them in Strasbourg were labelled 'Stalinist' in the same paper's editorial the following day.[66] Similarly much was made of the leader's denunciation of those behind the advertisement as 'infantile incompetents'.[67] By contrast to the impression given in the press, Alex Falconer, one of the MEPs Blair targeted, contended the meeting had not been so one-sided.[68]

Other stories appearing in the press helped strengthen the case presented by Blair. Towards the end of January, *The Observer* reported that Blair had been on the 'warpath' at a recent meeting of the Parliamentary Labour

Party.[69] The following day both the *Daily Mirror* and *The Guardian* ran features underlining Blair's belief that unless Clause Four was reformed the party would lose the next election.[70] Also significant was the selective reporting given different consultation results: whilst the Scottish party conference decision to support Blair made *The Guardian* front page and an editorial, the Greater London region vote against change two weeks later only merited a small item on the fifth page of the same paper.[71] Similarly, favourable coverage followed endorsements of change from other sectional groups, notably two major conference meetings of the national sections for youth and women. Despite the fact that both were representative rather than decision-making bodies, the results were interpreted by the press in an unambiguous way: 'Blair Wins Youth'[72] and 'Labour Women Vote Strongly for the New Clause 4'.[73]

In launching the debate over the Labour Party constitution in October 1994, Tony Blair could not be wholly sure his intention to re-write Clause Four would be successful. Modernizers' initial fears were confirmed when the Annual Conference voted to reaffirm the existing wording 48 hours later. Leadership anxieties were compounded by the decision of several CLPs, as traditionally represented by their General Committees, to vote against change. Nevertheless the leadership won its case in spite of these setbacks and the fact that they had been unable to promote a new Clause Four for fear of appearing to pre-empt a decision early on in the consultation period. At the special April 1995 meeting the vote registered in favour of change was 66 per cent to 34 per cent. The result overturned the previously binding 1994 conference decision which had supported the existing Webb version, albeit by a narrow margin of 51 per cent to 49 per cent.[74]

Arguably the new party structures created during the Kinnock leadership played an important role in enabling Tony Blair and his allies to revise the party's set of constitutional aims and values. Central to this and other internal debates were those influential agenda-setting mass media popular with the Labour membership and those increasingly powerful agents of the leadership belonging to Blair's office and core group of advisers. It was a combination of these aides, their contacts in the media and selected usage of opinion research findings which helped to reshape the perceptions of those participating in the discussion. Prior to winning the leadership Blair had expressed his ambivalence about the need to revise Clause Four not to mention the rest of the party's aims and values. In spite of having adopted a contradictory position within months of succeeding John Smith, Blair and his entourage were nevertheless able to govern the contours of the subsequent argument to the extent that they convincingly won it. In the process they were able to marginalize opponents as well as several plausible alternative viewpoints.

Conclusions

With the recent overhaul of party structures and the diminution of trades union input into policy decision, leadership elections and candidate selection, media and marketing driven agenda-setting have acquired greater importance in influencing the internal affairs of the Labour Party. This trend has been complemented by the introduction of party referenda during the Clause Four debate, the defining moment of Tony Blair's leadership whilst in opposition. The move, designed to facilitate discussion throughout the party and include the wider membership in the decision-making process, has afforded Blair and his aides even more control over debate.

The diminution in the party's representative democracy has enabled the leadership to mobilize support for its case. This has been achieved thanks in part to what Panebianco called 'electoral professionals', those specialist advisers charged with managing strategy. In turn these actors have been helped by their contacts in those media closely associated with the party and through judicious use of polling research which suggests the leadership's view reflects that of the 'opinion electorate', that is those voters deemed essential to any electoral success.

The emergence of the 'New', hierarchical Labour party is by no means an isolated development. In his original study Robert Michels identified the role the press could play in helping party leaderships to subjugate dissent and maintain control within their organizations. Similarly, in his pioneering study, Leon Epstein pointed to emergence of professionalism as a means of party governance. More recently Panebianco has highlighted the central importance of media strategists and the selected readings of public opinion to the structure and management of debate within parties. The thrust of these contributions, which have all been concerned with European cases, has been recently complemented by studies of British politics which have pointed to the growth of 'presidentialism'.[75] Arguably marketing and the media have been central to this development.

NOTES

1. Robert Michels, *Political Parties* (New York: Dover, 1959; first published 1915).
2. Robert McKenzie, *British Political Parties* (London: William Heinemann, 1963); Eric Shaw, *Discipline and Discord in the Labour Party* (Manchester: Manchester University Press, 1988).
3. Dominic Wring, 'From Mass Propaganda to Political Marketing: The Transformation of Labour Party Election Campaigning', in Colin Rallings *et al.* (eds.), *British Parties and Elections Yearbook 1995* (London: Frank Cass, 1996).
4. Bernard C. Cohen, *The Press and Foreign Policy* (Princeton, NJ: Princeton University Press, 1963), p.13, cited in L.J. Martin, 'Recent Theory on Mass Media Potential in Political Campaigns', *Annals of the American Academy of Political and Social Science*, No.427 (1976), pp.123–33.

5. M. McCombs and D. Shaw, 'The Agenda-setting Function of the Mass Media', *Public Opinion Quarterly*, Vol.36 (1972), pp.176–87.
6. Steven Lukes, *Power: A Radical View* (London: Macmillan, 1974).
7. Lewis Minkin, *The Labour Party Conference* (Manchester: Manchester University Press, revised edition, 1980); Thomas Koelble, *The Left Unravelled* (Durham, NC: Duke University Press, 1990).
8. Henry Drucker, *Doctrine and Ethos in the Labour Party* (London: Allen & Unwin, 1979).
9. In his pioneering study of political organisation, Ostrogorski used the phrase 'auxiliaries' in describing the newspaper allies of a party. See M. Ostrogorski, *Democracy and the Organisation of Political Parties* (New York: Haskell, 1902 reprinted 1970).
10. Leon Epstein, *Political Parties in Western Democracies* (London: Pall Mall, 1967).
11. Angelo Panebianco, *Political Parties: Organisation and Power* (Cambridge: Cambridge University Press), p.198.
12. *Tribune* (2 Sept. 1988).
13. Note the increasing prominence of the National Policy Forum, an organization which meets in between Annual Conferences to discuss party initiatives under direction from the leadership.
14. Lewis Minkin, *The Contentious Alliance* (Edinburgh: Edinburgh University Press, 1992), p.630.
15. Eric Shaw, *The Labour Party since 1979* (London: Routledge, 1994), pp.57–9.
16. Blair regularly attempts to neutralize the charge that he is an autocrat by attacking those who he believes preach about the politics of Labour leadership 'betrayal', *The Guardian* (27 July 1995).
17. Andy McSmith, *John Smith* (London: Mandarin, 1996).
18. Arthur Scargill, 'Future Strategy for the Left', unpublished paper, Nov. 1995.
19. The relationship between *The Guardian* and Labour has been examined in the left-wing satirical magazine *Casablanca* ('Who Guards the Guardian?: Part Two', Oct./Nov. 1992, p.7) and regularly by Hugh MacPherson in his parliamentary column for *Tribune*. Two recent studies also mention the link: Richard Heffernan and Mike Marqusee, *Defeat from the Jaws of Victory* (London: Verso, 1992), pp.219–20; Shaw, *The Labour Party since 1979*, p.126. That said, relations between the paper and Labour have been more strained since the promotion of Alan Rusbridger to the editorship in 1995.
20. *Daily Mirror* (5 Oct. 1995).
21. Patrick Seyd and Paul Whiteley, *Labour's Grassroots* (Oxford: Clarendon Press, 1992), p.37.
22. John Gorman, *Images of Labour* (London: Scorpion, 1985).
23. Richard Rose, *Influencing Voters* (London: Faber & Faber, 1967).
24. Nicholas O'Shaughnessy and Dominic Wring, 'Political Marketing in Britain', in Henry Tam (ed.), *Marketing, Competition and the Public Sector* (Essex: Longman, 1994).
25. Colin Hughes and Patrick Wintour, *Labour Rebuilt* (London: Fourth Estate, 1990).
26. Cited in Eric Shaw, 'Programmatic Change in the Labour Party 1984–94', paper presented at the Party Politics Conference, Manchester University, Jan. 1995.
27. Bob Wybrow, 'The 1992 General Election and Its Impact on the Image of Public Opinion Surveys', paper presented at the General Election Conference, Essex University, September 1992.
28. Brian Brivati, 'Clause for Thought', *History Today*, No.143 (October 1993), pp.7–10.
29. Steven Fielding, 'Mr Benn and the Myth of Clause Four', *Parliamentary Brief*, April 1995, p.38.
30. Anthony Crosland, *The Future of Socialism* (London: Jonathan Cape, 1956).
31. *The Guardian* (28 April 1992).
32. *The Times* (18 May 1992).
33. *The Independent* (2 Feb. 1993).
34. *The Times* (9 Feb. 1993).
35. Jack Straw, *Policy and Ideology* (Blackburn: Blackburn Labour Party, 1993).
36. Fabian Society, *A New Constitution for the Labour Party: The Report of the Archer Committee* (London: Fabian Society, 1993).
37. *The Times* (23 Feb.1993).

38. Neil Kinnock, *Tomorrow's Socialism, Part Two: Rethinking the Future*, broadcast on BBC2, 11 Feb. 1994.
39. B. Jones, 'Common Ownership: Relic or Asset?', *Renewal*, Vol.1, No.3 (July 1993), pp.55–61.
40. John Rentoul, *Tony Blair*, p.413.
41. *Breakfast with Frost*, broadcast on BBC1, 12 June 1994.
42. *New Statesman and Society* (17 June 1994).
43. *The Guardian* (8 Oct. 1994).
44. New Clause Four Campaign, *The New Clause IV*, campaign leaflet, 1995.
45. Tribune Group, *Beyond Clause Four* (London: Tribune Group of MPs, 1994).
46. John Solomon, 'Confused', *Fabian News*, Vol.107, No.4 (Aug. 1995), pp.22-23.
47. *Midnight Special*, broadcast on Channel Four, 4 Oct. 1995.
48. What's Left Network, *Network News*, No.1 (Jan. 1995).
49. *Tribune* (20 Jan. 1995).
50. Defend Clause Four Campaign, *Defend Clause 4, Defend Socialism Newsletter*, 1 (Winter 1995).
51. *The Guardian* (26 Jan. 1995).
52. *Daily Telegraph* (6 Feb. 1995).
53. *Daily Mail* (6 Feb. 1995), cited in Greg Philo 'Political Advertising and Popular Belief', in Greg Philo (ed.), *Glasgow Media Group Reader, Volume Two* (London: Routledge, 1995).
54. Tony Blair, *Face the Future: the 1945 Anniversary Lecture* (London: Fabian Society, 1995). The opening part of the series was widely commented upon in the media, for example see *The Guardian* (28 Sept. 1992). The first pamphlet was solely authored by Giles Radice and entitled *Southern Discomfort* (London: Fabian Society, 1992). The others, written with Stephen Pollard, were called *More Southern Discomfort* (1993) and *Any Southern Comfort* (1994). In an occasionally illuminating study of New Labour, former parliamentary frontbench researcher Leo McKinstry (*Fit to Govern?* London: Bantam Press, 1996, p.112) makes mention of the way the series had a marked influence on the Blair leadership.
55. Fabian Society, *The Fabian Society*, recruitment leaflet, 1995.
56. Labour Party, *National Executive Report* (London: Labour Party, 1992).
57. *Tribune* (3 March 1995).
58. *Daily Telegraph* (6 Feb. 1995).
59. *The Guardian* (22 April 1995); *Daily Mirror* (22 April 1995).
60. *Tribune* (10 March 1995).
61. *The Guardian* (25 Jan. 1995).
62. *Daily Mirror* (22 April 1995).
63. Labour Co-ordinating Committee, *Labour Activist*, Special Conference edition (29 April 1995).
64. *The Guardian* (3 Feb. 1995).
65. Incidentally a move later endorsed by an editorial in *The Guardian* (30 May 1995), a newspaper not generally thought of as required reading amongst the largely blue-collar membership of the union.
66. *The Guardian* (10 Jan. 1995). Interestingly, reflecting the notion that a sense of timing means everything, there had been remarkably little comment when the same advert appeared in *Tribune* the previous November. Certainly it did not lead individual signatories to ask for their names to be removed from the statement as happened on this occasion. Indeed the advert caused so much consternation amongst Labour MEPs that half of them immediately wrote a letter to *The Guardian* in support of Blair. This duly formed the basis of a frontpage story on the day the letter was published, the signatories' 30 or so names gaining a mention in the article as well as the actual correspondence section.
67. *The Guardian* (12 Jan. 1995).
68. *Socialist Campaign Group News* (Feb. 1995)
69. *The Observer* (22 Jan. 1995).
70. *Daily Mirror* (23 Jan. 1995); *The Guardian* (23 Jan. 1995).
71. *The Guardian* (11 March and 27 March 1995).
72. *The Observer* (5 Feb. 1995).

73. *The Guardian* (3 April 1995).
74. It should not be overlooked that the motions before the two meetings differed quite considerably: whilst the 1994 Annual Conference had called for a simple restatement of faith in the original Clause Four, the 1995 special delegate meeting was limited to speeches and a vote on whether to accept or reject the new version. Nothing was said of the older text. Blair had thus succeeded in turning the debate into a 'valence issue' rather than one of real contention. That said a noticeable and influential group of opponents including union leaders Rodney Bickerstaffe and Bill Morris held out against the change at the special conference staged on a Saturday afternoon which, underlining its high media profile, gained live coverage on BBC2.
75. Michael Foley, *The Rise of the British Presidency* (Manchester: Manchester University Press, 1993).

Privacy and Media Intrusion in a Democratic Society: Britain and the Calcutt Reports

MARTIN CLOONAN

This study deals with the right to privacy as it exists within a particular democratic society. Focusing upon two reports into privacy and the press in Britain in the early 1990s (the Calcutt reports), it illustrates how the issue of privacy can give insights into the type of democracy which exists within a society. The analysis falls into five parts. These deal with the Calcutt reports; the concept of privacy; the problem of regulating the press within a particular democratic society (Britain); the role of the press in defending British democracy; and the legacy of the Calcutt reports. In examining the right to privacy within the context of regulating the press in a democratic society, the account shows how the exercise of a particular right can be limited by the assertion that another right (in this instance freedom of expression) has precedence over it.

'The pluralistic society is the society of privacy *and* publicity',

Carl J. Friedrich[1]

Introduction

As this essay was being written British public life was settling down again after the death of Diana, Princess of Wales. In the aftermath, much attention was paid to the role the press[2] had played in bringing about the car crash in which the Princess died. While the death occurred in France, the British press was implicated as it had often paid handsomely for the photographs of the Princess with which foreign *paparazzi* supplied it. In the same month as the Princess died, pictures of her with Dodi Al Fayed were published in the British press, including ones which the *Daily Mirror* doctored in order to make it look as if the couple were kissing. At her funeral, Diana's brother, Lord Spencer, accused the press of having blood on its hands.

At one level the Princess's death was the story of a woman who died trying to escape the latest intrusion into her privacy. It can be seen as the climax to a series of events involving the British press invading the privacy of public figures. At times it appeared that elements within the press had concluded that those entering public life had given up *all* rights to privacy.

This essay examines an attempt to formulate a legal right to privacy – the Calcutt reports of the early 1990s. It falls into five parts. First, the Calcutt reports are introduced. Secondly, the concept of privacy is discussed. In the third part the problem of regulating the press within a democratic society (Britain) is addressed. The role of the press in defending British democracy[3] is discussed in the fourth part, while the fifth, and concluding, part, deals with Calcutt's legacy.

The analysis is based on the assumption that discussion of the right to privacy can give insights into the nature of British democracy in the 1990s. While exercise of the right to privacy can be beneficial to democracy if it enhances individual freedom, it can be detrimental if it leads to secrecy in the conduct of public duties and impinges upon the public's right to know how its officials are behaving. Being unable to discuss details of others' lives in print can also intrude upon freedom of expression. The need for a balance between conflicting rights is a central concern for democratic theorists and the Calcutt reports were an example of the quest for that balance. They sought to balance the right to privacy against the competing rights of freedom of expression and the public's right to know. The balance which resulted from Calcutt, it is argued, helps to illustrate the condition of Britain's democracy in the early 1990s.

Part I: The Calcutt Reports

The late 1980s saw a great deal of concern expressed about the behaviour of the British press. In particular, it was felt that, in an increasingly competitive market,[4] the tabloids were intruding too much into people's private lives. Such concern peaked with a famous remark by Lord McGregor, then chair of the Press Complaints Commission (hereafter PCC),[5] that the press' coverage of the breakdown of the Prince and Princess of Wales' marriage had led to them 'dabbling their fingers in the stuff of other people's souls'.[6]

There were a number of widely-publicized examples of press intrusion into the privacy of members of the general public in the 1980s. These included a *Sun* 'interview' with a Falklands war widow who never actually spoke to the paper, but whose story was based upon asking office secretaries how they would have felt in her place; a reporter who lied to the grandmother of a victim of the Hillsborough tragedy in order to get a photo of him which his parents wanted withheld; and the journalists: '... who broke down the walls of the intensive care unit which housed the captain of the *Herald of Free Enterprise* ferry'.[7]

Concern was also expressed about the practice of 'doorstepping' the families and friends of those who had been victims of crime or tragedy.

Often this concerned sensational murder trials such as the Yorkshire Ripper and Cromwell Street murders when members of the accused's family were subjected to press harassment. But while cases concerning members of the general public occasionally made headlines, the most highly publicised cases tended to involve one of three groups: celebrities, royalty and MPs. It was these groups who came to be the focus of Calcutt's attention.

Evidence of parliamentary concern about press behaviour is shown by the fact that in the 1988–89 session of the House of Commons two Private Members' Bills which sought to restrain the press came first and second in an MPs' poll for Private Members' Bills. These were Conservative MP John Browne's Protection of Privacy Bill and Labour MP Tony Worthington's Right of Reply Bill. Lacking government support, both Bills were defeated. But the government was aware of growing discontent on the back benches and sought to allay MPs' concerns about press intrusion into people's private lives by setting up a Committee on Privacy and Related Matters. This was announced by Home Office Minister Timothy Renton in the House of Commons in April 1989 and became known as the Calcutt Committee, after its chairman, David Calcutt.

Cause for Concern

As the Committee was deliberating there arose a case which seemed to encapsulate all the problems surrounding press behaviour. In February 1990, the television actor Gorden Kaye lay in a Charing Cross hospital bed after a road accident in which he sustained severe head injuries. A journalist and a photographer from the *Sunday Sport* newspaper ignored signs asking visitors to report to members of staff before seeing Mr Kaye, entered his room, chatted with him, and photographed him – apparently with his consent. But Mr Kaye's medical condition was such that 15 minutes after the 'interview' (and after security staff had been called to remove the journalists) Mr Kaye could not remember it. Court action was taken to prevent publication of the photos. But the Appeal Court ruled that this could not be done, although it did prevent the *Sport* from doing as it had intended and claiming in its story that the photos (and interview) were being published with Mr Kaye's permission. The *Sport* defended the Kaye story as an 'old-fashioned scoop'.[8]

Coverage of royalty, and particularly the breakdown of the Prince and Princess of Wales' marriage, also caused some concern. Incidents here included the *People*'s July 1991 publication of photographs of the Duke and Duchess of York's young daughter, Princess Eugenie, running naked in the high-walled garden of her home, which were taken without her parents' knowledge. The *People* used a censure from the PCC as a pretext for re-publishing the original photos. The Wales' extramarital affairs were covered by the press in the 'Squidgygate' tape (in Diana's case) and in the 'Camillagate' affair (in Charles' case) which both saw details of tapes of private conversations published in the press and in the *Times'* publication of extracts from Andrew Morton's book *Diana: Her True Story*. As the royals were highly reluctant to bring court cases against the press, it seemed as though their private lives were effectively unprotected from media intrusion.

Some MPs also voiced concern about press coverage of their own private lives. In February 1992 the Liberal Democrat Party leader Paddy Ashdown's affair with his secretary five years previously became known. The story was based on a document stolen from Mr Ashdown's solicitor. Although he was able to get a court injunction stopping the publication of the story in England, it appeared in Scotland which has a different legal system.

In July 1992 the *Independent* apologised to Secretary of State for Health, Virginia Bottomley, and her MP husband, Peter, for publishing the fact that she had been an unmarried teenager when she gave birth to their first son. The *Independent* justified publication on the grounds that earlier in the week the government had announced a campaign against teenage pregnancies. But it accepted that it had invaded the son's privacy by naming him in the article.

In the same month the *People* published details of an affair between David Mellor and actress Antonia da Sancha. Mellor was then Secretary of State for National Heritage – the department responsible for supervising the press. Details of the affair were gained by the paper bugging Ms da Sancha's rented flat – with the agreement of its owner – and wiring up the bed.

While many of these cases came after Calcutt's first report they are illustrative of problems surrounding the press at this time. It was in order to investigate such behaviour that Calcutt was set up.[9]

Calcutt 1 – The Committee on Privacy and Related Matters

The Privacy Committee followed previous Royal Commission reports on the press in 1949, 1962 and 1977 and the Younger Commission's report on Privacy in 1972. Its remit was:

> ... to consider what measures ... are needed to give further protection to individual privacy from the activities of the press and improve recourse against the press for the individual citizen ... and to make recommendations.[10]

The Committee began its work in May 1989, considered evidence up until August, and reported in June 1990. It noted that amongst the areas of complaint against the press were those of the harassment of individuals in private as well as in public, photographs taken without consent, publication of information about private lives, factual inaccuracies, the making up of comments, sensational reporting, untrue stories, publishing private photographs, references to individuals' criminal records which were irrelevant to the story being covered, and insensitive treatment of the victims of crimes.

Despite many instances of press misdemeanours, the Committee believed that the main problem was not that cases were particularly frequent, but that they tended to take a high profile. It was noted elsewhere that complaints about privacy formed only 8.7 per cent of those received by the PCC over a three year period,[11] although it was possible that many victims simply did not bother to complain. The Committee found it impossible to monitor the scale of such problems and so was unable to comment upon whether there was a growing problem.[12] It appeared likely that the debate was being fuelled in part by a growing demand for privacy from the public. Thus at one level the existence of the Committee reflected demands which were being made upon Britain's democratic institutions to protect people's private lives from undue media attention.

However, the Committee also sensed that the circulation wars between the tabloids had led to a situation where certain editors felt that they were 'off the leash'[13] and *none* of the witnesses appearing before Calcutt denied that matters had deteriorated.[14] The Committee examined various cases of intrusion into privacy and the role of the Press Council – the industry-financed body then responsible for the press' self-regulatory régime – in countering such invasions. Regulation is considered in some detail below,[15] and it is sufficient to note here that while the Committee acknowledged that victims of press intrusions often called for stricter, statutory controls, it believed that self-regulation should be given one final chance.[16]

However, the Committee also saw the need for reform and recommended the introduction of three new laws covering physical intrusion into private property (including placing surveillance equipment and taking photographs without consent) in England and Wales. This represented an attempt to shift the balance of power away from the press and back towards individuals, in all walks of life. In all these cases Calcutt believed that a number of defences were permissible. These were: the prevention, detection or exposure of crime or serious anti-social conduct; preventing the public being seriously misled; informing the public about matters relating to the effective discharge of any public function by the individual concerned; protecting public health or safety; and under lawful authority.[17]

Despite this the Association of British Editors (ABE) argued that the proposed new laws would hamper investigative journalism. It listed a number of cases which would have been difficult to research had the legislation been in place. These included reports that the Chancellor of the Exchequer, Norman Lamont, had exceeded his credit card limit 21 times; that Heritage Secretary David Mellor and his family went on a holiday paid for by the daughter of a prominent member of the Palestine Liberation Organisation; and that a surgeon had performed over 1,000 operations after being diagnosed as having AIDS.[18]

The Committee considered, but recommended against, the introduction of a statutory right of reply. Several witnesses to the Committee called for the introduction of a statutory tort of infringement of privacy as a means by which to establish a general legal right to privacy. But the Committee recommended against such a move. It also emphasised that its recommendations were to be taken as a package, and not as something from which the press could pick and choose.

Press reaction to the recommendations was almost uniformly hostile. The *Today* editor, David Montgomery, spoke of being sent to gaol to protect the Royals and the *Sun* also alluded to imprisonment (which was *not* mentioned in Calcutt). Professor David Flint, chair of the Australian Press Council, commented that it was ironic that just as Eastern Europe was emerging from years of state censorship, Britain should be moving toward it.[19]

In defence of the press, some commentators pointed to previous cases where apparent excesses had yielded important results with implications for British democracy. It was noted that Minister of War John Profumo's adultery with the mistress of a Soviet attaché, which helped bring about the Conservative Party's 1964 general election defeat, was disclosed because the tabloid press had been willing to pay for information. Similarly, readiness to pay informers led to the resignation of Tory junior minister Lord Lambton in 1973 because of his relationship with a call-girl and the disclosure in 1986 that Jeffrey Archer, then Deputy Chairman of the Conservative Party, had made payments to another call-girl.[20]

Importantly, the Committee itself argued that the right to privacy should be protected, in a context where 'freedom of expression is pre-eminent'.[21] Thus privacy was always a *secondary* consideration for Calcutt. Only in exceptional circumstances would it take primacy over free expression. Thus an official report concluded that British democracy would be more enhanced by protecting freedom of expression than it would by protecting privacy.

Following the Privacy Committee's report the Press Council was replaced by the PCC which came into existence on 1 January 1991. It was given 18 months to prove its worth. The government emphasized that: 'This was positively the last chance for the industry to establish an effective system of regulation'.[22] Calcutt was then asked to compile another report. This was the *Review of Press Regulation*, published in January 1993.

Calcutt 2 – The Review of Press Regulation

The second Calcutt report examined press regulation, protection of individual privacy and the possibility of a privacy tort. However, it was made clear that the main concern of *both* reports was the protection of privacy.

The second report was produced solely by Calcutt. He was not convinced that the PCC was an effective regulator of the press and recommended that it be replaced by statutory control. He also recommended that the new offences for intrusion onto property that the Privacy Committee had previously recommended become law and that the government give further consideration to the introduction of a privacy tort in order to establish a general legal right to privacy.

Press reaction to these proposals was again hostile. *Sun* editor Kelvin McKenzie declared that: 'I am not going to have some clapped-out judge... deciding what our readers want to read', while Sir David English, chair and editor-in-chief of Associated Newspapers likened the proposals to Nazi and Communist regimes.[23] Calcutt's opponents also argued that there were enough laws already in existence which curtailed freedom of speech. For example, the ABE noted that 46 laws already covered privacy in Britain.[24] However the question remained as to whether these laws were effective in protecting a developing right.

Part II: Privacy

The notion of individuals having a 'right' to privacy is comparatively recent. Its most famous modern declaration came in 1890 when an article by two lawyers from Boston, Massachusetts, Samuel D. Warren and Louis D. Brandeis, appeared in the *Harvard Law Review*. Entitled 'The right to privacy (The implicit made explicit)', it followed a series of press intrusions into privacy which culminated in the extensive coverage of Warren's daughter's wedding. Drawing upon British law, Warren and Brandeis wrote of the 'right to be left alone'. They urged that the courts should develop a civil law of damages for invasion of privacy and for the development of defamation law.

Many authors argue that talk of a right to privacy has gone hand in hand with the emergence of the individual as the locus of liberal (and capitalist) society. Thus Carl J. Friedrich argues that: 'The idea of the sacredness of privacy grew with the growth of individualism'[25] and Ferdinand Schoeman links the rise of concepts of privacy with the emergence of individualism in the seventeenth century.[26] Pointing out that many animals seek periods of isolation, Alan Westin, argues that there is thus a natural desire for privacy.[27]

While this shows privacy in a positive light, others have criticized privacy as a right to be secretive and anti-social. For example, Bruno Bettelheim argues that the demand for privacy comes from a propertied elite, and that as bourgeois individualism rose so did the desire to perform some functions in seclusion and the tendency to be ashamed of one's body.[28] Privacy has been seen as a severance of social relations which leads to a decline in responsibility. Marxists have attacked it for being a manifestation of alienated bourgeois society, while conservatives fear that it will lead to isolation and to the development of totally self-interested individuals.[29] As noted earlier, there have also been concerns that privacy can be used to cover up misdeeds in business or government.

Whatever its desirability, the concept of privacy has always been plagued with definitional problems. For example, the 1977 Royal Commission on the press had declared that the concept was 'not capable of a general definition'[30] and Judith Jarvis Thomson writes that the most striking thing about privacy is that 'nobody seems to have any clear idea what it is'.[31]

The Privacy Committee defined privacy as: 'the right of the individual to be protected against intrusion into his (sic) personal life or affairs, or those of his family, by direct physical means or by publication of information'.[32] It went on to suggest that a right to privacy *might* include protection from physical intrusion; publication of hurtful or embarrassing personal material; publication of inaccurate or misleading personal material; and publication of photographs or recordings taken without consent.[33]

A key question was the *amount* of privacy a given individual was entitled to. Privacy was seen by some as the means by which the rich and famous could avoid having to account for their misdemeanours, of concern only to the elite. The ABE accused Calcutt of being concerned only to protect the rich and famous and Calcutt himself was portrayed as part of an establishment which was keen to protect itself. The National Council for Civil Liberties (Liberty) agreed that privacy legislation would disproportionately benefit the rich and powerful about whom more, rather than less, needed to be known.[34] These people were more often in the news, but a certain loss of privacy seemed to be the inevitable price that was paid for being a celebrity.

The Privacy Committee had noted that 'not all people are entitled to expect the same amount of privacy',[35] especially if they chose to enter public life. Such people, said the Committee, did not give up all rights to privacy; however, 'we would expect that any conduct which impinges upon the public might reasonably be made public'.[36] But a sense of proportion was needed. As Calcutt noted, this reduction should *only* be to the extent 'that it is necessary for the public to be informed about the discharge of their duties'.[37]

Calcutt also concluded that, whilst the privacy of all those in the public eye was in need of protection, this was *especially* true of MPs and royalty, who were often subject to the most prurient reporting.[38] At times it seemed that these two groups effectively had no privacy, especially when the press used its stock defence when charged with intruding into private matters.

Public Interest

The notion of 'public interest' was the litmus test applied to identify articles which appeared to invade privacy. It provided an example of how the concept of privacy put a spotlight on to the state of British democracy. The way in which claims to privacy were countered by claims of 'public interest' raised the issue of how much information the public needed to know about the personal lives of those in key positions within the society. The Privacy Committee argued that 'public interest' was confined to matters relating to the detection of crime; protecting public health or safety; or preventing the public being misled by the individual's actions or statements.[39] In these cases investigating matters which would otherwise be private was permissible.

The Committee was adamant that 'public interest' was *not* the same as what is 'of interest to the public'; it did *not* equate with 'human interest' – which was the stock in trade of the tabloids.[40] The matter under investigation had to be relevant to the performance of public duties and go beyond mere prurience. But Calcutt's second report noted that: 'In the case of politicians, the public has a right to be informed about private behaviour which affects or *may* affect the conduct of public business'.[41] This was more liberal than the Privacy Committee's understanding and seemed to cover a very wide range of activities as practically *any* matter *might* affect public duties. Thus Robertson had argued some years earlier that the criterion for publication should be whether the matter actually *had* affected the ability to do a public job.[42]

In contrast, the ABE argued that some intrusions into personal lives *could* be in the public interest and that it was often necessary to invade a person's privacy *prior* to determining whether or not a story should be published in the 'public interest'. Often the very purpose of the invasion was to establish this.[43] Thus, argued the ABE, to do as Calcutt proposed and limit investigative journalism to those stories where public interest had *already* been established would result in a severe restraint on the press and, implicitly, upon Britain's democracy. Liberty agreed, arguing that subterfuge was often necessary in order to get stories as, for example, in investigating unsafe employment practices.[44]

However, it was also noted that the press were adept at using the phrase 'public interest' in order to excuse the most gross invasions of personal privacy. Calcutt received evidence that the press would *always* define 'public interest' as widely as possible.[45] He noted that: 'all too often … this justification for publication has been used by the press to seek to justify publication of any and all associated information and to regard any and every tactic to obtain such information as justifiable'.[46]

The question remained as to how far a definition of 'public interest' could be stretched. When the *People* bugged Antonia da Sancha's flat to get details of her affair with David Mellor the newspaper argued that this was in the 'public interest' as Mellor had been heard to say that the affair was leaving him 'seriously knackered' and so unable to write ministerial speeches.[47] In November 1993 the *Sunday Mirror*'s editor, Colin Myler, justified the paper's publication of photos of the Princess of Wales exercising in a private gym by claiming that there was a 'public interest' involved, since the ease with which the photographs were taken had implications for the Princess's security.[48]

Both these cases seemed to take 'public interest' beyond reasonable limits. As usual, they concerned a clash between privacy and two other 'rights' – those of free expression and the public's right to know. In these clashes 'public interest' emerged as the criterion by which the competing rights might be judged. But while Calcutt related public interest to public duty, the press often searched for public dirt. Notions of democratic accountability were used to justify prurience.

This had obvious implications for British democracy. It was widely held that those who volunteered to enter public life – politicians and, arguably, some members of the royal family – had given up some, almost intangible, amount of their right to privacy. In the case of MPs and other public officials there is an air of paradox about this. Whatever their motivations, MPs are people who have decided to enter public service, that is, to participate more than most in the democratic processes of their country. This undoubtedly aids the democratic process. But an inevitable price for such help is a certain loss of privacy. Thus in order to enhance democracy and, in certain senses, freedom, politicians have to surrender some freedom of their own. Whatever the rewards of office, the price is less freedom in one area than their fellow citizens have and expect.

The right to privacy is democratic in the sense that it applies to all, but, crucially, its *application* varies. Ironically those who have *chosen* to pay the fullest part in the democratic process (via public life) have *less* right to privacy than 'ordinary' people. Thus in Britain there is an *inverse* relationship between the amount of privacy one can expect and the extent of one's participation in the public democratic process.

Part III: Calcutt and the Limitations of British Democracy

Calcutt was very clear that he was dealing with the specific situation in England and Wales and commented that he was wary of learning from other countries' experience as 'measures adopted in one country might not travel well'.[49] This theme was taken up by Virginia Bottomley, in her new role as Heritage Secretary, when she rejected calls for French-style privacy laws on the grounds that 'few people would believe that they were appropriate *in this country'*.[50] The United States has also been dismissed as an appropriate comparison as it has a very different legal system and constitutional arrangements.[51] This echoes a familiar theme in the literature on privacy where the argument that privacy is relative to a given society is often put.[52]

As a particular society was under consideration, the constitutional arrangements of that society influenced the way in which the privacy debate was conducted. Thus while on the one hand the treatment given to the right to privacy provided insights into the nature of British democracy, on the other Britain's democratic institutions helped to determine the nature of that treatment. Britain is a constitutional monarchy, therefore anything which involved the monarchy could be argued, if somewhat tenuously, to have constitutional importance. Thus the *Sunday Mirror* could portray its invasion of the Princess of Wales' privacy in a private gym as a constitutional issue, because lax security had allegedly endangered the woman who was the wife of the heir to the throne and the mother of another.

That this was a spurious excuse does not alter the fact that the particular constitutional arrangements of Britain were what prompted the initial interest in Diana. Although the point could be made that, at the age of 19, Diana chose to enter public life (or, at least, to partake in it more fully), it is harder to argue that *anyone* could fully consent to the intrusive celebrity status which accompanied that decision. This is not to deny that Diana (and her husband too) later became adept at manipulating the press and was party to some invasions of her own privacy. Nevertheless, Diana's lack of privacy had its origins in Britain's constitutional arrangements.

These arrangements were beyond Calcutt's remit, but formed a backdrop to the reports. Ultimately, the surest way to protect the royals' privacy in the long term is to abolish the monarchy. This is far beyond Calcutt, but it is pertinent to ask whether a mature democracy wants to condone the press excesses that accompany royalty. It is possible that no future member of the royal family will create as much interest as Diana, but it is beyond doubt that while the monarchy remains in existence reporters will want to report on virtually *all* its activities. They can continue to try to justify their prurience by reference to the constitution and the fact that the British taxpayer still pays many of the monarchy's bills and therefore has the right to know everything the monarchy is doing.

In part this public interest may reflect a maturing democracy which is increasingly less deferential towards its representatives and more willing to ask questions – or have questions asked on its behalf – about them than it had previously been. Certainly the monarchy was open to public and press attack in the 1990s in a way that would have been inconceivable in earlier decades.

In terms of British democracy, the results of Calcutt were mixed. His remit was to investigate the status of privacy in a modern parliamentary democracy with particular characteristics. Britain has no laws which specifically relate to privacy and is also unusual in not having a Freedom of Information Act. The current (1998) Labour government has promised to implement Freedom of Information legislation.[53] It has also announced that the European Convention on Human Rights is to become part of domestic law. This has Articles on both privacy (Article 8) and free expression (Article 10) which will influence future debate. But Calcutt had to walk the line between privacy and free expression without specific legislation on either being in place.

However, a number of existing laws have implications for both privacy and free expression. In the case of privacy they include restrictions on the use of surveillance equipment, nuisance laws and laws covering data protection and breach of confidence. But remedies for breaches of such laws are often only available to those with considerable financial resources. The most obvious expression of this is the granting of court injunctions to rich and/or high-profile individuals to prevent unfavourable reports about them appearing in the press.

This illustrates that while it is the rich and famous who are most likely to have their privacy invaded, it is generally the same people who are most able to do something about it. In this respect privacy, like information, is merely another commodity. Whether the commodification of information which impacts upon the democratic process is desirable is, perhaps, a moot point. Meanwhile Calcutt's second report concerned the regulation of such information.

Regulation

One way in which the Calcutt reports shed light on British democracy was by showing the changing ways by which that democracy treated disclosure of information by the press over the years. Britain has never developed laws specifically covering the behaviour of the press, which has thus operated under the same laws as other organizations and individuals. But in order to placate public concern over its behaviour, the industry had introduced its own regulatory system. One of Calcutt's tasks was to make recommendations about whether this self-regulatory system should continue.

The press' first self-regulatory body, the General Council of the Press, was set up in 1952. Formed in response to a Private Member's Bill which threatened statutory regulation, it was composed entirely of members of the press. Following the second Royal Commission (1962) the General Council admitted some lay members and became the Press Council. It was still operative at the time of the Privacy Committee's report in 1990.

The Press Council saw its main role as being to defend press freedom in Britain – rather than dealing with complaints. However, it also sought to maintain ethical standards and part of this involved the consideration of readers' complaints. The Council's powers of sanction were limited to the publication of its adjudications, which the relevant newspapers were *not* obliged to publish. The problem of limited sanction was compounded by the fact that newspapers often used their publication of the Council's adjudications as an excuse to attack it.

The Council was also criticised for not publicizing itself widely enough and for not being truly independent of the industry. With these criticisms in mind, the Privacy Committee considered moving to a system of statutory control. Instead it called for a new self-regulatory body, to be called the Press Complaints Commission.

As noted earlier, the PCC came into being on 1 January 1991. Its first chair was Lord McGregor. The Privacy Committee expected it to be more concerned with acting on complaints than protecting press freedom and to include a wider range of lay members. However, there were a number of differences between PCC as envisaged by the Privacy Committee and the body that actually emerged. The most significant of these were that: it was less independent of the industry than was stipulated; it still asserted its role as a guardian of press freedom rather than concentrating solely on complaints; its Code of Practice was not produced by the PCC itself but by the industry; its Code watered down the Privacy Committee's recommendations; it would not operate a 'hot line';[54] and it was unwilling to initiate enquiries itself.[55]

In his follow-up *Review*, Calcutt concluded that the PCC was 'not the truly independent body which it should be'.[56] He expressed serious concern that the *Sunday Sport* (in the Kaye case) and the *People* (in the Princess Eugenie case) had both shown contempt for the PCC's decisions. He also disapproved of the way the PCC handled the publication by the *Sunday Times* of excerpts from Andrew Morton's book, *Diana: Her True Story* and the Mellor affair,[57] as well as its inaction in cases concerning other public figures.

The Privacy Committee had recommended that the PCC should be replaced by a statutory Press Tribunal in the event of self-regulation breaking down, or of maverick publications continually disregarding its decisions. While this had not happened, neither had the PCC been set up in the way that the Privacy Committee had recommended, so Calcutt's *Review* recommended statutory regulation. He intended that the new Tribunal would draw up a statutory code of practice, restrain publication of material in breach of it and investigate complaints both from the public and of its own volition.

Calcutt's opponents argued that any changes in the law which were meant to curb the excesses of the press would also be used against broadcasters and would be a threat to investigative journalism. Above all they argued that a statutory regulatory body was a move towards state censorship of the press. The ABE believed that ordinary people would be less likely to register complaints if this meant going through a complicated (and expensive) legal procedure rather than the relatively simple and free service provided by self-regulation.[58]

But while the Calcutt reports were often perceived in terms of a stark contrast between self-regulation or statutory control, the ABE noted that the reality was always a mixture of the two systems. The real question was, it argued, what the correct balance between the two should be[59] and it went on to argue for continuation of the self-regulatory system.

Debate on who should regulate the industry partly centred on the role of the judiciary – an appointed body with the role of interpreting Parliament's will as expressed in legislation. In this sense the debate over privacy was over which one of two unelected bodies – the PCC and the judiciary – could best protect it (accepting the ABE's point that the reality is always a mixture of systems). Calcutt rightly chose the judiciary. While neither has unblemished democratic credentials, it is the judiciary which has the longest tradition of interpreting the constitution. In contrast, the PCC was set up by the industry which also appoints its members and its independent status is still in dispute, although the PCC has reformed itself. It widened its membership to give it a lay majority in September 1993 and established a Privacy Commissioner in January 1994. In November 1994, Lord Wakeham replaced Lord McGregor as PCC chair.

The question Calcutt raised is what happens in British democracy when rights clash? If privacy clashes with free expression and/or the right to know, who, in England and Wales, is to decide the outcome? The answer Calcutt came up with was the courts, the traditional interpreters of the will of Parliament as enshrined in statute law. But Parliament itself decided otherwise. In July 1995, just two days before it decided to end its own self-regulatory practices as part of the reforms proposed by Lord Nolan,[60] Parliament decided that the press should continue to regulate itself. The penalty for those found guilty of abusing the right to privacy was to be censure from the PCC, not the full weight of the law (unless it could be proven that the rather flimsy protection of privacy laws provided in England and Wales had been broken).

The fact that a general election was looming might have influenced government thinking here, but the net result was a victory for the press and a defeat for the ideal of privacy. The debate had shown how British democracy stood at this point. The country's sovereign body had decided that an industry which had continually abused the right to privacy was to be allowed to continue regulating itself and deciding where to draw the line with regard to privacy. The nation's MPs decided that they were not fit to regulate their own affairs, but that the press was. Meanwhile parts of the press endeavoured to carry forward another ideal.

Part IV: The Role of the Press as a Guardian of British Democracy

The Calcutt reports also raised the question of how much information it is legitimate for the public to have about its public officials. Events before and after Calcutt highlighted such issues as: what does the public need to know in order to be able to cast its votes and have its confidence in public officials maintained? Furthermore, what provision of information does a democracy need? Ideally the role of the press here was to provide reports which helped the public to make informed choices. Unfortunately, at times it appeared as if the press placed prurience before propriety.

For example, in the Mellor case it is arguable that the fact that a Cabinet Minister was having an affair which was leaving him unable to perform his public duties *was* of concern to the public *if*, and *only* if, it was having an impact on the role which the taxpayer was paying him for. But this does *not* mean that the public had the right to know that Mellor allegedly made love wearing a Chelsea FC football kit, a 'fact' which was later exposed as a ploy to keep the story running.[61] This was *nothing* to do with his public duties. Mellor himself felt that the affair was not, in the 1990s, a resigning matter, and the pressure group Liberty rightly argued that if this was the case then reports of the affair were *not* in the 'public interest'.[62]

The Mellor case graphically illustrates the way in which the press, posing as guardians of democracy, can run prurient stories in their search for profit. The defence of 'public interest' is often spurious, a cover for the pursuit of profit via prurience.

In the broader context the Calcutt reports called into question the press's role within British democracy. They raised vexed questions about standards which were also being pursued elsewhere. In October 1994 the Nolan Committee on Standards in Public Life was set up. The fact that press coverage of a number of incidents had played a key role in the setting up of the Committee was acknowledged by Lord Nolan himself.[63] Its formation followed a series of allegations that Conservative MPs were willing to take sums of money in return for asking Parliamentary Questions. In its own way the setting up of the Nolan Committee was another reflection of the influence the press can have on the conduct of British democracy.

Implicit in the very title of the Committee's work was the idea that those entering public life had more of a responsibility than others to ensure that certain standards were met. The widespread belief that a number of MPs were not meeting these standards, as exposed by the press, became the trigger for the Nolan inquiry. The public demanded the right to know what its elected representatives' business dealings were. Men (and it overwhelmingly *was* men) in positions of public authority were held to account for actions which many of them considered to be private. The public's right to know eventually triumphed here as following Nolan's report MPs agreed to allow fuller disclosure of their business dealings and the appointment of a Commissioner for Standards – a move which ended the tradition of Parliament regulating its own affairs. In retrospect this can be seen as an unsuccessful attempt to deal with an issue which the press had highlighted and which came back to plague the Conservatives in the 1997 general election campaign.

The first two weeks of the official campaign in this election were dominated by what had become known as 'sleaze'. This generally involved financial or sexual impropriety amongst Conservative MPs. Press coverage of 'sleaze' made it difficult for Conservative Party representatives to discuss policy as the media continued to pursue a seemingly endless supply of 'sleaze' stories. Peccadilloes, not policy, became the dominant theme of the campaign. One result was a certain 'dumbing down' of political debate.

A key principle of democracy is that of participation in the political process. It is at least arguable that the behaviour of the British press and its concentration on sleaze contributed to disenchantment with the political process and thus less likelihood of participation. Voter turn-out at the 1997 general election was down on the 1992 figures and it is at least possible that press portrayal of politics added to a general cynicism and *dis*inclination to participate in the democratic process.

However, on balance, it appears that the press did democracy a valuable service here. The dogged pursuit of MPs such as Neil Hamilton and Jonathan Aitken led to the electorate being better informed. In the latter case *The Guardian* used a 'cod fax' by which to ensnare Mr Aitken. This involved the paper sending a fax purporting to come from Mr Aitken's office in order to confirm details of his stay at the Ritz Hotel in Paris. This action was described as 'an affront to the House' by the Commons Privileges Committee,[64] although no action was taken against the paper. However, while the case arguably invaded Aitken's privacy, it would have passed Calcutt's 'public interest' test as it showed Aitken to be seriously misleading the public. In general the light shed by the press undoubtedly contributed to an atmosphere where the Conservatives were seen as untrustworthy. The fact that they were heavily punished at the polls is surely not coincidental.

What do these cases tell us about the British press as a guardian of democracy? At one level, the press acts as spotlight, exposing those areas which various prominent public figures want to keep secret. There is a sense in which secrecy is the enemy of democracy and the press can perform a vital role in bringing to the electorate information which might otherwise be concealed. In this context the press *can* indeed be seen as a guardian of democracy. Without investigative journalism the electorate would have been much less well informed at the 1997 general election.

The other side of this is that the press can intrude too far into the private lives of individuals. At the time of writing the Conservative MP for Beckenham, Piers Merchant, has just resigned following *Sunday Mirror* exposures about his private life. This story first surfaced in the *Sun* during the run-up to the general election. It re-emerged following the Conservative Party conference in October 1997 after it appeared that Merchant was carrying on with the previously-exposed affair, a fact which he denied. He was caught out after the paper (with the connivance of its owner) set up a video camera in the flat where he was planning to meet his lover and after being followed by four reporters and two photographers for four days.

The 18-year-old woman involved in this story, Anna Cox, was taken to hospital in an ambulance following press harassment during her stay at Merchant's house. The truth about this particular case has yet to be established, but the fact that a young woman was taken to hospital as a result of press harassment is surely a matter of concern. The *Sunday Mirror* justified its story on the grounds that Merchant had lied to his constituents and party by saying the affair was over. How this affected the *performance* of his public duties was not clear.

The fact that this story broke just weeks after the public hand-wringing of the press over the death of Diana, Princess of Wales, shows that little has been learnt. A paper-thin 'justification' appears to be enough. Post-Calcutt it still appears that the price for information is invasion of private lives and prurient reporting.

The Merchant case clearly shows the dichotomous role of the press.

While the broadsheets may aspire to be informants of public debate, the tabloids have increasingly come to see themselves primarily as entertainers. The broadsheets report tabloid stories second hand to their readers. There has also been some 'dumbing down' of the broadsheets; the *Times'* publication of extracts from Morton's book on Diana is often cited as an example.

This raises the question of whom the press is ultimately meant to serve. As commercial enterprises they answer to owners and/or shareholders, but as public servants, their masters should be different. It is the relationship between these two sets of masters which is important. It might be a sad reflection on British democracy that one of its main protectors is an industry where disregard for vulnerable people has become the norm and where the truth is often secondary to the need to run an eye-catching story for as long as possible.

Much of this was again beyond Calcutt's remit, while forming the backdrop to his work. Calcutt was limited by a relatively narrow remit which excluded questions of ownership and the relationship between the press and British democracy. However, through the narrower spectrum of privacy Calcutt was able to shed further light on these complex issues. Once again the notion of privacy gave insights into the condition of British democracy. But that is only part of Calcutt's legacy.

Part V: Conclusion: The Calcutt Legacy

In July 1995 the government announced that the status quo would continue.[65] Virginia Bottomley told the Commons that self-regulation would continue and that no privacy legislation would be introduced as problems of definition, scope and possible defences had made it impossible to draft. This was not a view which Calcutt would have shared. It appears that, in the run-up to a general election the government was unwilling to confront a press which it still hoped would lend it support in the election campaign. If this was the case, then the gamble was miscalculated. The press largely turned against the Conservative Party and contributed to its biggest electoral defeat this century. Nevertheless, the non-implementation of Calcutt's recommendations is partly due to political timing.

However, Calcutt also contributed to his own downfall. The fact that the Committee gave primacy to free speech over privacy made privacy – the very reason for the Committee's deliberations – appear to be a secondary consideration. Calcutt offered little reason for the primacy of free speech, merely noting that one MP had queried it.[66] But if there is reason to doubt that free speech should automatically be given pre-eminence, then this is even more the case when the press is under consideration. As Geoffrey

Robertson has noted: '… there is an important distinction to be made between freedom of expression and freedom of the press, the former is an aspect of individual liberty, the latter a prerogative exercised by an industry'.[67] Calcutt erred in running the two together.

Furthermore, the fact that the reports tended to concentrate on the rich and famous and to underplay stories emanating from members of the general public played into the hands of opponents who could make the lazy accusation that it was only the elite whom Calcutt really wanted to protect. Although Calcutt had made it clear that it was wrong for the friends and family of those in the news to have their privacy invaded by the press, he gave primacy to the needs of royalty and MPs. This made it much harder for proponents of Calcutt to argue their case on egalitarian grounds and thus undermined Calcutt's democratic credentials. The ABE pointed out that Calcutt examined only three cases of 'ordinary' people[68] and Calcutt admitted that it was a case involving a pop star, Elton John, rather than a member of the public, which was the spur to action.[69] Thus *Sun* editor Kelvin McKenzie was able to describe the reports as a 'totally Establishment set-up'.[70]

But Calcutt ultimately *did* recommend placing press regulation onto a statutory footing, a highly significant change which would have made the press more accountable. There is good reason to be sceptical about the role of unelected judges in protecting British democracy, but there might be even more reason to doubt the power of the PCC in restraining the press. The fact that it is yet again redrafting its code of practice after the death of Diana shows merely that its previous efforts[71] have not been good enough. Just after the first Calcutt report David Mellor as National Heritage Secretary suggested that the press was drinking at the 'Last Chance Saloon'.[72] The problem is that last orders at this saloon seem to have been indefinitely suspended. Calcutt wanted to call time.

Perhaps the saloon is merely reflecting the circumstances in which it is placed. Another factor which Calcutt alluded to, but did not explore, is the nature of the market for newspapers. Calcutt noted that he was reporting at a time of unprecedented competition.[73] By the time of the reports the press was involved in a circulation war which included such gimmicks as bingo (a form of gambling), price-cutting and even free editions. This competition has continued, encompassing the broadsheets as well as the tabloids and led to an Office of Fair Trading investigation in July 1994. The press was also facing competition from a glut of new commercial radio stations and the advent of satellite television. In a tidal wave of news the need to stand out became ever greater. The result is, as a *Guardian* editorial reported after Diana's death, that news has become a commodity and 'The market simply rules'.[74]

Those working in the industry readily acknowledged this. Max Hastings, former editor of the *Daily Telegraph*, said of the tabloids: 'As long as people are making very large sums of money out of peddling rubbish, it seems reasonable to assume that they will go on peddling rubbish as long as they are allowed to.'[75]

A week after Diana's death, the experienced journalist Roy Greenslade placed the blame for the state of the press firmly on the patterns of ownership within the British newspaper market. He wrote: 'Driven by the profit motive, newspapers have lost sight of the reason they were founded in the first place; to inform, to educate, to guide, to offer communities a window to the world'.[76]

But that world was changing. Andrew Neil, editor of *The Scotsman*, argued that new privacy laws were irrelevant in an age of global communications in which national boundaries meant little.[77] At this level this was a challenge to the nation state to intervene in the global market – something for which the current Labour administration has shown little appetite. However, the alternative is to let both privacy and information become increasingly commoditized. The fact is that the state retains the power to intervene in the market and a government with a very healthy majority is in a good position to do so. Lack of political will is the only real constraint should the current administration wish to introduce privacy legislation. But one of Calcutt's weaknesses is that he looked at the international situation only as a potential source of new legislation, rather than as the marketplace where *paparazzi* photographs and newspapers themselves are traded freely.

Thus the legacy of Calcutt is somewhat mixed. As such it may be that he also erred in presenting his recommendations as an all-or-nothing package. He came to the conclusion that the press needed more legal constraint, but he made recommendations to a government that lacked political will to carry this through. He partly undermined his own case by seeing privacy as a right secondary to free speech and placing undue emphasis on the effects of the press on royalty and politicians. He was unable to comment on British constitutional arrangements and did not delve fully into questions of press ownership and the market.

Nevertheless, the debates around Calcutt also shed light on the condition of British democracy. The role of the press in exposing wrongdoing by public officials was cited as a reason for allowing self-regulation to continue. It was argued that self-regulation applied a lighter touch than the dead hand of the law which was seen as too inflexible to deal with complex privacy cases. Here one major part of Britain's constitutional instruments showed more faith in an extra-constitutional body, the self-regulation of the press, than it did in another constitutional body, the judiciary. Moreover, by allowing the press to continue with self-regulation while at the same time ending its *own* system of self-regulation, Parliament, the cornerstone of British democracy, demonstrated more faith in the good intent of the press than its own.

As noted earlier, at the time of writing it appears that the Labour government will incorporate the European Convention on Human Rights into British law. As this has provisions both for privacy and free speech, future clashes seem inevitable. Calcutt was aware of these clashes and tried to confront them. It may well be that in the clash between privacy and free speech, the British government should have looked for solutions in his reports, rather than in the European Convention. No government can doubt the seriousness of the matter.

In 1970 Brian Walden, then a Labour MP, introduced a Privacy Bill into the Commons in 1970. He commented that: 'The right to be left alone ... is the one which the British people care about most.'[78] In many ways, despite Calcutt's best efforts, the protection of that right within British democracy seems further away than ever 27 years later.

NOTES

1. Carl J. Friedrich, 'Secrecy versus Privacy', in J.R. Pennock and J.W. Chapman, *Privacy* (New York: Atherton Press, 1971), p.107 (added emphasis).
2. Throughout this article the term 'the press' refers to national daily and Sunday newspapers.
3. Calcutt's investigations covered England and Wales as Scotland has its own legal system and particular restrictions apply to Northern Ireland. Nevertheless, the reports have implications for the whole of Britain.
4. See conclusion.
5. See Part III.
6. David Calcutt, *Review of Press Self Regulation* (London: HMSO Cm.2135, 1993), 4.43.
7. David McKie, 'Self-Regulation and the Calcutt Report', *Index on Censorship*, No.7 (1990), p.2.
8. Raymond Snoddy, *The Good, The Bad and The Unacceptable* (London: Faber & Faber, 1992), p.93.
9. In addition to Calcutt, a Q.C. and Master of Magdalene College Cambridge, the members of the Committee were: Simon Jenkins, a *Times* journalist who became editor before the report was published; David Eady, a lawyer; John Spencer, lecturer in law at Cambridge University; John Cartwright, SDP MP; Sheila Black, a businesswoman; and Professor John Last, director of the Charities Trust and a former lay member of the Press Council.
10. Committee on Privacy, *Report* (London: HMSO Cm 1102. 1990), 1.3.
11. *The Guardian* (10 Jan. 1994).
12. Committee on Privacy, 4.8.
13. Snoddy, p.99.
14. Ibid., p.102.
15. See Part III.
16. Committee on Privacy, recommendation 11.
17. Ibid., 6.36.
18. ABE, *Media Freedom and Media Regulation* (London: Association of British Editors, 1994), pp.27/28.
19. See Snoddy, pp.105 and 107.

20. Alan Doig, 'The Double Whammy: The Resignation of David Mellor, MP', *Parliamentary Affairs*, Vol.46. No.2 (1993), p.171.
21. Committee on Privacy, 3.18.
22. Calcutt, 3.1.
23. *The Independent* (11 Jan. 1993).
24. ABE, p.26.
25. Friedrich, op. cit., p.115.
26. Ferdinand D. Schoeman, *Privacy and Social Freedom* (Cambridge: Cambridge University Press, 1992), p.121.
27. Alan Westin, 'The origins of the modern right to privacy', in Ferdinand D. Schoeman (ed.), *Philosophical Dimensions of Privacy* (Cambridge: Cambridge University Press, 1984), pp.56–9.
28. Cited by Michael A. Weinstein, 'The Uses of Privacy', in J.R. Pennock and J.W. Chapman (ed.), *Privacy* (New York: Atherton Press, 1971), p.90.
29. See ibid., pp.89-93.
30. Committee on Privacy, 3:2.
31. Judith Jarvis Thomson, 'The Right to Privacy', in Ferdinand D. Schoeman (ed.), *Philosophical Dimensions of Privacy* (Cambridge: Cambridge University Press, 1984), p.272.
32. Committee on Privacy, 3.7.
33. Ibid., 3.8.
34. Liberty, *Review of Press Self-Regulation: Submission to Sir David Calcutt QC* (London: Liberty 92/13, 1992), pp.7 and 17.
35. Committee on Privacy, 3.21.
36. Ibid., 3.24.
37. Calcutt, 4.37.
38. Ibid., 4.40.
39. Committee on Privacy, 12.23.
40. Ibid., 3.23.
41. Calcutt, 4.67, emphasis Cloonan.
42. Geoffrey Robertson, *People Against The Press* (London: Quartet Books, 1983), p.90.
43. ABE, 4.9.
44. Liberty, p.13.
45. Committee on Privacy, 13.8.
46. Calcutt, 4.34.
47. Doig, op. cit., p.173.
48. Roy Greenslade, 'Sneaky Look in the Mirror', *Guardian* (8 Nov. 1993), Part II, p.15.
49. Committee on Privacy, 2.6.
50. *House of Commons Debates*, 17 July 1995, col.1335 (added emphasis).
51. See, for example, *The Guardian* editorial (8 Sept. 1997) and Snoddy, p.16.
52. See, for example, W.L. Weinstein 'The Private and the Free: A Conceptual Inquiry', in J.R. Pennock and J.W. Chapman (ed.), *Privacy* (New York: Atherton Press, 1971), p.40. and Schoeman, p.166.
53. At the time of writing the government was proposing to introduce Freedom of Information legislation.
54. The idea of a 'hot line' was devised by the Committee as a means by which people who believed that a forthcoming press article would invade their privacy could ring up the PCC and inform them of this *prior* to publication. This was the only form of 'prior restraint' that the Committee was willing to endorse.
55. Calcutt, 3.94.
56. Ibid., p.xi.
57. Ibid., 5.23.
58. ABE, 5.12.
59. Ibid., 5.3.
60. See Part IV.
61. David Mellor, 'The Diet of Worms', *The Guardian* (14 March 1994), Part II, p.6.

62. Liberty, p.8.
63. Committee on Standards in Public Life, *Standards in Public Life Volume 1* (London: HMSO Cm. 2850-I, 1995), pp.15–16.
64. *The Guardian* (21 Jan. 1996).
65. See Department of National Heritage, *Privacy and Media Intrusion: The Government's Response* (London: HMSO Cm. 2918, 1995).
66. Calcutt, 3.3.
67. Robertson, p.63.
68. ABE, p.11.
69. Committee on Privacy, 1.5.
70. *The Independent* (22 Jan. 1993).
71. The PCC also redrafted its Code of Practice in July 1993 and April 1995. Every time the public has been assured that the new Code is the answer to press excesses. Every time those excesses have continued.
72. Calcutt, 2.7.
73. Committee on Privacy, 4.8.
74. *The Guardian* (8 Sept. 1997).
75. Snoddy, op. cit., p.109.
76. Roy Greenslade, 'Change the Front Page ... and Your Heart', *The Guardian* (8 Sept. 1997), p.7.
77. Andrew Neil, 'World Full of Hypocrisy', *The Guardian* (8 Sept. 1997), media section, p.4.
78. Cited by Mervyn Jones, *Privacy* (London: David & Charles, 1974), p.173.

Democratization and the Media in Poland 1989–97

FRANCES MILLARD

Poland constitutes a 'best case' example of post-communist media development. The emergence of a diverse media free of direct political interference can be analysed as both a cause and a characteristic of the democratization process. Although the media reflected and contributed to political turbulence, they performed significant functions of informing, investigating and agenda-setting. The diversity of the print media ensured pluralism of viewpoints, although the press remained generally partisan. The state broadcasting media did not fulfil their public service brief fully and they were subject to constant attempts at political manipulation and bitter controversy. Yet these developments did not work in the same direction; rather there were numerous crosscurrents and counter-tendencies.

Introduction

Dismantling the formal mechanisms of communist control of the media was the easy part for the New Democracies of Central and Eastern Europe after the 'revolutions' of 1989. Creating an institutional framework securing freedom of expression and responsible journalism proved a minefield of continuing political controversy everywhere. It could hardly have been otherwise. There is no universal template of press and broadcasting freedom to be stencilled mechanically on to different political-cultural configurations. Although freedom of expression is a universally acknowledged characteristic of liberal democracy, liberal democratic states offer different responses to conflicts between freedoms, and they employ varying mechanisms of formal and informal regulation of the media. In many respects debates in post-communist countries mirrored those in established democratic polities. In others they reflected the particular legacies of their own communist experience and the myriad objective difficulties of the process of transformation.

Poland, Hungary and the Czech Republic received the democratic seal of approval in July 1997 with the imprimatur of the North Atlantic Treaty Organization (NATO) and the European Union Commission's support for the inauguration of membership negotiations (along with Estonia and Slovenia); both these organizations had established certain general conditions for membership, including stable, democratic institutions.

Indeed, by 1997 few questioned the appropriateness of the 'democratic' label for these three of the four Visegrad states. Securing freedom of expression, including press and broadcasting freedom, was an important dimension of the democratization process. Free expression is both a prerequisite for and a characteristic of democratic, pluralist society. Without access to information, genuine debate, and the ability to disseminate different points of view other freedoms such as freedom of association and assembly and freedom of electoral choice cannot be realised. Representation itself and the deliberative processes of lawmaking require the exchange and sharing of information and opinion, while procedures for political accountability are negated or undermined by conditions and practices of secrecy.

In this context the Polish media represent a 'best case' example of the former communist states. Indeed Poland appears a paragon of virtue when contrasted with the scope of direct political control of the media in 'worst case' examples (Serbia, say, or Belarus). In terms of political manipulation and controversy the Polish case falls between the Hungarian, with its five-year 'media war',[1] and that of the Czech Republic.[2] This study examines how the media developed in Poland after 1989 and identifies the key political issues surrounding their de- and re-regulation. This also entails a brief examination of constraints on the media in the broad context of the development of civil liberties in post-communist states. Although not fully comparative, it does indicate the extent to which these developments have their counterparts elsewhere or alternatively should be understood as part of the specific Polish context. Its general thesis is that despite political turmoil and new commercial pressures, the mechanisms of authoritarian control were transformed after 1989 into a new hybrid media system which was both an index of and a contributing factor to the multi-faceted processes of democratization. Change occurred more rapidly in the print media than in broadcasting, but the media's imperfections, while manifold, were no more serious than those which may be identified in other democratic countries.

The broad context of media changes after 1989 was that of the multiple transition process experienced by post-communist states in their efforts to move to a liberal democratic system based on the market economy. The process of change in Poland was politically turbulent and punctuated by periodic crises and grave uncertainty. Poland was the first country in Eastern Europe to install a non-communist prime minister, the Solidarity intellectual Tadeusz Mazowiecki. This was a result of Solidarity's stunning performance in the partly competitive election of June 1989 and the defection of the satellite parties from the spurious Communist Party-led 'coalition' of the post-war period. The political consensus supporting Mazowiecki's government proved short-lived. The 'shock therapy' of

Finance Minister Leszek Balcerowicz traumatized the population with high inflation, deep recession and profound social dislocation. Solidarity began to fracture when its leader Lech Wałęsa launched his bid for the presidency in spring 1990 on a platform of painless acceleration of reform. Wałęsa's victory and Mazowiecki's defeat in the presidential election led to a minority government under Jan Krzysztof Bielecki from January 1991 up to the first fully competitive parliamentary election of October 1991. That election generated a highly fragmented parliament incapable of sustaining durable government. Jan Olszewski's clerically oriented coalition fell on a vote of no confidence in June 1992. The new prime minister Waldemar Pawlak, leader of the Polish Peasant Party (PSL), failed to form a government. Hanna Suchocka's seven-party coalition of 'Solidarity parties' survived for ten months but fell on a vote of no confidence in May 1993. The first period of Solidarity's tenure at the helm of Polish politics came to an end with the election of September 1993, when the Solidarity parties suffered a massive defeat.

From October 1993 to September 1997 the communist successor parties, the Social Democrats and the PSL, formed a majority coalition. Opposition was weak, not least because most self-styled right-wing parties and the Solidarity trade union were excluded from the *Sejm* (the lower house), having failed to cross the new electoral threshold. Yet the new coalition was beset with internal conflicts, magnified by President Wałęsa's hostile, obstructionist stance. Twice the coalition was reshaped under a new prime minister: Pawlak gave way to Józef Oleksy in March 1995 and after a spy scandal replete with accusations against the prime minister, Oleksy yielded to Włodzimierz Cimoszewicz in February 1996. The government found its position somewhat easier after the election of social democrat Aleksander Kwaśniewski to the presidency in December 1995, but severe tensions remained between the coalition partners. Kwaśniewski's election also marked a rapid polarization of Polish politics between the Left Democratic Alliance of the Social Democrats and Solidarity's new Solidarity Election Action (*Akcja Wyborcza Solidarność*, AWS). Although the Social Democrats increased their vote substantially in the 1997 election, AWS won a sweeping victory on an anti-communist platform stressing Catholic values and social doctrine. From November 1997 Solidarity Election Action led a coalition government with the Mazowiecki–Balcerowicz Freedom Union (*Unia Wolności*) under AWS premier Jerzy Buzek.

The development of the media thus occurred in a highly charged political atmosphere. The media reflected and often enhanced political divisions. Unsurprisingly, politicians saw them as a potent political resource and a weapon against their opponents. Much of the press was highly partisan and successive governments strove to maximize their influence on the broadcasting media. Yet overall the media fulfilled the functions of investigating, informing and educating both the elites and the attentive public.

The Media after 1989

The Press

Communist Party control of the Polish press weakened substantially in the 1970s after earlier bouts of periodic liberalization, with another hiatus of increased central direction during martial law (1981–83).[3] The gathering strength of the underground press provided alternative sources of information not only on current politics but also on key events in Polish history and access to literary works frowned on by the regime. Blatant propaganda diminished in the officially sanctioned press as did the obligatory nods in the direction of Marxism-Leninism. Specialist journals of limited circulation were more or less left alone by the censor and, equally important, the Press Department of the Party's Central Committee. Access to Western newspapers and journals also became easier in the large cities. In these respects Poland resembled Hungary. In both the pluralism of media expression and the scope of permitted debate created a qualitatively different situation from that in the Soviet Union and other members of the Warsaw Pact; from the mid-1980s Soviet *glasnost* enhanced and legitimized this liberalism.[4] The independent Catholic press in Poland, albeit constrained by censorship and the central allocation of paper, remained without parallel elsewhere. Television was more tightly controlled, especially its news and information programmes; but it attracted large audiences with high quality Polish drama and Western films, soaps and documentaries.

As a result of Round Table negotiations between government and Solidarity in 1989, the independent trade union regained its legal status and gained some limited access to radio and television. Mistrustful of the official press, Solidarity created its own; this was possible because restrictions on private economic activity had been relaxed, and it was sanctioned by explicit decisions of the Round Table. The first issue of Solidarity's newspaper *Gazeta Wyborcza* (*Election Gazette*) on 8 May 1989 under the editorship of the prominent dissident Adam Michnik assumed a symbolic importance of massive dimensions; *Gazeta* rapidly became (and remained) the most widely read of all Polish dailies. Following Solidarity's electoral victory in June and its assumption of a dominant role in a Grand Coalition under Tadeusz Mazowiecki, two sets of factors influenced developments, particularly of the print media.

First, prior censorship by the Central Bureau for the Control of the Press and Public Performances (*Główny Urząd Kontroli Prasy i Widowisk*) effectively ceased to operate. In its early months *Gazeta Wyborcza* had some battles with the censor, whose stamp was necessary for the printer to start the machines rolling; the Soviet Union and the other fraternal allies proved the most sensitive subject.[5] However, after the installation of the new government the Censor became increasingly irrelevant. By the time Parliament abolished the Bureau in April 1990, it was effectively moribund.

The changed political and economic environment facilitated the emergence of an avalanche of new publications, with over a thousand new titles registered, but no longer licensed by the state, between May and December 1989. The Communist Party's giant conglomerate RSW (*Robotnicza Spółdzielnia Wydawnicza*, Workers' Publishing Co-operative), which had controlled the production, distribution and retail sales of virtually the entire press, effectively lost its monopoly of publishing (the privatization of its distribution arm, Ruch, was announced in 1997). Some of the 'new' press came from the underground, but much was genuinely new. As elsewhere in Eastern Europe, every permutation of political stance found expression, but the new publications filled numerous other gaps in the market, with a proliferation of erotica and soft pornography, the appearance of publications for national minorities, gays and lesbians, vegetarians, computer enthusiasts and the like. Two political weeklies made a particular splash, the serious Poznan-based *Wprost* (*Directly*), modelled on the *Time/Newsweek* format, and the lewd, anti-clerical satirical *Nie* (*No*), edited by the notorious former communist press spokesman Jerzy Urban.

Secondly, the economics of publishing changed virtually overnight as the press now had to compete for readers. Despite economic reforms promoting 'self-financing' in the 1980s, the disappearance of subsidies and the introduction of market prices for paper (December 1989) sent prices up dramatically, while the rise in the general price level resulting from Balcerowicz's 'shock therapy' forced them still higher in the early months of 1990. The Ministry of Culture continued to subsidise certain literary and cultural journals and publications serving the tiny Belorussian and Ukrainian minorities. However, numerous publications folded, among the earliest of which were the Communist Party's own periodicals, including *Życie Partii* (*Party Life*) and *Myśl Marksistowski* (*Marxist Thought*) and finally, with the Party's dissolution, its major theoretical organ, *Nowe Drogi* (*New Roads*). Others transformed themselves more or less successfully, changing their format and layout and seeking advertising revenue, often for the first time. The day of the Communist Party's dissolution, 29 January 1990, saw the final appearance of the previously ubiquitous slogan 'Workers of the World Unite ...' emblazoned under the title of the Party's national daily *Trybuna Ludu* (*The People's Tribune*, subsequently *The Tribune*) and many of its numerous provincial papers.

Amendments to the Press Law in June 1989 made foreign investment in the media possible, and major international corporations made their appearance. Foreign firms set up new publishing houses, established journals modelled on successes elsewhere, and purchased existing publications, sometimes with Polish partners. Foreign capital was welcome in view of the urgent need for modernization. Foreign ownership increased with the law on the liquidation of RSW in March 1990, followed by the establishment of the RSW Liquidation Commission to oversee the privatization of its remaining 176 newspapers and periodicals. Prime Minister Mazowiecki's critics cited slow progress in disbanding the communist media empire as evidence that he was 'soft on communism' and that a new de-communizing broom (that is, Solidarity leader Lech Wałeşa) was necessary to accelerate the transformation process.

No less than 90 titles were sold by auction to foreign owners or joint stock companies, 72 were given to journalists' co-operatives, and the ownership of the remainder passed to the State Treasury. The French press magnate Robert Hersant 'emerged as the clear victor', purchasing – in partnership with co-operatives and the Solidarity trade union – seven daily papers from RSW and also a share of the former government organ *Rzeczpospolita* (*Republic*)[6] which remained (and remains) the effective paper of record.

Although it aroused anxiety, foreign ownership of the media never reached Hungarian proportions: in Hungary by 1990 70 per cent of the national daily press was owned by foreign firms, leading the state publishing house to repurchase several dailies and weeklies.[7] In Poland the distinctive mechanism of transferring papers free of charge to co-operatives, coupled with the fact that Poland's large population could sustain a greater variety of publications than that of Hungary, allayed concerns of a wholesale foreign takeover. This did not prevent significant controversies over particular newspapers. It also fed anxieties of the xenophobic and clerical right-wing, not only for political reasons but also because of 'threats to national culture', including the 'moral pollution' of Western influence.

The transfer of ownership to labour co-operatives proved still more sensitive. Bearing the hallmarks of Solidarity's long-standing focus on self-management and in the absence of capital for management or labour buy-outs, the RSW law provided that the Liquidation Commission should give preference to co-operatives comprising at least half the staff of a given paper. The 50 per cent requirement paved the way for two competing co-operatives to seek control in a number of cases. Trade unions and the emerging small political parties battled for employee support and/or bid to purchase the most popular papers. The Solidarity trade union, for example, bought the popular Warsaw evening paper *Express Wieczorny* (*Evening Express*) and *Gazeta Wspólczesna* (*The Contemporary Gazette*). The National Audit Committee (*Narodowa Izba Kontroli*, NIK) identified 'significant irregularities' in the work of the Commission and accused it of handing over assets to co-operatives lacking the financial resources to continue publication. Indeed, few co-operatives survived as such, some transforming themselves into limited companies immediately following the transfer of ownership, some selling out as financial problems overwhelmed them.[8] According to NIK 45 per cent of co-operatives sold out quickly to private firms.[9] Press ownership formed one aspect of wider allegations about the economic penetration of '*nomenklatura* capitalism', partly because groups of journalists often had links with the Communist Party. When firms associated with members of the old *nomenklatura* bought press titles, they were accused both of using economic power to seek political influence and of laundering ill-gotten gains.

The question of the political colouring of the press was often linked to its ownership. At the end of 1996 five firms controlled 71.6 per cent of the daily newspaper market in Poland.[10] The German Neue Passauer Presse, which bought out Robert Hersant, controlled 12 dailies, with minority holdings in others. The Norwegian firm Orkla Media controlled nine daily papers, including a 51 per cent stake in *Rzeczpospolita*; and the Swiss Jörg Marquard Group four. Tidnigs Marieberg, part of the Bonnier concern, owned 50 per cent of the Media Express Group which published *SuperExpress* and *Express Wieczorny*. The American firm Cox Enterprises had a small share (12.5 per cent) of Agora-Gazeta, publishers of *Gazeta Wyborcza*.

Interference with editorial policy was not reported frequently, but Polish firms were as, if not more likely, to stand accused as their foreign counterparts. Orkla-Media was criticised for political interference in the editorial line of *Slowo Polskie* (*The Polish Word*), the largest newspaper in Lower Silesia (40–50,000 issues daily), and indeed the paper's editor was removed in April 1997. During the 1997 election campaign its German owner was accused of successful pressure on *Dziennik Bałtycki* to withdraw allegations made against President Kwaśniewski. However, *Rzeczpospolita* retained its high reputation; it had early problems with governments rather than with its French or Norwegian owners. Its editor Dariusz Fikus commented that Olszewski's government (1991) thought that *Rzeczpospolita* was 'still a government organ' (as it had still been in 1989–90) whose editor could be carpeted for unfriendly articles,[11] while the Pawlak government (1993–95) made an abortive attempt to renationalize it, as well as exploiting the availability of a free 'government column' for polemics rather than information (as a result, the column was cancelled).[12]

Życie Warszawy (Warsaw Life), associated after 1989 with Mazowiecki and then with more right-wing elements of Solidarity, continued a conservative line after its purchase in 1993 by Sardinian businessman Nicola Grauso. Grauso appeared to lose interest in *ZW* after he failed to win a licence for his illegal television channel Polonia 1, and he aroused criticism on that score.[13] However, when he sold ZW in spring 1996 to Zbigniew Jakubas, head of the firm Multico and owner of *Kurier Lubelski* (*The Lublin Courier*), some 50 journalists left in protest claiming that its purchase was 'part of the government coalition's offensive against the media'.[14] They established a new conservative daily *Życie* (*Life*) which attracted a loyal readership in its early months.

Press ownership thus proved complex and fluid, as the print media changed hands rapidly. The diversity of the press was unquestionable, however. In 1995 despite a general fall in circulation, 63 daily newspapers remained, including strong regional and provincial papers. The major political weeklies survived (though heavily outranked by the popularity of the women's press). In the highly regarded Estymator survey of May 1997 the left-wing *Polityka* and the liberal-centrist *Wprost* jointly occupied eighth place with 5.4 per cent of respondents reading each of them over a six-week period. The scurrilous, gossipy *Nie* followed with five per cent.[15] Specialist publications proved more ephemeral, with large numbers of closures and ownership transfers. The economic press, for example, was far weaker in its penetration than in Hungary and the Czech Republic, both with much smaller populations. The Swiss-owned *CASH* ('the Weekly of the Polish Middle Class') folded in Poland in January 1997 while thriving in its Czech version.[16] The religious press was also in difficulties, with the editor of *Słowo – Dziennik Katolicki* (*The Word – the Catholic Daily*) attributing its closure to perverse Catholics reading *Nie* and *SuperExpress*. Yet the regional press remained strong, and there was a ferment of activity at local level, with vast numbers of small local papers and parish newsletters: in Katowice province in 1997 48 communes had their own papers.[17] By 1997 no organ of the press could be regarded as a government mouthpiece, and the political diversity of the press was unquestionable. Decline in circulation as overall readership fell in line with trends in other European countries was a greater problem than overt political interference.

Broadcasting

The position of the broadcasting media was slower to change and still more controversial. A few commercial radio stations, including the popular Radio Zet, obtained permission to broadcast before June 1991, when Parliament suspended the issuing of broadcasting frequencies pending new legislation. Several draft bills fell foul of the breakdown in the broad parliamentary consensus after Wałęsa's election to the presidency. From autumn 1991 the Catholic hierarchy also began to express concern about the media, perceived as lacking objectivity and deeply imbued with anti-clericalism. The Church achieved a major success with the broadcasting law of December 1992:[18] after its difficult passage through the *Sejm*, the Senate succeeded in restoring a controversial clause requiring broadcasters to 'respect the religious feelings of their audience and especially to respect the Christian value system' (Art.18, §2).

The law's main thrust was the transformation of state radio and television into public service broadcasting agencies. This was also the case in the Czech Republic (1991), Slovakia (1991) and Hungary (1995), and all four drew on their admiration for the BBC as the epitome of public service broadcasting. The new Polish institutions were also similar to those of their neighbours. The law provided for a National Broadcasting Council (*Krajowa Rada Radiofonii i Telewizji*, KRRiTV) of nine persons 'outstandingly knowledgeable and experienced in the sphere of mass communications' (Art.7 §1): four appointed by the *Sejm*, three by the President and two by the Senate for six-year terms, with one-third of the membership renewed every two years. Members were to resign from political parties and from positions of authority in national associations, trade unions, employers' associations or religious organizations. The Council's main task was 'to guard freedom of speech in radio and television, to secure the independence of broadcasters and protect the interests of their audience, and to ensure the open and pluralistic character of broadcasting' (Art.6). The Council controlled the licensing of private radio and television stations on the basis of commitments regarding programming, finance and technical preparedness.

The Council had oversight over the Supervisory Boards of Polish Television and Polish Radio, which each assumed the status of a trading company excluded from certain provisions of commercial law. The rights of their owner, represented by the Finance Minister, were limited to receiving the companies' balance sheets, allocating profits and appointing one member of the Supervisory Boards (the others appointed by the Broadcasting Council).

Immediately, there were strong positive and negative reactions to the law, with many civil libertarians deploring the possibility of any return to censorship.[19] However, the Broadcasting Council did not become 'in effect a censoring agency'.[20] The 'Christian values' clause appeared increasingly irrelevant. Although with the clerical bent of the new 1997 coalition it could assume some political importance, the requirement that the Council's decisions be taken by absolute majority reduced the likelihood of moral intervention.

The Broadcasting Council however remained the object of ceaseles political controversy, as did the arrangements for managing Polis Television. Despite attempts to ensure the expert, non-partisan compositio of the Council and to secure its independence, it did not achieve this statu in the first years of its operation. In many respects little seemed to hav changed. Andrzej Drawicz, a celebrated scholar of Russian literature an Solidarity activist, had assumed the chairmanship of the old State Radio an Television Committee in 1989. Drawicz reported few problems with th Communist Party or its associated trade union but 'the honeymoon wit Solidarity was brief': Solidarity tried to assume the former Party role, t behave as 'a sort of political police' and it demanded a voice in th appointment of key personnel.[21] Drawicz's close association with Prim Minister Mazowiecki led to accusations of broadcasting bias and behaviou 'worse than that of the communists' as Solidarity's 'war at the top intensified between Mazowiecki and Lech Wałęsa. According to Drawic supporters of Wałęsa's presidential candidacy were not slow to register the discontent and made persistent 'demands for special treatment in reportin the appearances of the accelerator' (that is, Wałęsa).[22]

Successive governments brought frequent changes to the Committee personnel; but battles to place partisan sympathizers in positions o influence equally characterised the new Broadcasting Council and th Supervisory Board for Polish Television. Between 1993 and 1997 th Council had five chairpersons. President Wałęsa in particular demonstrate his continued determination to secure favourable reportage. The first majo upheaval concerned the president's nomination of Solidarity journalis Marek Markiewicz as Chairman in March 1993 and his even mor controversial, illegal dismissal of Markiewicz as Chair in 1994. This wa only the first instance of dubious presidential actions vis-à-vis th Broadcasting Council. Later that year Wałęsa (unsuccessfully) ordere Markiewicz's dismissal (he had remained a Council member) and that o another of his own nominees.[23] In May 1995 in nominating a leadin Christian nationalist as Chairman of the Council, Wałęsa refused to obtai the prime minister's counter-signature (required by the Little Constitutio of December 1992). Wałęsa's interference never matched the intensity o conflict between president and government of Hungary's 'media war'; bu it constituted one element of his relentless search for political resource especially after the victory of the successor parties in 1993. Yet in Octobe 1994 it was not the government but the opposition Freedom Union (UW which sponsored a parliamentary 'appeal' to the President, arguing (inte alia) that his violation of the Broadcasting Council's independenc constituted a source of destabilisation and a danger to Polish democracy.[24]

The Council was contentious in its own right too. Its supposed politica balance led to stalemate rather than efficient dynamism. Its licensing decisions were seen as dubious and lacking transparency. The Council compounded its award of a satellite licence to the controversial firm PolSat in October 1993 by issuing PolSat a terrestrial franchise in January 1994. It stood accused of insufficient research of PolSat's financial position and of relying on Zygmunt Solorz's personal assurances without supporting documentation. For many Solorz, PolSat's owner, was doubly suspect: at the time of the second concession he was wanted by the Austrian police[25] and he enjoyed close links with the Social Democrats.[26] A consortium of other firms complained unsuccessfully to the Supreme Administrative Court over the creation of PolSat's 'new private monopoly', but the Court upheld the legality of the licensing decision. A licence to the elite pay channel CanalPlus (November 1994) also aroused condemnation because expert consultants had advised against the decision. If the Council was damned by its decisions, it was also damned by its indecision and delay.

The management of Polish Television was another area of unceasing criticism, both of the Broadcasting Council and PTV's Supervisory Board. Television audiences were growing rapidly; by 1997 virtually all Poles (99 per cent of households) had access to at least four channels, the two state-owned channels (TVP1 and TVP2), one regional channel and Polsat. About 35 per cent had access to numerous others via cable or satellite, with PolSat 2 and the Luxembourg-based entertainment channel RTL-7 proving the most popular. Poles watched some 3.5 to four hours a day on average (five hours during the Pope's visit in June 1997[27]), mostly concentrated from five o'clock in the evening to ten o'clock.

Modern techniques for monitoring television audiences provided the basis of competition for viewers. After the discovery of 'prime time', programmers vied to provide the most attractive programmes, notably feature films, serials, and light entertainment. News programmes, documentaries, and political speeches and debates also attracted quite large audiences. Viewing figures for May 1997 showed most people watching TVP1 (82.8 per cent had watched it), PolSat (70 per cent) and TVP2 (66.2 per cent).TVP1 still attracted the largest share of evening audiences (7:30 p.m.to 11:00) with 35.8 per cent (spring 1997), but PolSat gained 31.2 per cent and TVP2 17.1 per cent.[28]

Criticisms of Polish Television escalated in 1996 and 1997 as the parliamentary elections of September 1997 approached. They centred on the absence of a coherent strategy for public television, incompetence and financial mismanagement, and undue politicization. *Wprost* referred to the situation as a 'telecatastrophe' and media correspondents and politicians alike spoke freely of the 'crisis' of public television. Although political to its core, the crisis could not be linked straightforwardly to conflicts between president and government (during Wałęsa's tenure to December 1995) or between government and opposition. We have already seen that Wałęsa was critical of his own appointees to the Broadcasting Council, and his persistent criticism often focused on television coverage of his office.[29] This in turn was partly a reflection of the president's battle on two fronts: against the anti-Wałęsa wing of Solidarity and the equally hostile followers of former prime minister Jan Olszewski and against the Social Democrat-Peasant coalition (from autumn 1993).

Without doubt the arrival of Wiesław Walendziak as head of Polish Television led to huge changes in personnel (the youth and brash confidence of the young arrivals earned them the sobriquet 'pampers' after a brand of disposable nappy) and a visible presence of journalists closely associated with the political right. Jacek Kurski, for example, became a familiar figure to viewers. As spokesman for Olszewski's Movement for Rebuilding Poland (ROP), Kurski was noted for his attacks on the Freedom Union and for suggesting that Solidarity trade union leader Marian Krzaklewski might be aptly described as a 'floppy dame' (*rozlazła baba*) hanging on Wałęsa's lapel.[30] He had also co-edited a diatribe against Wałęsa following the fall of Olszewski's government in June 1992.[31] Elżbieta Isakiewicz provided another example; known for her rabid Catholic nationalism, she was a highly partial television presenter. Whether this mattered much is extremely doubtful in one sense: the public was certainly used to political tendentiousness and was quite capable of making their own judgment on the performances.

However, Walendziak came under unrelenting pressure, as politicians monitored their television coverage down to the last second and complained vociferously about inadequate access. He also stood accused of managerial incompetence. Walendziak submitted his resignation at the end of February 1996 on the grounds that he was exhausted by political infighting. The divided Television Supervisory Board did not accept his resignation; but nor did it accede to his demand for the removal of two managers involved in dubious financial arrangements. After Walendziak finally departed, the Audit Commission's report for 1994–96 revealed at best a catalogue of inefficiency and waste, at worst extensive corruption in the awarding of unprofitable contracts, failure to observe internal procedures, losses on sales of films and videos, an incoherent remuneration system, and inconsistencies in financial documentation.[32] If Walendziak had not caused all these failures, neither had he remedied them. Yet the Commission (NIK) itself was regarded as deeply politicized, and *Wprost* attacked *Polityka* for its 'inexcusable attacks' on Walendziak and for publishing a 'wholly uncritical' series of extracts from the draft NIK report.[33]

Walendziak's successor Ryszard Miazek fared little better, though controversy over the political bias of television veered to the left as the more controversial figures of the right departed. Indeed, by August 1997 the Television Supervisory Board was dominated by members identified with one or other coalition partner, as the two 'opposition fig leaves' resigned in protest. Miazek himself was a politically inspired appointment (associated with the Peasant Party, PSL) and he was not up to the job either. Miazek even lost the support of the PSL, furious at the lack of coverage of Firefighters' Day and the Peasants' Holiday (*Święto Ludowe*) on the evening television News.[34] Even the Broadcasting Council criticised the 'chaos' and 'crisis' in TVP 1.

Allegations of overt political bias continued unabated, with accusations and denials flying fast and furious from all directions. Solidarity's electoral arm AWS threatened to rewrite the broadcasting law to undermine the security of tenure of PTV's 'supervisors' and to require the public media to propagate 'pro-family values' as well as Christian ones. In fact the official figures issued by PTV's management to rebut claims of unfair access did not confirm either set of allegations, though they conveyed nothing of the content of news coverage. In news reporting in May 1997 the Social Democrats (including government ministers) got five minutes 20 seconds, AWS four minutes four seconds, the Freedom Union three minutes 52 seconds, the PSL two minutes 58 seconds, ROP one minute 15 seconds, and the Labour Union (UP) one minute ten seconds.[35]

Politicians may have placed undue stress on the importance of television, but it was easy to see why they were so obsessive about questions of access. Given their general impoverishment, the provision of free access to the media only at election time, and an exaggerated belief in the power of television as a medium of political influence, they saw it as their main means of reaching the public. Their concern was also closely linked to the character of much Polish news reportage, which consisted largely of giving politicians airtime to express their own convictions. The major news programmes included little which could pass for analysis. Indeed, a monitoring exercise by the Broadcasting Council (4–10 September 1996) found 'errors' in ten per cent of TVP's reports in its three major news programmes. The most complex issues were handled worst and the viewer received insufficient information to enable independent judgements 'on vital political issues'. Failing to ask pertinent questions was 'passive journalism' and public television risked becoming 'the mouthpiece of politicians'; selecting 'witty or coquettish sound bites' served merely to 'sensationalize and dramatize political events'.[36]

Not surprisingly, television coverage of elections was particularly controversial. Yet even in this sensitive arena a marked improvement was evident. In 1991 journalists shied away completely from election comment, leaving the voters to the mercies of the parties' own rather dreadful propaganda efforts. In 1993 television was similarly unadventurous, with relatively little analysis or debate. One commentator viewed the campaign on state television as 'so sluggish as to be almost invisible'.[37] By the presidential election of 1995 however the situation had changed, with far greater provision of opportunities for debate and hard searching of candidates. Partisan questioning by biased journalists was evident, but by and large the respective sympathizers had similar opportunities to grill opposing candidates. Ironically perhaps private channels displayed less tendentiousness than the public sector. Progress was not linear, however. The referendum campaign was a television disaster. However, state television did quite well during the 1997 parliamentary election, when journalists facing politicians appeared rather more successful in curbing their partisan zeal. None the less, political parties submitted bitter complaints to the Broadcasting Council; at least some of which, it must be acknowledged, were well founded.[38]

If Polish Television was in a state of permanent flux and the subject of bitter polemics and acrimonious conflict, Polish Radio escaped largely unscathed. Partly this was because it adhered seriously to its complex public service brief, partly because of the diversity of alternative radio. The first commercial station, Radio Zet, offered a combination of serious political broadcasting, popular music and middlebrow entertainment. It grew rapidly, leading the radio rankings with 28.7 per cent in mid-1997 (Polish Radio's First Programme had 27.4 per cent, RMF FM 26.2 per cent and the Catholic Radio Maryja nine per cent).[39] Polish Radio retained considerable cultural importance for its associated orchestras and its long-standing support of concerts, music festivals and competitions. The main bone of contention was the Broadcasting Council's failure to provide frequencies enabling it to reach the entire country, while handing out desirable frequencies willy-nilly to commercial firms with few public service obligations.

The most interesting development in the field of radio was the rise of Radio Maryja, a specifically Polish cultural, spiritual, social and political phenomenon. Initiated in 1991 and financed mainly by listeners' donations, Radio Maryja reached about 40 per cent of the population by 1997 and had a faithful audience of some five million.[40] Its listeners were distinctive in listening longer each day than other radio listeners and only to Radio Maryja. Its diet of religious homily and nationalist rhetoric not only inspired committed listeners but also mobilized political and social activism. Its guiding force, Father Rydzyk, was a controversial figure and a frequent source of embarrassment to the Church hierarchy, not least because of his anti-Semitism – the Episcopate had 'considerable reservations, especially over the use of … unChristian and dishonest language'[41] – but his ability to inspire his audience was not in doubt. Radio Maryja generated a deep response in the traditional Catholic element of society. Its strident calls to political action met with massive enthusiasm and it took a stand on key political events: urging listeners to vote for Lech Wałęsa, to protest to the State Election Committee over Kwaśniewski's electoral victory, to join anti-pornography campaigns, to picket parliamentary deputies who supported liberalization of the abortion law, to contribute funds to save the Gdańsk Shipyard from liquidation, to vote 'no' in the constitutional referendum, to vote for Christian candidates in the 1997 election, and to support RM itself: Radio Maryja mobilized some 600,000 letters to the National Broadcasting Council demanding the allocation of a frequency to reach Silesia; it also persuaded many listeners to transfer their privatization shares to its coffers. Its social arm was 'Families of Radio Maryja', a loose social movement based on the parish. 200,000 people took part in a 'pilgrimage of the Families' in August 1996 and despite its lack of formal organization, membership or statute, 600 bureaux functioned in almost half the parishes reached by RM.[42] In September 1997 20 deputies entered parliament with the endorsement of Radio Maryja.

Civil Liberties and Media Regulation

If the broadcasting law was the key piece of legislation in the period 1989–97, numerous other statutes (or their absence) were also relevant to the media's role in the democratization process. Freedom of the press requires safeguards for journalists but also constraints on their actions. Constraints are always controversial; they may result from broader issues of freedom of expression (the question of a right to reply, prohibition of incitement to ethnic hatred); personal liberties (privacy, redress for defamation, the naming of defendants); or the physical security or moral fabric of society and its state. The 1997 Constitution did not include a specific clause securing press freedom but rather subsumed it under the general right to free expression (though Article 54 explicitly prohibited prior censorship of the media). This is unusual; but rarely outside the United States is the concept of press freedom so libertarian as to equate it with virtual absence of restraint.[43]

There is no 'right to reply' in Poland, although the issue of protecting people from intrusive journalism surfaced in such fora as the Centre for Monitoring Press Freedom. Various proposals were mooted – a British-style Press Council or a Media Ombudsman[44] found favour in some circles – but no consensus emerged. Suits for defamation of character became common, but they were used largely by politicians and journalists themselves rather than by 'ordinary', non-political citizens. It is difficult to judge the impact on investigative journalism, since most cases appeared to involve insulting epithets rather than matters of serious public interest. However, the editors of *Gazeta Wyborcza* were vindicated from accusations that they had set it up with Solidarity's money and then lined their own pockets with the proceeds, and litigants against *GW* lost a case involving allegations of police corruption in Pozna. However, Polish libel law is explicitly biased against the media, with a view 'more sensitive to reputation than to freedom of speech …'.[45] Since the police do not automatically follow up implications of wrong-doing suggested by media reports, the two factors together could discourage investigative reporting.

Polish journalists came into conflict with the state over the issues of official secrets and protection of their sources. Only one, the notorious Jerzy Urban, was convicted (February 1996), for publishing in *Nie* in 1992 copies of documents dating from 1958; they confirmed the collaboration with the security services of the former director of the Polish section of Radio Free Europe.[46] In September 1994 the *Sejm* passed a draconian law listing more wide-ranging categories of secrecy than those adopted during martial law[47] and providing penalties of up to ten-years imprisonment for journalists, even when revealing matters of public interest. The ensuing storm of protest led to a sudden about-face by the Social Democrats, and the Senate roundly rejected the law.[48] Thus at the beginning of 1998 this important area was still subject to 'communist law'. Nor had progress been made on a new Press Law.

The ruling coalition proceeded cautiously during the Oleksy Affair, which saw its own then prime minister (inconclusively) accused of spying for Russia. From December 1995 the press rushed to provide further details on the basis of an avalanche of confidential leaks which further called into question the role and political orientation of the security services. The media appeared to be not at all intimidated even after Urban's conviction and a series of unexplained attacks on *Wprost* journalist Jerzy Mac. Indeed, the Procuracy dropped charges against two *Życie Warszawy* journalists for publishing a secret 'Oleksy' document after they refused to testify. This was clearly a political decision: the (1984) Press Law broadly guaranteed confidentiality of journalists' sources, but not for spying, treason or homicide.

The new Penal Code reached the end of its long legislative process in mid-1997. It contained two relevant sections: first, the Court may release journalists from the requirements of professional secrecy 'when that is essential in the cause of justice'; the second specifies imprisonment from three months to five years for revelation of official secrets (still undefined by new legislation). The need for a new Press Law, Law on Official Secrecy, and Code of Criminal Procedure (expected to incorporate qualified privilege for doctors, lawyers and journalists)[49] was keenly felt by journalists who saw the existing situation as a serious potential threat to their independence.[50] On the other hand, the overt party-political activities of many journalists and/or their association with highly partisan papers or television programmes made it more difficult for the profession to escape its communist legacy of (partial) subservience and redefine itself as genuinely independent.

Public Order and Morals

The 1977 Constitution envisaged the circumscribing of civil liberties in the democratic state 'when and only when necessary for its security or public order, whether for the protection of the environment, health or public morals or for securing the rights and freedoms of other persons' (Art.31 §3). There were no signs after 1989 of precedents for such restrictions in relation to the media. Urban's 1991 acquittal for disseminating 'pornography' demonstrated the reluctance of the courts to venture into this charged area. No prosecution of pornography was successful up to 1997, despite church-inspired campaigns to force the procuracy to take action.[51] This seemed unlikely to change, since the new Penal Code removed almost all anti-pornography provisions.[52] Nor were media organs prosecuted for incitement to racial or ethnic hatred, despite potential candidates among the fringe press (comparable to the Czech Republic's anti-Semitic *Politika,* which was banned in 1994) and Radio Maryja with its vituperative anti-Semitism. The political fallout clearly did not seem worth the candle.

Democratization and the Media

Many developments reported here have their counterparts in other post-communist countries. Appointment and dismissal of media personnel provided a spectacle of political infighting almost everywhere. Privatization was difficult and links between politicians and media owners were commonplace. Allocation of radio and television frequencies caused political storms. No country escaped allegations of political bias of state broadcasting media. Foreign investment generated anxiety. The process of legal regulation remained incomplete. Yet in Poland, as in Hungary and the Czech Republic, these developments showed crosscurrents and counter-tendencies; they did not all work in the same direction, whether to generate a cohesive political economy of the media[53] or a consistent pattern of neo-authoritarianism. Governments sought advantage in their continuing domination of the broadcast media, but governments changed hands in Poland and Hungary and were bound to do so again. Indirect methods of influence replaced direct political control. By contrast in the fourth Visegrad country, Slovakia, Vladimir Mečiar effectively dominated the political scene for most of the period from 1989–97 and his government 'increasingly sought to stifle and control the media'.[54] While not wholly lacking tendencies to media diversification and pluralisation, Slovakia saw a more persistent and uni-directional authoritarianism, in regard to the media and more generally. Meciar dismissed 17 of the 18 members of the state broadcasting councils (November 1994) and over six years Slovak state television (STV) had nine directors and six senior editors of the main news programmes in quick succession.[55] Programming became more pro-government, more 'Slovak', and less accessible to the opposition to the point where STV could be described as 'a government mouthpiece'.[56]

Mečiar's party, the Movement for Democratic Slovakia (HZDS), owned and subsidised part of the press, such as the nationalist pro-government Slovak daily *Slovenská Republica*, while TV Dolina and TV Markíza and the national cable channel VTV were also said to have strong links to the party.[57] Journalists assumed political functions such that the 'overlap between state functions and media functions has in some instances become extreme, and is not limited to the state-run media'.[58] It was the cumulative effect of such developments and the wider political context in which they operated that distinguished Slovakia from its close neighbours. Yet even in Slovakia one would be hard pressed to deny the extent of media transformation; the fact that Mečiar's actions have not gone uncontested is itself an indicator of profound change.

Unsurprisingly then, media developments in the first post-communist decade displayed both strong similarities and culturally specific particularities. In Poland the print media from 1954 onwards were a significant indicator of liberalization and provided a mirror of change as well as constituting an agent of change, whether above or below ground. After 1989 the process intensified and extended to the broadcasting media. The media's role in democratization is impossible to disentangle from other factors working in the same direction, but their atmospheric qualities, agenda-setting potential, ability to call government to account, and provision of opportunities for multi-faceted debate make their role considerable. At its best the Polish press fosters democratic ideals, informs, analyses and reveals corruption and undemocratic practices; is interesting, erudite and enlightening. At its worst the press undermines democratic ideals by preaching intolerance and conformity, attacking or supporting government regardless of merit; it is tendentious, intolerant, parochial, ill informed and distasteful. Television by contrast remained less diverse. State television largely failed to come to terms with its public service remit and its political coverage was uninspiring, though election coverage improved significantly. Some commercial stations provided some counterbalance (often as controversial, as when PolSat showed a film favourable to

Kwaśniewski during the 1995 presidential election). The notion of an independent expert Council overseeing the broadcasting media also seemed utopian, especially given the polarization of the political scene after 1995. With both highly imperfect, a continuing state sector enabled resistance to some of the pressures of commercialisation, while the commercial sector mitigated the pressures of political bias of state broadcasting.

NOTES

1. Ildikó Kováts and Gordon Whiting, 'Hungary', in D. Paletz, K. Jakubowicz and P. Novosel (eds.), *Glasnost and After: Media and Change in Central and Eastern Europe* (New York: Hampton Press, 1995), pp.97–208; András Lánczi and Patrick H. O'Neil, 'Pluralization and the Politics of Media Change in Hungary', *The Journal of Communist Studies and Transition Politics*, Vol.12, No.4 (1996), pp.82–101.

2. See, for example, Steve Kettle, 'The Development of the Czech Media since the Fall of Communism', *The Journal of Communist Politics and Transition Studies*, Vol.12, No.4 (1996), pp.42–60; Frank Kaplan, 'Changes in the Czechoslovak and Czech Mass Media since 1989: An U.S. Perspective', *East European Quarterly*, Vol.XXX, No.1 (1996), pp.115–29.

3. A. Remmer, 'A Note on Post-Publication Censorship in Poland', *Soviet Studies*, Vol.XLI, No.3 (1989), pp.415–25.

4. Kovats and Whiting, 'Hungary', pp.103–6; Karol Jakubowicz, 'Poland', in D. Paletz, K. Jakubowicz and P. Novosel (eds.), *Glasnost and After: Media and Change in Central and Eastern Europe* (New York: Hampton Press, 1995), pp.133–4.

5. Ernest Skalski, 'Pięciolecie Gazety Wyborczej', in Alina Słomkowska (ed.), *Pięciolecie Transformacji Mediów (1989–1994)* (Warsaw: Dom Wydawniczy Elipsa, 1995), p.340.

6. Zbigniew Bajka, 'Kapitał zagraniczny w polskich mediach', in Alina Słomkowska (ed.), *Pięciolecie Transformacji Mediów (1989–1994)* (Warsaw: Dom Wydawniczy Elipsa, 1995), p.97.

7. Agnes Gulyás, 'Media and Politics in the Transformation Period: the Case of Hungary', paper presented to the Political Studies Association Specialist Conference, South Bank University, 8 Feb. 1997, pp.9–10.

8. Elżbieta Ciborska, 'Pięciolecie transformacji prasy postpezetpeerowskiej (1989–1994)', in Alina Słomkowska (ed.), *Pięciolecie Transformacji Mediów (1989–1994)* (Warsaw: Dom Wydawniczy Elipsa, 1995), p.197.

9. *Rzeczpospolita* No.182, 3 Aug. 1992; Piotr Skórzynski, 'Smutna twarz mediów', *Lad*, No.4 (23 Jan. 1994).

10. Mieczysław Prószyński, '50 milionów czytelników czasopism', *Rzeczpospolita* No.296 (20 Dec. 1996); this is comparable to the 70 per cent cited by Tomasz Goban-Klas, 'Politics versus the Media in Poland: A Game without Rules', *The Journal of Communist Studies and Transition Politics*, Vol.12, No.4 (1996), p.27.

11. Dariusz Fikus, 'Od Sztandaru Młodych do Rzeczpospolitej', in Alina Słomkowska (ed.), *Pięciolecie Transformacji Mediów (1989–1994)* (Warsaw: Dom Wydawniczy Elipsa, 1995), p.157.

12. Dariusz Fikus, 'Dlaczego nie chcemy kolumny rządowej', *Rzeczpospolita*, No.37 (13 Feb. 1995).

13. Joanna Kraszewska-Ey and Mariusz Janicki, 'W papierowym walcu', *Polityka*, No.5 (4 Feb. 1995).

14. Grzegorz Sieczkowski and Anita Blaszczak, 'Przeciek sterowany', *Rzeczpospolita*, No.207 (5 Sept. 1996).

15. Jerzy Baczynski, 'Co się czyta', *Polityka*, No.24 (14 June 1997).

16. Adam Grzeszak, 'Tytuły na straty', *Polityka*, No.5 (1 Feb. 1997).

17. Barbara Cieszewska, 'Jeden przeciw wszystkim', *Rzeczpospolita*, No.278 (29 Nov. 1996).

18. The text of the Law is in *Rzeczpospolita*, No.17 (21 Jan. 1993), and *Rzeczpospolita*, No.18 (22 Jan. 1993).
19. Father Adam Boniecki, 'O Katolickiej cenzurze i wartościach chrzescijańskich', *Tygodnik Powszechny*, No.4 (24 Jan. 1993); see also M. Pęczak, 'Swoboda i dyktat', *Polityka*, No.7 (13 Feb. 1993).
20. Goban-Klas, p.30.
21. Andrzej Drawicz, 'Byłem prezesem TVP', *Polityka*, No.19 (13 May 1995).
22. Ibid.
23. A. Kublik and D. Wielowieyska, 'Rado, Czuj się odwołana', *Gazeta Wyborcza*, No.223, (24–25 Sept. 1994).
24. *Rzeczpospolita*, No. 239 (13 Oct. 1994).
25. Beata Modrzejewska and Anna Wielopolska, 'Organ pod własnym nadzorem', *Rzeczpospolita*, No.97 (25 April 1995).
26. Sieczkowski and Blaszczak.
27. *Rzeczpospolita*, No.140 (18 June 1997).
28. Miroslaw Pęczak, 'Polak przed ekranem', *Polityka*, No.25 (21 June 1997).
29. Miroslaw Pęczak, 'Czyja telewizja?' *Polityka*, No.21 (21 May 1994).
30. *Rzeczpospolita*, No.105 (7 May 1996). Wałęsa always wore a miniature Madonna on his lapel.
31. Jacek Kurski and Piotr Semki, *Lewy czerwcowy* (Warsaw: Editions Spotkania, 1993).
32. NIK referred 19 issues to the Procuracy as a consequence of its investigation into Polish Television between 1994 and 1996; Piotr Sarzyński, 'Zgniła równowaga', *Polityka*, No.24 (14 June 1997).
33. Stanislaw Janecki, 'Bez znieczulenia', *Wprost*, No.5 (2 Feb. 1997).
34. *Gazeta Wyborcza*, No.135 (12 June 1997).
35. Ibid.
36. Beata Modrzejewska, 'Najwięcej potknięc w najważniejszych informacjach', *Rzecz-pospolita*, No.276 (27 Nov. 1996).
37. J. Mac, 'Telewizja wyborcza', *Wprost*, No.37 (12 Sept. 1993).
38. For example, ROP's complaint was quite rightly upheld by the Broadcasting Council against 'Candidates on 2' (*Kandydaci w dwójce*), TVP2, 11 Sept. 1997, when journalist Barbara Czajkowska's questioning lasted far longer than the time permitted for Senator Romaszewski's answer.
39. Baczyński, op. cit.
40. Boguslaw Mazur, 'Polska Partia Rydzyka', *Wprost*, No.19 (11 May 1997).
41. Bishop Tadeusz Pieronek, quoted in Maciej Luczak, 'Holding Maryja', *Wprost*, No.14 (6 April 1997).
42. Małgorzata Subotic, 'Alleluja! - i do przodu', *Rzeczpospolita*, No.113 (16 May 1997).
43. Wojciech Sadurski, 'Freedom of the Press in Postcommunist Poland', *East European Politics and Societies*, Vol.10, No. 3 (1996), pp.440–1.
44. Grzegorz Sieczkowski, 'Inicjatywa w rękach dziennikarzy', *Rzeczpospolita*, No.276 (27 Nov. 1996).
45. Sadurski, p.446.
46. *Rzeczpospolita*, No.32 (7 Feb. 1996).
47. 'Komitet Helsinki: Zagrożenia dla praw czlowieka', *Rzeczpospolita*, No.215 (15 Sept. 1994).
48. *Rzeczpospolita*, No.235 (8–9 Oct. 1994).
49. Sadurski, p.448.
50. Grzegorz Sieczkowski, 'Inicjatywa w rękach dziennikarzy', *Rzeczpospolita*, No. 276 (27 November 1996).
51. Miroslaw Usidus and Michal Janowski, 'Przed sądem ostatecznym', *Rzeczpospolita*, No.185 (9 Aug.1996).
52. Sadurski, p.450.
53. Denis McQuail, *Mass Communication Theory: An Introduction* (London: Sage, 1987), 2nd edn, p.64.
54. Andrej Školkay, 'Journalists, Political Elites and the Post-Communist Public: The Case of

Slovakia', *The Journal of Communist Studies and Transition Politics*, Vol.12, No.4 (1996), p.72.
55. Školkay, p. 77.
56. *OMRI Daily Digest*, No.210, Part II (30 Oct. 1996).
57. Sharon Fisher, 'Slovak Media under Pressure', *Transition*, Vol.1 (6 Oct. 1995), p.7; Sharon Fisher, 'TV Markiza', *Transition*, Vol.2 (18 Oct. 1996), p.48.
58. Školkay, p.77.

Regime Transition and the Media in Taiwan

GARY D. RAWNSLEY and
MING-YEH T. RAWNSLEY

Taiwan's recent experience of political regime transition suggests the existence of a strong correlation between the promotion of free and diverse media and the level of political change. The government's efforts to create a more liberal media environment are commendable, but, owing to the structure of the market and ownership patterns, the party of government (the Kuomintang) maintains a powerful influence over television and major newspapers. This makes the so-called new media, especially cable television and talk radio, particularly important to democratization in Taiwan. So far, however, they have tended to promote a divisive and adversarial political culture rather than true democratic consolidation.

Introduction

On 23 March 1996, the people of Taiwan were given the opportunity for the first time in their history to participate in democratic elections for their President and Vice-President.[1] Although this does not imply that Taiwan's transition is complete, it has nevertheless made remarkable progress since the process of political reform began in 1986. Not surprisingly, it has therefore been the subject of renewed interest as suggested by the sudden proliferation of English-language studies on Taiwan's political transformation.[2] Yet most of these fail to devote sufficient attention to the role of the mass media;[3] and this is curious given that the media have been a powerful force for weakening authoritarian rule, have helped to structure participation and competition within the political arena, and have thus made a positive contribution to the consolidation of democratic procedure. It can be convincingly argued that those features of Taiwan's transition that have contributed to its unique character and success – a smooth and gradual liberalization characterized by rapid economic growth, a remarkable degree of inclusiveness, and an almost complete absence of violent confrontation between the government and opposition[4] – were served by a highly-developed mass media and one of the most literate societies in Asia.[5] In short, Taiwan's recent experiences of regime transition suggest the existence of a strong correlation between the promotion of free and diverse media and the level of political change.

This account seeks to add to the literature on the media and political transition[6] by first considering the process of Taiwan's liberalization. This will be followed by an investigation of how well Taiwan's media have served and furthered the two remaining criteria of democratic consolidation – participation and competition.

The government of Taiwan itself accepts that free and diversified media are essential components of democratic change. Former director-general of the Government Information Office (GIO), Jason C. Hu, has described the 'unfettered flow of information' as a 'prerequisite for democratic development':

> Deregulating the news media allows media professionals to handle information according to the best of their ability and free judgement. It is extremely important for the media to make information available, serve as a government watchdog, make social assessments, and resolve conflicts. Therefore, the government as well as the public should respect and safeguard the independence of the media in their role as a fair and impartial fourth estate that checks and balances the executive, legislative and judicial branches of the government.[7]

But while the government's many efforts to create a more liberal media environment are certainly commendable, ownership patterns that distort the political agenda still restrict participation and political competition. These patterns focus on, and thereby promote, the Kuomintang (KMT) party of government. The party's influence over three of the current four network television channels, together with the most influential and widely read newspapers, remains a hindrance to the attainment of full democracy. This has made the so-called 'new media', especially cable television and talk radio, particularly important, and their role in Taiwan's political transition needs to be assessed. Nevertheless, although liberalization has reduced political control of the media, the diversification and commercial competition present in the market have imposed their own limitations on the contribution which the media can make to political life in Taiwan. In addition, Beijing's extraordinary influence over developments in Taiwan presents its own challenges, not least in defining the political, and therefore news agenda which the media are obliged to follow.

The Media and Authoritarianism

To understand fully the role that the media have played in Taiwan's political transition, it is necessary to offer a brief survey of the media environment before martial law was lifted in 1987. This history will then demonstrate precisely how dramatic, yet at the same time how smooth, that transition has been compared to other experiences of regime change.

Prior to 1987, Taiwan was an authoritarian state which had successfully combined economic openness with centralized political authority, and was characterized by one-party tutelage and limited political participation. As Steven J. Hood has observed, 'Democracy was at best a long-term goal, secondarily important to recovery of the mainland and economic development'.[8] At the centre of this political edifice was the Nationalist Party, the KMT, which since 1924 has been organized according to Leninist principles. Its cellular and cadre-led basis granted the KMT enormous power and leverage over every aspect of life in Taiwan, and its structure enabled a highly efficient system of political communication to mature: 'Party cells and local party branches permeate Taiwan society, monitoring the mood and social ties of local residents village by village and ward by ward'.[9] Not only has the KMT been the party of government since 1947, but it has also been responsible for the formation of Taiwan's political culture. Its functions have included political recruitment, socialization, mobilization and social control.[10] This environment formed restricted mass media which tended to act as transmission belts on behalf of the KMT – the 1976 Broadcasting and Television Law gave the GIO the power to instruct all stations to broadcast 'such programs as news and publicity of governmental orders and policies'[11] – thus granting it a monopoly on information which was crucial to its exercise of authority.

By 1987, the KMT owned four national daily newspapers; the government owned two, and the military five.[12] Since the KMT dominated the government, and therefore had absolute control of the military, the party enjoyed overwhelming authority over the activities of the print media. The remaining 20 newspapers were privately owned, but the majority tended to have close corporate ties with the KMT. Indeed the owners of the two newspapers with the highest circulation, the *China Times* (*Chung Kuo Shih Pao*) and the *United Daily News* (*Lien Ho Pao*) were members of the KMT Central Standing Committee. Nevertheless, the *Independent Evening Post* (*Tzu Li Wan Pao*) and the *People's Daily* (*Min Chung Jih Pao*) were owned and controlled by native Taiwanese (as opposed to Chinese who had come to Taiwan after the Communist victory on the mainland) without close connections with the KMT.[13] The *Taiwan Times* (*Taiwan Shih Pao*), located in Kaohsiung in the south of the island, was also privately owned and independent, publishing what Bruce Jacobs called 'strongly worded editorials and comments'.[14]

This is significant, for it suggests that even in a politically restricted media environment, the KMT was prepared to tolerate a degree of press independence. Steven J. Hood has noted that while the KMT was 'obsessed' with 'controlling dissent', the party nevertheless made a 'modest effort to ease some restrictions' long before it decided to lift martial law:

The press called for greater Taiwanese representation in government. By 1956 newspapers began to print some stories the KMT previously considered dangerous for public consumption ... Newspapers in Taiwan called on the government to reform the system and pay decent wages to promote efficiency and to relieve the temptation for official corruption.

Although Hood speculates that such developments may have been a reaction to the Hundred Flowers movement on the mainland, this nevertheless indicates that a level of public criticism was accepted, and even encouraged.[15] Even the *China Times* and the *United Daily News*, while broadly supporting the government, were able to be more editorially independent than newspapers published by the government or party precisely because they were privately owned, and were therefore in competition with each other. Those published by the authorities, however, did enjoy a circulation advantage because all public institutions were required to subscribe to them.

Even though market competition played a significant role in circumscribing editorial autonomy, the print media were still subject to an extensive body of laws and regulations which were designed to reinforce the KMT's power. Copy was never scrutinized by a censor before publication, although Articles 22 and 23 of the National Mobilization Law bestowed upon the government powers of confiscation after publication if newspapers printed anything considered to be threatening to political or military interests. The vague and arbitrary wording which left such laws open to interpretation, gave the government enormous latitude in exercising its jurisdiction over the media. Other laws were more specific; the Publication Law, for example, regulated the registration of publications (restricting ownership to 'reliable' persons[16]) and restricted the number of pages they could print.[17]

Despite all of these restraints on their activities, the print media were the main and most popular source of political information and opinion, especially as the national literacy rate hovered around 94 per cent. In his 1976 essay on Taiwan's press, J. Bruce Jacobs presented a picture of an industry that was of critical importance in the political life of the nation. 'At all levels of Taiwan's political system', he wrote, 'politically-interested persons read the daily press regularly ... To be politically *au courant* in Taiwan, one has to read the daily press'.[18]

In addition the party-state enjoyed major ownership of the three main television networks (local stations did not exist until 1995): the Taiwan Television Company (TTV, established in 1962), whose principal stock owner was the Taiwan Provincial government; the China Television

Company (CTV, established 1968), owned in large part by the KMT; and the Chinese Television System (CTS, established 1971), owned by the Ministry of National Defence.[19] They were regulated by the Broadcasting and Television Law of 1976 which not only controlled their ownership, finance and structure, but also governed their programming. For example, it stipulated that the entertainment output of these stations should promote the Chinese culture; should be broadcast mainly in Mandarin (Taiwanese dialect programming was discouraged because of its association with the outlawed independence movement); and should not conflict with 'official policies'.

Thus the KMT has been using its monopoly of the electronic media as a critical part of its machinery to maintain sovereign power and to promote its own very distinct world-view. As the late President Chiang Ching-kuo once observed:

> Among all the means of mass communications television is the most effective. Thus the production of television programmes must not be profit oriented. Only when television carries out the spirits of the Three Principles of the People,[20] can it be said that our television industry fulfils its social responsibilities as a medium of mass communications.[21]

In other words the leaders of the KMT embraced the idea that all forms of mass communications, especially television, had identifiable 'social responsibilities'. For the KMT this involved making a positive contribution to social control and national reconstruction. This was strengthened by the almost complete penetration of Taiwan's daily life by television: in 1990, television sets in use numbered almost six million, while there was an average of 98.8 colour television sets per 100 households. There is reason to suggest these figures are conservative – in 1995, 95 out of every 100 persons watched the television news on one of three network stations, while variety shows were viewed by 90 per cent of the population.[22]

Although the television industry was ostensibly not motivated by the pursuit of profit, the three stations nevertheless competed intensively for advertising revenue; however, competition did not extend to programme quality. As Kuo Li-hsin has noted: 'Television's responsibility of "mass communications" in the ROC has been minimized to just one function, "mass consumption"'.[23] Such observations are reinforced by the proportion of the weekly television schedule (55 per cent) devoted to entertainment.[24]

The three commercial television organisations were unadventurous, producing programmes for the 'middle ground' market with 'mass' tastes in order to attract as many viewers as possible, thereby eroding the diversity of programming. Commercialism, together with Chiang Ching-kuo's vision of the role that television might play in society, created an industry which, in structure and output, reflected the utilitarian character of Taiwan that had been formed over four decades of martial law: programmes shied away from controversy; they completely avoided political subjects, and concentrated instead on providing information and entertainment which would not upset the *status quo*.

It can be seen, therefore, that with few exceptions the mass media were in no position to scrutinize the decisions and actions of the government, or challenge the legitimacy of its platform. The idea of an independent and critical Fourth Estate was anathema to Taiwan. Instead, the media were politically 'guided' on what stories to cover and how, so that their work might meet the objectives of the regime, defined by the KMT as the economic and political development of Taiwan, and the reunification of Taiwan with mainland China. In addition, editors were members of the KMT, thus placing 'gatekeepers' in prominent and powerful political positions, and compelling their independence and professional integrity to be questioned. The role of the media did not extend beyond framing and interpreting for the people of Taiwan the government's actions and decisions.

Severe political control of the media environment meant that the opposition had a more difficult time than the KMT, but was no less successful in finding a channel to voice its convictions. To clearly understand the role of the dissident media, it is crucial to appreciate that since 1951 the KMT did allow at least a semblance of electoral democracy to flourish, albeit only at the local level and subject to strict political control. Nevertheless, a high level of popular participation and competition was encouraged. Independent candidates[25] were permitted to run against KMT candidates in local elections, and were allowed to criticize and actively campaign against the government during brief 'democracy holidays'. Yet while their indiscretions were overlooked in victory, election defeat carried severe penalties, including the possibility of imprisonment. There was thus a strong imperative for independents to fight and win elections, to mobilize their supporters, and build and maintain a solid institutional base at the grass-roots level. As C.L. Chiou has asserted, 'To win elections thus literally meant political survival for the opposition members and their democratization campaigns'.[26]

Yet campaigning was extraordinarily difficult; the 1980 Election and Recall Law prohibited all candidates standing for election from using the regular mass media, but did allow the use of party-owned media, a clause which clearly benefited the KMT. Thus the opposition had to develop alternative methods of getting its messages across to the electorate, and did so primarily by relying on interpersonal communication and rallies, but also by organizing an innovative yet illegal media system as an alternative to the

KMT dominated media. As C.L. Chiou has observed, although opposition elites 'were not great in number in the 1950s and the 1960s, and under the "white terror" of the martial law government of the Nationalists, they could not get much popular support among the severely intimidated Taiwanese people ... their achievements were ... very important in terms of sustaining the opposition campaigns and establishing operational models for the following generations'.[27] Their participation in these local elections provided both candidates and voters with valuable experience of electoral democracy.

The evolution of an alternative media followed a similar pattern: as the independents began to coalesce into the Tangwai (literally meaning outside the party) movement in the late 1970s, and formed the Democratic Progressive Party (DPP) in 1986, magazines and political journals provided their foremost channel for expressing grievances and offering alternative political information. Although they articulated views which were prohibited by the myriad of laws created and administered by the KMT, their publication was tolerated until they began to engage in more concerted and organized activity, such as the formation of parties. Then the government would intervene and suppress them, often gaoling the publishers or contributors. The life of such magazines was very short, but their publishers never ceased in their efforts to find an audience.[28] In other words, the government was prepared to endure the advocacy of critical opinion, but was not prepared to allow such opinion to form the basis of actual political activity.

As Taiwan entered the age of the electronic media, the opposition discovered a new method of disseminating alternative opinion and information, but were nevertheless inspired by their predecessors' experience of publishing. Thus the underground radio and cable television systems which were established in the 1990s bore more than a passing resemblance to the political journals of previous generations. The dissident media played a crucial role in the opposition's fight for survival, and acted as one of many sources of pressure on the government to democratize Taiwan.

In short, Taiwan's authoritarian political system did allow for democratic procedure – electoral competition and high levels of participation – at the local level which, although restrictive, did at least provide the basis for the future consolidation of democracy. It could be argued that the pressures for democratization grew despite restricted access to the media, not because of it.

The Media and Democratization

The process of democratization in Taiwan has been far from linear; the boundaries between liberalization and political reform were often blurred and difficult to identify. Nevertheless, reforming the media environment was definitely part of the liberalization that occurred with the lifting of martial law in July 1987, even though it was slow – restrictions on the publication of daily newspapers were not suspended until January 1988; and there were still areas of the electronic media which were only liberalized *after* political reform[29] – receiving and transmitting cable television broadcasts was illegal until as recently as 1993, while call-in radio stations were only legalized in 1994 due to their association with the underground media. Even now, a decade after the reform process began, the KMT still enjoys considerable influence over the three network television stations and national radio networks.

Media liberalization, then, allowed the more tangible political reforms to be widely publicized; it increased popular awareness of the agenda for change, and of course granted the opposition a more powerful means of expression. Since free and open elections help to define democracies, and are the periods in the calendar when the benefits of political communication are most clearly realized, their discussion is inevitable. After all, Taiwan holds more elections than any other state except the United States and Switzerland. The role of the media during such political flashpoints has been well summarized by Vicky Randall: 'The media must inform people about the different parties and candidates and help them to choose from among them. They should also be the watchdogs, exposing instances of electoral malpractice. At the same time they must help to keep up the pressure for change.'[30]

Previously, winning elections had been a matter of survival for the opposition: defeat in the polls meant severe punishment for candidates who had dared to stand against the official KMT platform. The legalization of the opposition movement, together with a freer media environment, prompted a significant change in electoral practices, including the use of those methods of mobilization normally associated with western (specifically American) election campaigns. However, difficulties prevail: recent research has suggested that many of these techniques (such as negative campaigning, the professional organization of campaigns) either did not work in recent elections, or were rejected altogether, while the mainstream media remain dominated by images of KMT candidates (magnifying the importance of incumbency), and are therefore unable fully and freely to inform the electorate about alternative candidates and platforms. In addition the often vicious, and usually uncorroborated, personal attacks on candidates suggest that Taiwan's political culture has yet to grasp the existence of the fine line between freedom of speech and the responsibilities that accompany electoral democracy.

Nevertheless, the rapid growth of cable broadcasting and talk-radio have provided the opposition candidates with an opportunity to target their political propaganda for specific audiences, and thus appeal to the voters most sympathetic to their platform. In addition, the media have been central in exposing electoral malpractice and corruption, and in stimulating the movement against such behaviour. Yet while the use of the media is growing, recent elections clearly demonstrate that traditional forms of mobilization (primary groups, sound-trucks, rallies, and *guanxi*, or strong personal relationships and patron–client networks) remain significant, while voters are beginning to decipher the superficiality of such features of media-dominated campaigns as the photo-opportunity.[31]

However, the opportunities that are presented by political liberalization are tempered by other factors, most notably market forces, which are more or less beyond the control of any one individual or group; and these forces play a role of comparable power to political restrictions. After all, political involvement in the media is a recognised enemy; the political environment is structured in such a way that interference can be resisted by institutionalized checks and balances, and by the emergence of strong forces of opposition. The effects of commercialism are more subversive and sinister since they legitimately erode the quality of programming via reference to such notions as 'free market forces', and 'value for money'. For example, the print media remain dominated by a small assortment of powerful corporate interests which own and control groups of newspapers. In 1993, the consortia owning the three most important newspapers in Taiwan – the *China Times*, the *United Daily News* and the *Liberty Times* (*Tzu You Shih Pao*, a new title which entered the industry in the post-reform era) – dominated the market with a combined share of 54 per cent.[32] Since the groups owning these three newspapers have close links with the KMT, the political significance of this market superiority cannot be overlooked.[33]

Nevertheless, it cannot be denied that the print media now enjoy greater editorial independence despite the persistence of traditional ownership patterns. But the role of censor is now played by the market, rather than the government. Fierce competition for advertising revenue and readers has forced the print media to converge on the middle ground. This is clearly illustrated by the short-life of the *Capital Morning Post* (*Sho Tu Tsao Pao*) which was established and financed by Kang Ning-hsiang, a prominent DPP politician. It was forced to close down not because it advocated the opinions of the opposition, but because it captured an unsustainable share of the market.

Competition in the market, which forces the press to concentrate on attracting the largest number of readers by consolidating their position on the middle ground, has also tempered the radicalism of previously dissident print media; the principal political journals which survive either are sponsored by big patrons who have the financial resources to support such ventures, or are small collections of articles by politically active intellectuals and require little financial assistance.[34]

Liberalization of the media was clearly not a panacea for the problems faced by the industry; indeed, reform in some areas heightened popular dissatisfaction with the limited changes being effected in others. Media issues in particular have become sensitive and highly politicized, and struggles against those unreformed sectors of the electronic media have been frequently organized as a method of mobilizing opposition against the government, as the following case clearly demonstrates.

Feeling that their legal rights had been neglected by the government for long enough, 5,000 farmers from the central and southern parts of Taiwan staged a demonstration in Taipei on 20 May 1988.[35] The demonstration soon turned into a violent confrontation with the police, resulting in more than 100 protesters being arrested, 90 per cent of whom were later charged. The three network television stations all portrayed this incident as a 'riot', which is, of course, a term of reference laden with political meaning. Their news reports broadcast images of an hysterical public attacking the Legislative Yuan, parked cars being set on fire, policemen wounded by flying stones, and the streets of Taipei city left in disarray.

In order to provide an alternative representation of events from that being broadcast on the national television stations, two small private organizations, the 'Green Group' and the 'Third Image', captured a visual record on their own camcorders and edited them into short factual videos. Both of these tapes, but especially that produced by the Green Group, suggested that the police and soldiers had started the riot by attacking the protestors, that they chased and hit runaway students and farmers, and emphasized the way the demonstrators had stood up against authority. In other words, they offered a very different interpretation of events from that provided by the mainstream media. Although the quality of these videos could not compete with the professional television cameras, and despite the fact that they could not be legally sold, rented or even shown in public, black market copies proved extremely popular. Perhaps this was a sign that many people in Taiwan were eager to seek out alternative truths, as well as a demonstration that they did not trust the three national television networks to present an objective portrait of political and public issues. It also explained why the Department of Cultural Affairs (DCA) of the KMT felt it necessary to later produce and distribute another video by re-editing news material collected from the networks. Although this official account of the incident expressed precisely the same viewpoint as that told by the three television enterprises, such an action implied that the KMT government had sensed the pressure generated by the movement against the mainstream electronic media and felt that it had to respond.[36]

The event which had sparked the demonstrations was commemorated in 1995 by a march to reform the media which demanded that the KMT, the government, and the military withdraw from involvement in all television enterprises. It served as a reminder of the apparently partial and highly negative way that the news broadcasts of the networks reported political and social movements in a period of supposed democratization.[37]

These are just two examples (from the many which could be cited)[38] which illustrate not only the level of popular disappointment with the performance of Taiwan's national television, but also (i) how the media themselves have become an issue in the opposition's struggle for further reform, and (ii) how the framing of events by the mainstream media is also politically significant since it defines how the audience will interpret any given news story.

The Media and Democratic Consolidation

So technological developments, market competition, and the convergence of the print media on the political middle ground in an era of ever greater dependence on television for information, have all encouraged the opposition to explore alternative methods of political communication. Their use of radio and cable television has been particularly successful, and this is significant for Taiwan's social and political transformation. John Keane has identified the need for the development of a 'plurality of non-state media' in democracies 'which both function as permanent thorns in the side of political power ... and serve as the primary means of communication for citizens situated within a pluralistic society'.[39]

In Taiwan, the task of satisfying Keane's condition has been bestowed upon the new media. The three main network television stations are still in no position to 'act as permanent thorns in the side of political power' due to prevailing patterns of ownership and influence. For example, just prior to the election for the Legislative Yuan in 1992, the KMT's Department of Cultural Affairs was accused of demanding that these stations refrain from broadcasting anything relating to the DPP's platform, or providing information about that party's candidates. These accusations were fiercely contested by the DCA which claimed it would never issue such instructions. This may be true; but it can be argued that given the government's long involvement in the three television stations, the KMT no longer needs to issue formal instructions. Instead, there is a tacit understanding that the networks will act as their own censor. Such an environment does not provide for the development of an independent and objective Fourth Estate which is obliged to be critical of the government when necessary. Nor does it allow for the expression of a plurality of opinion. Hence the new media –

and cable in particular – are providing the people of Taiwan with alternative information, opinion and, via the popularity of call-in programmes, greater opportunities to participate in the political process. In turn this will have long-term benefits for the consolidation of democracy.

As Sheila Chin has noted, cable television in Taiwan 'originated from regular Common Antennas Television (CATV) systems and the activities of "Fourth Channels" set up by cable television pirates and political opposition'.[40] The term, the 'Fourth Channel' was used by the public in Taiwan to refer to its status as an illegal addition to the three official television stations. The CATV system first appeared in Taiwan in 1969, and 'while the outlines of the technical, economic and regulatory framework were beginning to emerge, the spread of CATV remained relatively minor, serving only 400,000 households by 1991'.[41] However, as the political liberalization and the strength of the opposition movement intensified, the cable television industry grew rapidly during the 1990s; just prior to the passage of the Cable TV Law in 1993, cable had already penetrated nearly 50 per cent of Taiwan's households, and rose to 70 per cent in early 1996.[42]

Cable television has been increasingly important in strengthening the growth of Taiwan's civil society. Because of the local character of cable programming, primarily due to the limited range of frequencies allocated to broadcasters, programmes can be tailored to accommodate the diversity of Taiwan's modern society. But we would argue that the new media should not be a substitute for the national broadcasting systems because narrowcasting creates its own problems. In particular, narrowcasting only serves to divide the audience even further, since they will seek out those programmes which correspond to their own political orientation, and thus insulate them further from alternatives. As James Robinson notes, 'cable news coverage and talk shows did not make for notably more objective comment. They promoted competition in bias'.[43]

The creation of a new media environment which will take its rightful place in a democratic Taiwan requires more than the opening of a plurality of channels catering for minority interests. Further liberalization of the existing mainstream television system is crucial if the limitations of narrowcasting are to be avoided, and if the consolidation of democracy is to be successful. The current danger is that the legalization of the new media has softened the demand for further liberalization of the mainstream television stations. Neither has Taiwan's cable television industry been in a position to resist the concentration of ownership which characterizes other forms of media. Immediately after legalization, the KMT ensured that it would have as big a stake as possible in the new television market, and mobilized its legislators to amend the Cable and Television Law to allow political parties to invest in the cable industry.

Moreover, the principles of market capitalism within the cable and satellite industry create the problems which are associated with commercialism. A national survey revealed in 1995 that cable channels broadcast more entertainment shows than the three national television stations in order to attract the largest possible advertising revenues.[44] Cable operators compete not only with themselves, but also with satellite owners, and the three networks. The result of this fierce competition is that the quality and content of many locally produced entertainment and niche market programmes on the cable channels suffer. High production costs and market competition inhibit the diversity which the cable system was meant to provide; by law they are required to produce a fixed quota of locally-produced programmes – 20 per cent in 1993, rising to 25 per cent in 1996[45] – but they often meet this by creating low-quality productions or by simply copying the formats of successful programmes on other channels.

Some have also identified problems associated with the non-dialogical character of call-in programmes and talk radio, and have suggested that, contrary to opinion, they contribute little to popular participation.[46] Those who have studied the phenomenon in the United States have had reason to be cynical about its use and value. It is closely associated with the growing dissatisfaction with politicians and politics in general across the United States (borne out by David Mervin's examination of the news media in the US, in this volume), and with what has been described as a national obsession with 'rant and rave time'. Edwin Diamond and Robert A. Silverman have concluded that 'the best thing that can be said about talk radio may be that it provides an outlet for venting some of the anger endemic in America', and their cynicism undermines their confidence in the medium's democratic potential:

> In the wired nation, the call-in programmes and the talk-show hosts present themselves as facilitators of the 'power of the people'. In grandiose fashion – the normal mode of such discourse – their shows are described as 'democracy in action'. The existence of new outlets for the exchange of political beliefs and the expression of self-interest *sounds* like a positive, bracing development; it can be taken as self-evident that public policy counts. In practice, the talk-show culture too often exchanges only the mutual ignorance of listeners and hosts who share mainly a taste for ranting and raving.[47]

It is difficult to be this sceptical of Taiwan's experience with call-in programmes. Here, the medium's role and influence suggest that systems in transition value the opportunity to 'rant and rave' as symbolic of their newly discovered freedom of speech: 'Listeners are eager to express their views about national developments and question over the air officials who appear at the studios to answer questions.'[48]

Commenting on the role of call-in programmes during the 1994 elections, Professor Hu Fo said that 'many people felt much more involved in the elections.'[49] This is an encouraging sign that the so-called new media will open spaces for political debate, and thus foster the further consolidation of Taiwan's democratic culture. Indeed the government itself has recognized the contribution which call-in programmes can make to democracy. In October 1993, the national Broadcasting Corporation of China established a 'Minister's Hotline' which allowed government officials to be scrutinized by the public. As a national event, this was an exception; most call-in shows are broadcast on those radio stations which form part of the new media. It is true that these do experience many of the same problems as cable television in terms of narrowcasting, and in heightening popular expectations of what can be achieved; moreover, the national radio spectrum is still dominated by the KMT.

However, it cannot be denied that through a multiplicity of new channels, an increasingly informed citizenry are given greater opportunities to participate and compete in the political process. Their role in the consolidation of democracy is much more difficult to determine; the new media are in an enviable position to encourage the growth of civil society, but until Taiwan's media environment is reformed to allow the mainstream media to perform the functions expected by democracy, the new media only serve to maintain the divisive and adversarial political culture.

Conclusions

Taiwan's recent experiences of regime transition suggest the existence of a positive correlation between the promotion of free and diverse media and the level of political change. Liberalization of the media is definitely a requisite for democratization but, as happened in Taiwan, it may either precede or follow the introduction of more tangible political reform and thus give the process a much sharper focus.

Democracies are defined by the level of popular participation and competition allowed, and are therefore given form by a plurality of free and open media. Occupying a central position within democratic societies, the media act as mirrors of ideas and the catalyst for serious public debate. As many views and opinions as possible are discussed in order that individual citizens might make a full and worthwhile contribution to the political process. As Taiwan continues on the path towards full democracy, the role of the media will undoubtedly increase; an efficient, independent and diverse media system is crucial for the successful consolidation of democratic procedure, and to protect the system against the possibility of decay. The new media do allow for the expression of views which are absent in the mainstream, but until the mainstream itself is liberated to accommodate such opinion, then the process of consolidation is in danger. As Vicky Randall noted in her 1993 paper on the media in the Third World: 'If the media are to make their full contribution to democracy, there needs to be democracy *within* the media, dispersal of control over and access to the media to the whole range of local communities, minority groups and so on.'[50] Some state regulation is advisable; a completely commercialized media only serves to devalue their role as agents of political change and education. A concentration of private ownership can be just as dangerous as a state/party monopoly, while market competition focuses attention on seeking profit and audiences, rather than on the quality of output.

Particularly close attention needs to be devoted to monitoring the output and impact of the Formosa Television Corporation, Taiwan's newest television station which went on the air in June 1997. This is a welcome development which will inevitably encourage further democratization; it is Taiwan's first fully private network station, and is located in Kaohsiung in the south of the island; it guarantees a large number of programmes in the Taiwanese dialect; it holds out the prospect for greater competition within the media à la Randall; and although it promises that its Board of Directors, primarily drawn from the ranks of the DPP, will not influence its political coverage, it is highly probable that it will be seen as a force to counter the other network television stations.[51]

Perhaps one solution to the problems currently challenging Taiwan's television system lies in the development of a public service broadcasting station, free from both political and commercial pressure and ultimately accountable to the people. In 1991, John Keane passionately described his ideal public service television system which should, he said,

> facilitate a genuine commonwealth of forms of life, tastes and opinion to empower a plurality of citizens who are governed neither by despotic states nor by market forces. It should circulate to them a wide variety of opinions. It should enable them to live democratically within the framework of multilayered constitutional states which are held accountable to their citizens, who work and consume, live and love, quarrel and compromise within independent, self-organizing civil societies which underpin and transcend the narrow boundaries of state institutions.[52]

There is no reason why Taiwan could not support such a system provided it is responsive to indigenous requirements; variations of the ideal have been adopted in other countries, including the United States, Japan and Britain, and Taiwan has studied these models with interest.[53] Taiwan is certainly in need of a genuine national public television institution which will function as a Fourth Estate, and would go some way towards allowing the people themselves, rather than the politicians, to define the agenda. Although we are not suggesting that such a station would necessarily cure all the problems facing modern Taiwan, it would at least provide an open forum in which problems and possible remedies can be discussed, problems which perhaps both the political establishment and the mainstream media currently prefer to ignore.[54]

However, the successful consolidation of democracy – if by consolidation we mean 'the peaceful transfer of power from one democratically elected government to another'[55] – is challenged by forces which are much more powerful than any of those so far discussed. The People's Republic of China continues to exert a considerable influence over the transition to democracy and the agenda which is followed by the media. This was clearly illustrated during the 1996 Presidential election.[56] Issues which are bound up with Taiwan's relations with China – national identity, the level of threat from Beijing – structure Taiwan's political life in such a way that the probability (though not possibility) of a change of government is unlikely in the short-term. In turn these very important issues frame the methods and content of political discourse in Taiwan, and thus drive the media's agenda. In other words, the media will never be completely independent until the complex issue of identity is resolved.

NOTES

1. On this election, see Yun-han Chu, 'Taiwan's Unique Challenges', *Journal of Democracy*, Vol.7, No.3 (1996), pp.70–82; John Fuh-sheng Hsieh and Emerson M.S. Niou, 'Taiwan's March 1996 Elections', *Electoral Studies*, Vol.15, No.4 (1996), pp.545–9; Gary D. Rawnsley, 'The 1996 Presidential Election Campaign in Taiwan', *Harvard International Journal of Press/Politics*, Vol.2, No.2 (1997), pp.47–61.

2. In his most recent book, *The Taiwan Political Miracle: Essays on Political Development, Elections and Foreign Relations* (Langham, MD: University Press of America, 1997), pp.9–12, John F. Copper suggests reasons why Taiwan has tended to be neglected by scholars.

3. Stevan Harrell and Huang Chun-chieh (eds.), *Cultural Change in Postwar Taiwan* (Taipei: SMC Publishing Inc., 1994) is an excellent study of Taiwan's culture, though it only offers a brief discussion of the media.

4. 'In fact while the transition in Taiwan has been long in coming, it has nevertheless been one of the smoothest transitions among newly democratized countries.' Steven J. Hood, *The Kuomintang and the Democratization of Taiwan* (Boulder: Westview Press, 1997), p.10. This stands in marked contrast to the record of success in those states which have experienced abrupt change. See Samuel P. Huntington, *The Third Wave* (Norman, OK: University of Oklahoma Press, 1991), pp.142–51. However, Taiwan *is* familiar with violent confrontation, and all the best political histories of Taiwan will discuss the 1947 February 28th Incident, the Chungli riots of 1977, and the Kaohsiung incident of 1979.

5. In 1995, the national literacy rate was 94 per cent. *Republic of China Yearbook, 1997* (Taipei: GIO, 1997), p.293.

6. See Lucien Pye (ed.), *Communications and Political Development* (Princeton, NJ: Princeton

University Press, 1963); D. Lerner and W. Schramm (ed.), *Communications and Change in Developing Countries* (Honolulu, HI: East–West Center Press, 1967); T.E. Skidmore (ed.), *Television, Politics and the Transition to Democracy in Latin America* (Baltimore, MD: Johns Hopkins University Press, 1993); E. Fox (ed.), *Media and Politics in Latin America: The Struggle for Democracy* (Beverly Hills, CA: Sage, 1988); Vicky Randall, 'The Media and Democratisation in the Third World', *Third World Quarterly*, Vol.14, No.3 (1993), pp.625–46.

7. Jason C. Hu, 'Freedom of Expression and Development of the Media', in Jason C. Hu (ed.), *Quiet Revolutions on Taiwan, Republic of China* (Taipei: Kwang Hwa Publishing, 1994), p.500.

8. Hood, p.31.

9. Hung-mao Tien, *The Great Transition: Political and Social Change in the Republic of China* (Taipei: SMC Publishing Inc., 1989), p.72.

10. Ibid., pp.71–2. Steven J. Hood's volume, *The Kuomintang and the Democratization of Taiwan* is an excellent history of the KMT.

11. *Broadcasting and Television Law 1976*.

12. Tien, p.197.

13. 'Taiwanese' refers to the Chinese who have lived in Taiwan since the sixteenth century; the 'mainland' Chinese are nationalists who only arrived in Taiwan in large numbers after their defeat by the Communists.

14. J. Bruce Jacobs, 'Taiwan's Press: Political Communications Link and Research Resource', *China Quarterly*, Vol.68, No.4 (1976), pp.778–88.

15 Hood, p.37.

16. Jacobs, p.785. See also Edwin A. Winckler, 'Cultural Policy on Postwar Taiwan', in Stevan Harrell and Huang Chun-chieh (eds.), p.38.

17. In 1988, the number was increased from 12 pages to 20.

18. See Jacobs, pp.778–9.

19. CTS was previously the Educational Television Station (ETV). The ownership percentages have altered slightly over the years, although the basic pattern has remained the same: according to material published in 1993, 48.95 per cent of TTV belonged to the Taiwan Provincial Government, 26.94 per cent to domestic trading companies, 19.98 per cent to Japanese business (Fuji, Hitachi, NEC, Toshiba), and 4.13 per cent to a number of individuals. 60.27 per cent of CTV's stock belonged to cultural enterprises established by the KMT, and 39.73 per cent of its stock belonged to domestic business. For CTS, 40.15 per cent of its stock was owned by the government (29.76 per cent by the Ministry of National Defence, and 10.39 per cent by the Ministry of Education), 13.55 per cent was owned by domestic industry, and the remaining 46.3 per cent was owned by a number of quangos (30.66 per cent by a KMT cultural enterprise, 10.26 per cent by a foundation related to the Ministry of National Defence, and 5.38 per cent by the CTS Foundation). See Chen-huan Wang, 'The Control of Broadcasting and Television Media', in Jui-cheng Cheng *et al.* (ed.), *Deconstructing Broadcasting Media: Establishing the New Order of Broadcasting Media* (Taipei: Cheng Society, 1993), pp.88–109.

20. The Three Principles of the People (San Min Chu I), credited to Dr Sun Yat-sen, were included in the ROC's Constitution. These principles are Nationalism, Democracy, and Livelihood – in other words government of the people, for the people, and by the people. See Sun Yat-sen, *San Min Chu I: The Three Principles of the People* (Taipei: China Cultural Service, undated), and *The Teachings of Sun Yat-Sen: Selections from His Writings* (London: The Sylvan Press, 1945).

21. Chen-huan Wang, p.77.

22. *A Brief Introduction to the Republic of China* (Taipei: GIO, 1990), p.82; and *A Brief Introduction to the Republic of China* (Taipei: GIO, 1995), p.151.

23. Li-hsin Kuo, *Criticism of Television and Observation of the Media* (Taipei: China Times Culture Publication Ltd., 1990), p.8.

24. According to an interview with the GIO's Mrs. Ching-Wen Lu (Leeds, December 1991), the three national television stations provided an average of 55 per cent of entertainment programmes per week. This figure coincided with Ming-yeh Rawnsley's calculation based

on TTV, CTV, and CTS's timetable in February 1996.

25. The KMT prohibited the formation of political parties.

26. C.L. Chiou, *Democratizing Oriental Despotism: China from 4 May 1919 to 4 June 1989, and Taiwan from 28 February 1947 to 28 June 1990* (Basingstoke: Macmillan, 1995), p.81.

27. Ibid., p.75. A similar pattern was followed in Brazil. See Guillermo O'Donnell and Philippe C. Schmitter, *Transitions from Authoritarian Rule: Tentative Conclusions about Uncertain Democracies* (Baltimore, MD: The Johns Hopkins University Press, 1993), pp.22–3.

28. Chien-san Fang, *The Political Economy of the Broadcasting Media's Capital Movement: The Analysis of the Changes in Taiwan's Broadcasting Media During the 1990s* (Taipei: Taiwan Radical Quarterly in Social Studies, 1995), pp.123–75. Also Hood, p.66.

29. For example, the DPP was legalized in 1989, which was also the first year when genuine multi-party elections began. Since 1991, elections have been held for the entire Legislative Yuan and National Assembly, thus terminating their domination by members elected in 1947.

30. Randall, p.639.

31. For a more comprehensive discussion of recent election campaigns in Taiwan, see Gary Rawnsley, 'The 1996 Presidential Campaign in Taiwan: Packaging Politics in a Democratizing State', *The Harvard International Journal of Press/Politics*, Vol.2, No.2 (1996), pp.47–61.

32. Shieu-chi Weng and Hsiu-hui Sun, 'How Media Use Influences Voters Political Knowledge, Party Preferences and their Voting Behaviour in Taiwan's 1993 General Voting', *Journal of Electoral Studies*, Vol.1, No.1 (1994), pp.1–25.

33. Yet the *China Times* and the *United Daily News* are still unable to prevent their readership from falling in a period of greater media diversity and competition, and especially a greater dependence on television as a source of news and information. In contrast, the readership of the *Liberty Times* is rising. This can be explained by the fact that its owners have corporate interests in a number of other profitable ventures, thus allowing the *Liberty Times* to develop and withstand the shock to Taiwan's press industry. It can also be explained with reference to the remarkable number of activities which are used to promote the newspaper, many of which are familiar to readers of the British tabloid press (television advertisements, the giving away of 'scratch' cards, offers tied to subscription and, of course, a low cover price).

34. The only exception in Taiwan is the weekly magazine, *Journalist*. This is a wholly independent and therefore objective publication which engages in investigative journalism. We freely admit to our inability to reconcile complete freedom from state control over the press and the dangers inherent in commercialization and market competition. More research is required.

35. The farmers' grievances have deep roots. The main explanation for this particular protest, organised by the Yunlin Farmers Rights Promotion Union, was the government's effort to acquire Most Favoured Nation Status from the United States (US), which prompted the Legislative Yuan to loosen the restrictions on the importation of fruit and vegetables. The farmers worried about the effects this would have on their livelihood.

36. Tsung-Chi Lin, 'Both Cable and Non-Cable Media Have Limits, but People's Protests Have No Limits', *The Journalist*, 3 May 1990, pp.84–6.

37. *Central Daily News* (International Edition), 22 May 1995.

38. More examples are available in Ming-Yeh Rawnsley, 'Public Service Television in Taiwan' (University of Leeds doctoral thesis, 1997), pp.28–37.

39. John Keane, 'Democracy and the Media – Without Foundations', in David Held (ed.), *Prospects for Democracy* (London: Polity, 1993), p.238.

40. Sheila Chin, 'Broadcasting and New Media Policies in Taiwan', Anabelle Sreberny-Mohammadi *et al.* (eds.), *Media in Global Context: A Reader* (London: Arnold, 1997), p.82.

41. Ibid.

42. *Free China Review* , Feb. 1996 (Vol.46, No.2), pp.1–5.

43. J.A. Robinson, 'Taiwan's 1995 Legislative Yuan Elections: Appraising in Democratization', *The American Asian Review*, Vol.14, No.3 (1996), p.112.

44. Jim Hwang, 'Cable Cat's Cradle', *Free China Review*, Feb. 1996 (Vol.46, No.2), p.7.

45. Fang, p.44.

46. John B. Thompson, *The Media and Modernity: A Social Theory of the Media* (London:

Polity Press, 1993), p.246.

47. Edwin Diamond and Robert A. Silverman, *White House to Your House: Media and Politics in Virtual America* (Cambridge, MA: MIT Press, 1995), p.141.
48. *Republic of China Yearbook, 1996* (Taipei: Kwang Hua Publishing, 1996).
49. *Free China Review*, Vol. 45, No.2, (1995).
50. Randall, p.644.
51. See the *Free China Journal*, 20 June 1997, p.4.
52. John Keane, *The Media and Democracy* (Oxford: Polity, 1991), p.126.
53. Much more information and discussion of Taiwan's Public Service Television system is provided in Ming-Yeh T. Rawnsley, 'Public Service Television in Taiwan' (University of Leeds doctoral thesis, 1997).
54. The law to establish a Public Television Station was passed in 1997.
55. Ming-Yeh T. Rawnsley, p.642. Also see Huntington, op. cit., Ch.5.
56. See Ming-Yeh T. Rawnsley, op. cit., pp.50–54.

Asia and the International Press:
The Political Significance of Expanding
Markets

GARRY RODAN

The rapid capitalist industrialization of East and Southeast Asia is viewed by many as a force for greater political liberalization. Try as they may, it is argued, authoritarian leaders will be unable to contain the social and political forces unleashed by the very economic transformation they have championed. In particular, effective media censorship is regarded as an unavoidable casualty of development. In addition to social changes increasing the level and diversity of demand for news and information, there is also the difficulty of restricting the impact of new electronic technologies. Moreover, a free flow of information is depicted as a functional requirement, indeed imperative, of further market development.

However, this study of the international press and its reporting on Singapore, Malaysia and Hong Kong reveals that the expansion of markets in East and Southeast Asia is not an unqualified force for liberalization. Indeed, market expansion can be as much a force for self-censorship as a force for wider and more critical reporting. Conflict with authoritarian governments over reporting runs the risk for media organizations of being denied access to increased circulation and advertising revenue. It also runs the risk of expensive legal actions, a measure deployed with considerable effect by the authorities in Singapore. Neither consideration can be ignored by commercial media enterprises. Furthermore, the continued success and increasing sophistication of the Singapore economy has been reconciled with extensive political censorship of the media. This experience not only encourages other authoritarian regimes, but also calls into serious question the assumption that mature capitalist development in Asia necessarily requires a free press.

Introduction

The consolidation and extension of capitalist markets in developing countries is popularly viewed as a force for liberal social and political change. In particular, the contemporary version of modernization theory contends that diverse social groups and interests resulting from economic change exert pressures for liberalism or pluralism at the expense of authoritarian regimes. Failure to respond to these pressures threatens the

---

Thanks to Robert Roche for his research assistance in the preparation of this contribution and to Vicky Randall for constructive criticisms on an earlier draft of this work.

legitimacy of such regimes, not least because social and political change is both a consequence and necessary precondition for sustained and sophisticated market development on which the credibility of these regimes so heavily rests.[1] This argument is complemented by the views of various liberal economists who emphasise the importance of a free flow of information to the future of market economies in Asia.[2] As they see it, in a modern, industrialized economy, the volume and range of information essential to conduct business and make informed investment decisions defies tight official control. New technologies – such as fax machines, satellite television and the Internet – also greatly increase the difficulty of official censorship and limit the ability to obstruct views which challenge those of authoritarian regimes.

Yet the experience in East and Southeast Asia poses serious challenges for the association of capitalist market development with the emergence of liberal institutions in general and liberal media institutions in particular. Indeed, as will be demonstrated via an examination of the international press and electronic wire services, the dramatic expansion of circulation and advertising markets in the region has also been a force for extensive self-censorship as organizations attempt to safeguard increasingly important and profitable commercial footholds and avoid costly legal and other battles with authoritarian regimes. Moreover, the most rapidly expanding reporting involves electronic business information services. While the nature of this information is not completely unproblematic for authoritarian regimes, it is generally less contentious than the overtly political reporting in newspapers, which has aroused greatest consternation in the past.

The major focus here is on Singapore, with some consideration also of Malaysia and Hong Kong. There are good reasons for this emphasis. Singapore is the most advanced economy aside from Japan in the region, and thus the best test of the proposition that successful market development undermines authoritarian control over information. Singapore's authoritarian leaders have also embarked on the most concerted attempt to institutionalize limits on international press reporting, their attempts serving as a model for other authoritarian leaders in the region. While the experiences and directions of the international press are not identical in the cases of Singapore, Malaysia and Hong Kong, it will be seen below that economic development has not been an unambiguous force for liberal information flows or political liberalism in any of these countries.

Expanding Markets in Asia

Newspaper circulation and market share of advertising is generally in decline in the established, industrialized countries of the world, most notably in the United States and Europe. But in the developing and recently-industrialized countries in much of East and Southeast Asia the situation is very different. Emerging middle classes engaged in business and professional activities represent both larger English-educated audiences for international newspapers and targets for advertising companies through those newspapers. Daily newspaper circulation levels between 1991 and 1995 grew by as much as 15 per cent in Singapore and 24 per cent in Malaysia.[3] The pattern among established Asia-oriented international press publications such as the *Far Eastern Economic Review (FEER)* the *Asian Wall Street Journal (AWSJ)* and *Asiaweek* mirrors this trend.[4] Meanwhile, publications with a wider global spread of readers such as *The Economist, Time, Newsweek, Businessweek* and the *Financial Times* are also producing more copy on Asia and/or increasingly competing for circulation in Asia.[5]

Circulation increases and the growing purchasing power of readers have meant substantially improved opportunities to attract advertising revenue in industrializing Asia. Singapore, for example, experienced a 47 per cent increase in newspaper advertising revenue between 1994 and 1995, while it jumped as much as 121 per cent in Malaysia.[6] Advertising companies conceptualise the region in terms of bands of markets. Malaysia, Indonesia and Singapore, for instance, are seen as a single band making up a critical mass of English language readership and potential consumers for the same products. Losing circulation access to any one of these three markets thus has important implications for attempts to attract advertising. Table 1 below provides some indication of the extent to which different elements of the international press have been able to boost advertising revenue in the 1990s. While the increases vary, they are all significant.

Expanding press circulation and advertising revenue markets in Asia are increasingly developing alongside, or in conjunction with, other information services. In particular, electronic business information services have expanded dramatically in the region, under the aegis both of the established news agency wire services as well as some of the comparatively new, more specialist electronic media companies, such as American-owned Bloomberg Business News. Business information services are especially attuned to the needs of investors in financial, commodity and equity markets. Companies compete on the basis not just of the quality and reliability of information, but of the speed with which it can be delivered to assist investment decisions. While many stock markets have either slowed or are in decline in parts of Europe and North America, they have expanded rapidly in Asia in the last decade. Interest from international investors outside the region has combined with local demand from multinational companies already operating in Asia, and rising local business groups and institutional investors, to generate a substantial volume of media business.

TABLE 1
INTERNATIONAL BUSINESS PRESS IN ASIA :YEARLY ADVERTISING REVENUE
BY TITLE AT RATE CARD PRICES (US DOLLARS)

	1992	1993	1994	1995	% increase 92/95
Asiaweek (weekly)	19,276,102	18,759,427	20,232,700	25,502,468	32
AWSJ (daily)	18,789,549	21,570,073	27,494,408	34,430,840	83
BusinessWeek (weekly)	10,240,819	8,713,427	10,646,400	14,494,511	42
Economist (weekly)	8,409,461	8,460,835	8,525,391	10,029,626	19
FEER (weekly)	11,613,657	13,598,119	17,857,530	21,782,204	88
IHT (daily)	12,932,188	14,663,602	18,359,831	18,427,855	42
Newsweek (weekly)	30,306,622	27,135,936	34,150,449	40,857,188	35
Time (weekly)	32,856,789	32,716,951	41,209,603	51,677,409	57

Source: SRG Research Services (Hong Kong).
Notes: Figures are for Asia, Pacific and Australasia.

Sharp increases in the number of correspondents and editorial staff based in the region have been necessary to keep up with this demand.[7]

Authoritarian governments in East and Southeast Asia have generally been less sensitive to the activities of traditional wire services and the more recent electronic business information services.[8] Reports are brief, highly focused and much more matter of fact than customary news stories and opinion pieces in the printed media. Importantly, the shifting pattern of demand towards business information services is taking place alongside the development of media and business conglomerates with diverse interests across, and sometimes beyond, various forms of reporting and publication. This raises the possibility that such organizations may be increasingly forced to weigh up the commercial costs of pursuing too critical a line of political and social inquiry in traditional printed press reporting as its relative contribution to overall profits diminishes.

Singapore: Tightening the Screws on the International Press

Despite its size, Singapore represents a prize market for English-language publications in Asia, and its government has ambitious aims of establishing Singapore as a prime regional and global information hub. At the same time, Singapore authorities have embarked on the most deliberate action to bring international press reporting into line with domestic press practices. This strategy has produced results too: extensive self-censorship characterizes international press reporting on Singapore, yet the city-state is increasingly adopted as a reporting base for the region.

Although at no time after taking office in 1959 was the ruling People's Action Party (PAP) under Lee Kuan Yew comfortable with criticism from the press, it was not until the early 1970s that attention turned to the international press. By this time, the Singapore government had comprehensively nullified the domestic press, and media in general, as a critical and independent force.[9] A number of incidents involving the international press occurred in the early 1970s,[10] but it was the Hong Kong-based *FEER* which became most deeply embroiled in ongoing friction with Singapore's authorities.[11] A meeting in Singapore between *FEER* editor Derek Davies and Lee Kuan Yew in 1976 failed to produce a lasting truce. Instead, despite a comparative lull in disputes through to the mid-1980s,[12] an uneasy relationship continued. In 1985, Davies found himself yet again meeting with Prime Minister Lee who reiterated that his government would not tolerate foreign correspondents 'meddling in Singapore politics'.

This heightened conflict in the 1980s was not unrelated to the December 1984 election result, which involved a 13 per cent drop in the government's share of the vote. Subsequently, the government became even more sensitive to international press reporting – especially as it related to the analysis of the government's treatment of political opponents. The *FEER* was soon joined by a number of other international publishers in dispute with the Singapore government. This included the owners of the *FEER* and *AWSJ* – Dow Jones & Co. – after the latter was fined S$6,000 by the Singapore High Court over an article concerning the treatment of lone opposition member of parliament (MP), Joshua Jeyaretnam.[13] This marked a move away from simply exerting direct pressure on journalists and editors in favour of broader legal and financial penalties on the publisher and other parties to the production of a publication.

It was an approach which would soon be developed and refined, starting with amendments in 1986 to the Newspapers and Printing Presses Act (NPPA). Under these changes, the Minister of Communications and Information could restrict the local circulation of newspapers published outside Singapore considered 'engaging in the domestic politics of

Singapore'. There was no definition of either 'engaging in' or 'domestic politics' provided in the 1986 amendment. This was instead left to the Minister's discretion.[14] The Act was further amended in January 1988 to allow the reproduction and sale of restricted, or 'gazetted', publications in Singapore,[15] provided advertisements were deleted.[16] This enabled the Singapore government to claim that it was not attempting to totally obstruct the passage of critical comment. Instead, it was insisting newspapers not be allowed to profit commercially from 'engaging in the domestic politics of Singapore'. Before long most major international publications dealing with current affairs had been netted under the new legislation.

Time was the first victim of the amendments following its failure to print a letter from James Fu, the Press Secretary to the Prime Minister, in response to an article in the 15 October 1986 edition entitled 'Silencing the Dissenters'. The article focused on the plight of Jeyaretnam. Circulation, which was then 18,000 copies per week, was reduced to 9,000 as of 19 October, to be further reduced to 2,000 as from 1 January 1987. *AWSJ* was next in line, with circulation limited to just 400 copies per day, down from 5,000, in the wake of an article on 9 February 1987, 'Singapore Exchange Puzzles Financiers'. Again, the conflict was exacerbated by the disinclination of the newspaper to publish the Singapore government response. This was followed by circulation reductions for *Asiaweek,* down to 500 copies per week, for refusing to print un-edited letters on behalf of the Singapore government. Authorities were unhappy with an article published on 7 October 1987 which alleged mistreatment of some of the 22 Singaporeans held under the Internal Security Act (ISA). Before the year was out, the *FEER* had its circulation curtailed as well to 500 copies per week, following a 17 December article concerning the ISA detentions and lay Catholic Church workers caught up in the swoop.

With the exception of the *FEER* case,[17] the government's claim to a right of reply was a recurring theme in these disputes.[18] This pattern would only be consolidated in the years ahead. In 1988, *AWSJ*'s Fred Zimmerman summarized the problem this posed for himself and other editors among the international press: 'It is a fundamental condition of a free press that newspapers should be free to decide what they will print without fear or favour from any external source, and that it is the judgement of the editor and not the dictates of any government which should determine what appears in the newspaper.'[19]

The late 1980s not only witnessed the expulsion of various foreign correspondents, and threats thereof, and visa denials to various journalists,[20] but further legal actions, including a lengthy exchange of writs between Lee Kuan Yew and Dow Jones & Co.[21] Dow Jones also unsuccessfully challenged the circulation restrictions imposed on the *AWSJ* through

Singapore's Court of Appeal.[22] Further amendments to the Newspaper and Printing Presses Act in 1990 tied foreign publications even closer to the jurisdiction of the local courts. An annual permit system was introduced for foreign publications which involved a hefty bond that could be drawn on to cover any legal liabilities that might be incurred. Furthermore, each publication was now required to appoint an agent in Singapore to receive legal notices — a safeguard against legal action failing to net the publisher along with other parties in a suit..[23]

From Protest to Resignation

Not surprisingly, the hostile climate for the international press in Singapore forced a rethink within some publications. The *FEER* had decided in December 1987 to cease all circulation in Singapore rather than operate at the restricted circulation rate of 500 copies per week. As a result of the additional 1990 rules, the *AWSJ* also suspended its 400-copy circulation in Singapore. The *AWSJ*'s 16 October 1990 editorial explained: 'What worries us is the purpose to which, five years experience warns us, these powers will be put. We have concluded that trying to meet the conditions being imposed by the government of Singapore would degrade the product we offer readers throughout the world.' However, by this time there was already a discernible trend towards accommodation by much of the international press to the Singapore government's rules. *Time* printed in full the Singapore government response to the October 1986 article two weeks after being gazetted and by the middle of 1987 circulation restrictions had been lifted. *Asiaweek* was also allowed to increase circulation to 5,000 per week from October 1988 after printing an unedited version of a letter from a Singapore official and the editor-in-chief gave an undertaking not to allow 'personal views or value judgements' of his correspondents to influence articles.[24] *Asiaweek* was further rewarded in September 1990 when circulation limits were increased to 7,500. Into the 1990s, the Singapore government continued to dangle the carrot of incremental increases in circulation rates, and this proved an effective discipline.[25]

   After a short period, even the *AWSJ* had a change of heart. In search of a truce, in early 1991, Dow-Jones & Co. Vice-President, Karen Elliot House, wrote to Lee Kuan Yew offering to withdraw an appeal against an earlier judgement on the condition Lee withdrew his cross-appeal. Lee accepted the offer subject to Dow Jones & Co. paying his legal costs. A statement by Dow Jones President, Peter Kann, that he 'never meant to defame Mr Lee in any way' further smoothed relations. This was viewed less charitably in the *New York Times,* which reported with apparent disappointment that Dow Jones 'threw in the towel'.[26] But it paid commercial dividends for the *AWSJ,* with a partial restoration of circulation – up to 2,500 copies per day – declared in September 1991. This was increased further in July 1992 to 3,500 copies and then to 5,000 copies in May 1993. A comment towards the end of 1992 by Minister for Information and the Arts, George Yeo, that the *AWSJ* had been 'fair and balanced in its reporting over the last two years' explained the relaxation. Singapore authorities were sufficiently satisfied that this trend had been sustained to permit an increase in circulation to 9,000 per day in July 1996.

The same course was charted by the *FEER,* which Dow Jones & Co. took full control of in 1987. This marked a shift from an independently-run operation out of Hong Kong to the adoption of an American corporate approach involving closer links between the business and reporting arms of the company. Under this arrangement, regional managers would be more accountable for profits. Lee Kuan Yew's sparring partner, Derek Davies, was subsequently replaced in 1989 as editor by Philip Bowring, another previous combatant in the *FEER's* clashes with Lee. However, Bowring was removed from that position in 1992 to make way for Gordon Crovitz. Crovitz, who had a legal and business background, was appointed as both editor and publisher. Suspicion that changes at the *FEER* were part of a deal between Dow Jones and the Singapore government were denied by George Yeo.[27] Yet in 1994, authorities lifted the ceiling on the *FEER's* weekly circulation to 2,000 copies and this was further raised to 4,000 in May 1995. During this time, *FEER* reporting on Singapore had been minimal.[28] That which did take place was uncharacteristically bland and unanalytical — a description which equally applied to the accounts in the *AWSJ* during the early 1990s. In 1997 the *FEER* was finally permitted by the Singapore government once again to station a full-time correspondent in the city-state.

The International Herald Tribune (IHT), by contrast, had distributed in Singapore without serious problem for decades. Nevertheless, it recently became a victim of Singapore's clamp on critical press reporting so that virtually all major international press organizations have now borne the brunt of official disapproval in one form or another. The *IHT,* jointly owned by the prestigious *New York Times/Washington Post* groups, had a daily circulation in Singapore of 4,000 at the time. However, it did not suffer circulation restrictions but hefty financial penalties as a result of defamation suits and contempt of court charges brought by Lee Kuan Yew and other senior government figures.

The first of these cases stemmed from an article by regular columnist Philip Bowring, formerly of the *FEER,* entitled 'The Claims About Asian Values Don't Usually Bear Scrutiny' published on 2 August 1994. Lawyers for Lee Kuan Yew and his son and Deputy Prime Minister, Lee Hsien Loong, complained to the *IHT* about the suggestion of nepotism involved in

Lee junior's political rise. Despite the *IHT*'s published apology, it did not meet the Lees' satisfaction, nor that of Prime Minister Goh Chok Tong who also took offence at the piece. The upshot was a High Court order on the *IHT* to pay S$950,000 in total damages to the trio, a decision which was not contested by the *IHT*. From the outset, it appeared, the *IHT* placed a premium on not aggravating Singapore's leaders.

Another article in 1994, published in the 7 October edition and entitled 'The Smoke Over Parts of Asia Obscures Some Profound Concerns', was reacted to with equal indignation. Written by American academic at the National University of Singapore, Christopher Lingle, this was a response to an earlier article in the *IHT* written by Singapore diplomat Kishore Mahbubani which favourably contrasted Asian political trends with those of Europe. Lingle's observation that some authoritarian regimes in the region use 'a compliant judiciary to bankrupt opposition politicians' was interpreted by Lee Kuan Yew as an oblique reference to Singapore. Following a police visit that included the seizure of materials from Lingle's office and home, the academic departed Singapore. In November, the Singapore government instigated legal action for contempt of court against Lingle, the *IHT* and associated parties. The *IHT* subsequently published in its 10 December edition what it referred to as a 'clarification', which stated that: 'We apologise unreservedly to Lee Kuan Yew and the Singapore judiciary,' pointing out that it was never the paper's intention to imply Singapore had a compliant judiciary. Yet this was followed in December with civil suits by Lee Kuan Yew for libel damages against Lingle and the executives of the *IHT*.

IHT Asia editor, Michael Richardson, mounted his defence around the argument that he did not understand Lingle's reference to refer to Singapore, but possibly the regimes in Burma, North Korea, China or Vietnam. The *IHT* defence did not draw on the fact that there were instances in other Southeast Asian countries of political persecution through the courts leading to the bankruptcy of oppositionists. However, it was the *IHT*'s apology and failure to contest the action on the basis that it was fair and reasonable comment which attracted most critical attention. This position was deplored by leading international jurist and human rights activist, Michael Kirby.[29]

Once again, the courts showed little mercy on the *IHT* for 'coming quietly'. All defendants in the first case were found guilty of 'contempt of court by way of scandalising the Singapore judiciary', fined various amounts, and ordered to pay the government's legal costs, totalling in excess of S$100,000.[30] In a separate libel action brought by Lee Kuan Yew, a further S$100,000 damages was awarded.[31] Yet in the face of these outcomes, the *IHT* announced that it would co-sponsor a world trade conference in April 1996 with the Singapore government. The meeting was the precursor to the December 1996 World Trade Organization (WTO) Ministerial Conference in Singapore. *IHT*'s chief executive, Richard McClean, declared at the time that he was gratified at Singapore's 'demonstration of commitment' to the newspaper adding that the *IHT* intended to print and operate in Singapore 'for many more years to come'.[32] Business conferences involving high-level government officials and business people are also held by Dow Jones and are an important exercise for media organizations to consolidate and extend strategic contacts. They also symbolize the fundamentally commercial nature of the media enterprise.

In the *IHT* case, internal divisions publicly surfaced over the appropriate response to problems in Singapore. *IHT* President, Richard Simmons, appeared at odds with people responsible for the news and editorial content when he expressed the view that the paper could operate successfully in Singapore with judicious editing. *IHT* editor, John Vinocur, forthrightly dismissed this option: 'To hell with it. We'll not trim our sails for that crowd. If they don't like it, they can lump it and we'll pull out.'[33] Sidney Gruson of *The Washington Times,* a director emeritus of the *IHT,* also weighed in with the view that (with a few defence-related exceptions) nobody but the paper's editors should be allowed to dictate the content of a newspaper. The likelihood is that such internal division is not peculiar to the *IHT,* but common to most media organizations contending with the same problem.

Institutionalizing Self-censorship

However harsh the penalties may be through legal actions against the international press, this is not the preferred mode of discipline by authorities in Singapore. Rather, the legislative framework is designed to promote self-censorship which avoids open confrontation. The nebulous legislative phrase 'engaging in the domestic politics of Singapore' appears designed to foster self-censorship as those seeking to avoid trouble interpret this cautiously. Periodic difficulties arise when the margins of tolerance are misjudged, or special sensitivities are aroused. In the recent *IHT* cases, probably the two most sensitive topics were involved; inferences of nepotism or executive influence over the judiciary are taken most seriously and personally by Lee Kuan Yew. Since the mid-1980s, it has become standard practice for most international publishers to treat copy on Singapore with special care, increasingly drawing on legal advice before publishing reports on sensitive matters. More often, editors and correspondents have learnt to limit or avoid overt criticism or scrutiny of Singapore's political leaders or institutions.

Apart from the fear of expensive penalties via Singapore's courts, there are other techniques meant to induce self-censorship. Employment passes are renewed on an annual basis, with an official policy of two to three years' maximum stay. However, this maximum is waived selectively so that 'well-behaved' journalists do have a chance of staying longer. Correspondents are also made very aware at the outset of their stay that their reporting is being closely scrutinized and some energy goes into educating them about 'no go zones'. The Media Division of the Ministry of Information and the Arts (MITA) has an extensive infrastructure keeping tabs on what is being written or broadcast and responding to reports it takes exception to. Letters and phone calls from the Press Secretary to the Prime Minister and Director of the Media Division of MITA – throughout most of the last decade, Chan Heng Wing – have been common. This communication may be couched in terms of the need to correct a matter of fact, but can quickly digress to broader ideological and philosophical critiques of a piece. It soon becomes clear to correspondents that there is a range of sensitivities to be very carefully navigated, or avoided altogether. These include questions about official corruption, the independence or otherwise of the judiciary and race relations. Even the tone of report can result in castigation.[34] Whatever the complaint and however seemingly trivial the issue may be, the impression reporters are left with is that everything they write is examined in extremely fine detail.

What then is the impact of all this attention and pressure? Editors of international press organizations invariably contend that despite the difficulties there is no compromising in the reporting of news. But this claim does not hold up to scrutiny and self-censorship appears, if anything, to be consolidating rather than whittling away in Singapore. Brief examination of some recent stories illustrates the point.

The first of these concerns the coverage in 1996 of an incident involving the Senior Minister Lee Kuan Yew and his son, the Deputy Prime Minister Lee Hsien Loong, both of whom had received substantial discounts on expensive private condominium purchases from HPL Limited. The reporting of this by the major international press publications was conspicuously unanalytical and pieces on it were remarkably brief, given the importance of the story. The first report by the *FEER*, for example, was not until 6 March, even though the filing of suits began in early January. The format of the report departed from its normal highlighting of the significance and implications of the event in the opening paragraph. Instead, it ran a straight news report in the style of a wire story which was only about 600 words long. A correspondent from another publication, and based in Singapore, admitted in interview that the HPL affair presented a major dilemma. While he knew he was dealing with a political scandal, he was not sure how to handle it. He opted to report on it quite differently from if he had been outside Singapore: no consideration at all was given to the political morality of the discounts, only whether or not they were legal. This approach was almost universally adopted by the international press, rendering it virtually indistinguishable from the government-controlled domestic press.

A similar pattern is to be found in the coverage of legal actions taken by senior government ministers against political opponents in early 1997. A total of 21 defamation suits were taken out against two Workers' Party candidates in the January election by PAP leaders – Tang Liang Hong and Joshua Jeyaretnam. The allegedly defamatory remarks by Tang were in repudiation of claims by government ministers that he was a Chinese chauvinist and a threat to racial harmony. These claims, described by Tang as 'lies', were largely based on comments by Tang about the disproportionate representation of the English-educated and Christians within the government which were made well before he joined the Workers' Party and ran as a candidate in the election. It appeared as though the government had baited Tang.

Although the suits began piling up in early January, the *AWSJ*'s first story on the topic did not come out until 11 March. It was simply taken from Associated Press News Service rather than compiled by its own Singapore correspondent and it was limited to a description of the High Court decision to throw out Tang's defence for failing to comply with court orders to submit a list of his assets. This was followed up by an editorial on 12 March, which in itself amounted to an admission of the importance of the court actions. However, the most critical content involved direct quotes from an earlier editorial in *The Straits Times* and sections of a human rights report by the US State Department. The *FEER*'s first piece took the form again of a brief, straight wire service format story which appeared as late as 6 March. *Asiaweek,* by comparison, had published three separate stories and another three brief items on the topic in this time. These pieces were all, however, conspicuously restrained in their descriptions, let alone evaluations, of law as a form of political control in Singapore. In interview, one foreign correspondent who covers Singapore for a different publication volunteered the view that, on the coverage of the Tang/Jeyaretnam writs, 'the international press has been cowered. No question'.[35]

Similar cases are observable among the news agencies. The way they dealt with a press conference called by opposition political figure Chee Soon Juan in October 1996 provides one illustration. Chee called this to raise questions arising out of an Australian Special Broadcasting Service (SBS) television current affairs programme, 'Dateline', concerning investments in Burma of public money by the Singapore Government

Investment Corporation (GIC). The programme made connections between GIC investments and those of Burmese drug lords and drew attention to the apparent freedom of Stephen Law, who is denied access into the US because of suspected drug dealing, to move in and out of Singapore. By any measure the story was significant. However, although there were various news agency correspondents and bureau chiefs present at the press conference, only one person actually filed a story. According to that correspondent, though, it was a decision over which he agonized for fear of adverse reaction from authorities. It was a great relief when, after having filed the report, he watched the late news on the Television Corporation of Singapore (TCS) which had a report on the issue not dissimilar from his own.[36]

Importantly, while the major international press organizations may have adopted a decidedly restrained reporting approach in Singapore, they have at the same time continued to endorse the city-state as a reporting base for covering the Southeast Asian region – especially for business information services.[37] The quality of infrastructure and efficient bureaucracy render it more attractive a base than neighbouring countries. Reuters news agency has even moved its entire Asian production desk and management personnel from Hong Kong to Singapore, a decision it has explained in terms of cost advantages. Amid questions about how such a trouble spot for the international press could be a viable editorial base, Reuters' Asia News editor, Rodney Pinder, explained that 'Singapore has given us certain guarantees that they will not interfere with our handling of news from other Asian countries'.[38] Yet this is the same government which, shortly after Pinder's statement and in August 1997, requested the Foreign Correspondents' Association (FCA) in Singapore to abandon a forum it was organising involving Indonesia Democratic Party (PDI) leader, Megawati Sukarnoputi.[39] The FCA promptly ceded to the request and rescinded its invitation to Megawati.[40]

Clearly, media organizations have been able to thrive commercially in Singapore by concentrating activities on less contentious areas. In some cases, though, this even includes direct co-operation with Singapore's government. Dow Jones, for example, has a 29.5 per cent share in a joint venture project, which includes the Singapore government-owned Temasek Holdings group, providing Asia's first business news satellite service – Asia Business News (ABN).[41] ABN beams its 24-hour business, financial and economic news services throughout the region. In the lead-up to ABN's services being provided in Singapore, programme managing editor Christopher Graves commented: 'Instead of browbeating people to change their ways, we've decided to play ball.'[42] Playing ball with the authorities is precisely what an assortment of international companies are also doing in Singapore to get a share of the markets for other satellite services beamed from Singapore, as well as cable television targeting Singapore's domestic audiences. These 'infotainment' companies have been especially responsive to overtures about the need to avoid critical social and political content, concentrating instead on sports, music, family-oriented soap operas and other safe material.[43]

We see in the Singapore case, then, that the expansion of business opportunities in the city-state has coincided with a moderating of critical reporting by the international press, rather than a loosening of effective controls. This is not just in response to the negative sanctions imposed on publications deemed to have 'engaged in domestic politics'. It is also a measure of the seduction of Singapore as both a market in its own right and a reporting base for servicing other markets in the region.

Malaysia: The Importance of Mahathir's Comfort Zone

The international press has had its difficulties in Malaysia too. In addition to periodic rebukes of the international press from Prime Minister Mahathir, correspondents have been expelled or barred from government press conferences, subscriptions to publications have been withdrawn by government ministries, advertising bans by government departments have been imposed on particular publications, and threats of publication bans have also been issued. As in Singapore, there are also certain sensitive topics – some of which are spelt out in law in Malaysia – and the government continues to pay close attention to if and how they are reported.

Nevertheless, by comparison with Singapore, surveillance of the activities of the international press is much less systematic and intense. Indeed, in some respects the margin for critical reporting has increased in the 1990s, a period when the market economy has grown and become more sophisticated. The Malaysian government's Multimedia Super Corridor (MSC) plans – involving a 9-by-30 mile zone near Kuala Lumpur promoted as a regional base for the creation and distribution of multimedia products and services – have even led some observers to assert that the economic forces for comprehensive censorship relaxation are rapidly gathering momentum. One writer depicts Malaysia as a model of how policy makers 'should embrace the role that multinational corporations may play in fostering democracy'.[44]

However, as will be shown below, this perspective ignores the critical importance of political factors, notably Mahathir's more secure position within the ruling United Malay National Organization (UMNO), in shaping the environment for international press reporting and the limits of this apparent loosening up by the authorities. Ironically, it also downplays the difficulties the international and domestic press are facing from the business sector as legal actions are increasingly employed against journalists. Finally, Malaysia too demonstrates that there are still striking cases where sections of the international press are prepared to make adjustments at the editorial level in an attempt to advance broader commercial interests.

Press reporting is legally circumscribed in various ways in Malaysia. Under the Sedition Act, for example, the special rights of Malays, language policy and privileges of the royalty must be respected. In the wake of the 1969 racial riots which resulted in 1,000 civilian deaths, any comment that can be interpreted as questioning or criticizing Malay privileges and associated policies has remained especially sensitive. The 1984 Official Secrets Act further impedes investigative or critical journalism through its requirement for journalists to prove that information contained in a story was not classified prior to the story's publication. The same act severely blocks access to documentation of state-owned companies and departments. This poses special problems for attempts to expose government corruption. The Printing Presses and Publications Act of December 1987 also gives the Minister for Home Affairs the power to ban publications deemed contrary to Malaysian interests, national security or public morality. Following the Singapore example, the Act further requires publishers to apply for annual licences which can and have been refused.[45] Importantly, alongside the legal 'black zones' which are spelt out in legislation (and not always strictly enforced, it should be noted), there are various other political sensitivities that journalists have come to understand and which guide self-censorship.

During the mid-to-late 1980s, life for both the international and domestic press in Malaysia was especially difficult. This was a direct reflection on the state of national politics at the time. Mahathir's hold on power within UMNO was uncertain and he was not keen on the press adding to this problem. Major government policy blunders and financial scandals were also occurring and the press was writing forthrightly about them – especially the international press. The *AWSJ*, in particular, was devoting critical attention to these stories, so much so that in 1987 it was required to present its edition each day to the Special Branch before distribution. This resulted in lengthy delays in getting the publication onto the streets. In 1986, the Malaysian authorities also expelled *AWSJ* correspondent Raphael Pura following their dissatisfaction with a series of critical pieces. He was given short notice by the Minister to leave the country. However, following legal appeal, it was ruled that a visa amounted to a legal contract and that Pura had been denied due process to account for his actions before the Minister's decision.

Then in 1987 the Internal Security Act and Sedition Act were deployed in a crackdown known as 'Operation Lallang' which not only involved mass detentions but the closure of three major domestic newspapers for alleged subversion, by reporting on racial aspects of political conflict between two government parties. The crackdown on dissent encompassed intellectuals, environmentalists, and other elements of an incipient civil society about which the government felt nervous. These newspapers reopened in 1988 after changes in editorial management and a not coincidental dramatic moderation in critical reporting. Another important related development occurred in 1988 when Mahathir dismissed all senior judges after a series of findings in preceding years went against the government. All three judges who had earlier ruled in favour of Pura were removed. Hereafter, the judiciary has shown little of the previous independence that frustrated the government's attempted political exercises through the law.

The situation became less dangerous for the press as Mahathir consolidated his power within UMNO and the economy strengthened through the 1990s. The legislative and judicial changes during the late 1980s also added comfort to the political leadership. With the domestic press essentially tamed, periodic brushes between authorities and the international press continue but these have not been as serious or as systematic as in the past. The *AWSJ* is not only freed of the routine presentation of copy to the Special Branch, it now uses Malaysia as one of its printing bases in Asia. With aspirations to compete with Singapore as a regional publishing centre, Malaysian authorities have taken a more pragmatic view on how to deal with the international press. The government has even indicated it may recall a law requiring foreign news agencies, such as Reuters, Associated Press and UPI, to distribute news through the state news agency, Bernama.

The theme to disputes that have occurred between authorities and the international press in the 1990s has been the 'Mahathir factor': Prime Minister Mahathir provides the cue that a particular article might warrant some sort of punishment of a journalist or publication. This is usually taken up by government departments and state-owned companies. An article during 1993 by Kieran Cooke in the *Financial Times,* for example, made mention of a minister having failed to return commemorative gold coins received from the Standard Charter Bank. When Mahathir publicly commented on his disapproval of the article and the damage it did Malaysia's reputation, this attitude quickly percolated through the public sector. It resulted in an unofficial advertisement ban by state-owned companies, which were among the most powerful and profitable in the Malaysian economy, on the *Financial Times.* The *IHT* had a similar experience following the publication of a supplement on Malaysia. The cover page carried a picture of a Malaysian woman smoking which Mahathir thought depicted Malaysians in a poor light. Following his rhetorical question of 'why should we advertise with such a publication?', government departments and state-owned companies ceased advertising with the *IHT* for a few years.

In a February 1996 case involving *Asiaweek,* the Home Ministry actually issued a directive that all ministries cease subscriptions to that magazine – which amounted to 138 subscriptions. Mahathir's annoyance with the publication was evident in reaction to a journalist's question on whether he would be carrying out a cabinet reshuffle – the subject of speculation by *Asiaweek*'s Roger Mitton in the 23 February edition. Mahathir commented: 'I am not saying whether a reshuffle is in store or otherwise. I will ask *Asiaweek* first'.[46] According to Mitton, though, it was possible that an earlier piece he had written about the power play between Mahathir and Deputy Prime Minister Anwar Ibrahim may have been the principal source of irritation.[47]

These cases of conflict between the international press and the Malaysian authorities are indicative of two patterns in the 1990s. First, it is clear that Mahathir's sensitivities are paramount in the determination of action against the international press for its reporting. The biggest risk for journalists appears to be that of personally offending Mahathir – especially if this occurs in the context of dealing with issues like corruption or racial politics. Second, the sort of retribution meted out to publications and journalists by the government is less severe than in Singapore and far less resources go into the surveillance and scrutiny of journalists and their articles.

The less intense and less systematic scrutiny of the press in Malaysia, when compared with Singapore, cannot solely be explained in terms of Mahathir's political security. After all, the PAP is probably the most politically secure of regimes in Asia. To some extent, the logistics of a city-state renders surveillance more effective than in a regionally diverse and more expansive territory. More than this, however, the PAP and its relationship to state and society differs from that of UMNO. The PAP is a more unified and coherent political force presiding over extensive and institutionalized corporatist structures. The political reach of the state is thus more comprehensive and the capacity to exert this unambiguously is more developed.

The importance of Mahathir's, and indeed UMNO's, sense of political security and its relationship to economic growth has significant implications for the future. It means that the margin for tolerance of critical reporting may prove highly conditional, a point that the financial crisis surfacing in 1997 and affecting Malaysia and other economies in the region appeared to indicate. It is noteworthy that both Prime Minister Mahathir and Deputy Prime Minister wasted little time in condemning the international press for coverage of this crisis. The former contended that: 'Quite a few people in the media and in control of big money seem to want to see South-East Asian countries, and in particular Malaysia, stop trying to catch up with their superiors and to know their place';[48] while Anwar argued that the foreign media are especially sympathetic to the international corporate sector and thus unable to provide a balanced analysis of the crisis.[49] Mahathir also depicted US-based currency speculator and international financier, George Soros, as a chief culprit in the collapse of Malaysia's currency. Interestingly, Soros not only dismissed Mahathir's remarks as 'using me as a scapegoat to cover up his own failure', but added that the Malaysian Prime Minister 'couldn't get away with it if he and his ideas were subjected to the discipline of independent media inside Malaysia'.[50] Soros's open advocacy and support for free media to combat authoritarianism stands in sharp contrast with the general position of business taken in East and Southeast Asia in recent times, as will become clear below.[51]

The sensitivity of authorities either to critical accounts of government economic policy or to negative projections about the Malaysian economy quickly generated a sense of caution in some professional quarters. Speculation about official retribution for acts of 'economic sabotage' translated into self-censorship among brokerage houses, many of whom kept the lid on some of their reports, published watered-down versions, and prevented their analysts from speaking to the media.[52] The government also announced the establishment of a committee to screen all foreign media reports on the Internet about Malaysia, and called on the local media to refrain from negative writing that could be used by the foreign media to tarnish Malaysia's image.[53] In addition to this, Information Minister, Mohamad Rahmat, warned American broadcaster CNN that continued negative reporting on Malaysia might result in the end of its access to the local market.[54]

In conjunction with the reporting of problems with the Malaysian economy, dangerous levels of smoke covering much of Malaysia as a result of fires from neighbouring Indonesia elicited further expressions of concern about the international media. The Malaysian government issued a directive to academics banning them from making public statements on the smoke problem, for fear that comments about the environmental and health threat would adversely affect the tourist industry.[55] This was followed by the use of the Internal Security Act (ISA) to detain ten people for religious activities considered by authorities to be detrimental to national security. These people were Muslims practising Syiah teachings, which a government spokesperson contended were against the Government, the monarchy system and the Constitution.[56] Though this incident did not directly relate to the press, it could be interpreted as symptomatic of a rising concern by the government about the potential of its detractors to profit politically from the economic downturn.

Interestingly, if the degree of government anxiety about press reporting has generally been less acute in the 1990s compared with a decade earlier, this is not apparently the mood in the private sector. One of the most striking developments in recent years has been the increasing recourse to legal actions against journalists and publishers from the Malaysian private sector, as if inspired by the success of this technique by the Singapore government. Both local and foreign correspondents have been the subject of writs, including Raphael Pura of the *AWSJ*. In the most recent case, *FEER* correspondent, Murray Hiebert, was convicted of contempt of court and sentenced to three months' gaol, a decision he is appealing against.[57] In handing down his decision in the Hiebert case, justice Low Hop Bing said that contemptuous attacks on the Malaysian judiciary by the media had gone on for far too long. The questioning of the independence of the judiciary, to which Justice Low was referring, has evolved since the changes to the judiciary by Mahathir in the late 1980s. Hiebert, incidentally, is the first foreign journalist to be sentenced to gaol for committing contempt in the normal course of his duties.[58]

In broad terms, then, the climate for the international press has improved over the last decade, although the legislative and licensing conditions under which they operate have been tightened to promote self-censorship. However, business has become more sensitive to critical reporting and is apparently encouraged by the changed complexion of the judiciary in its prosecution of journalists. Yet it is not just business interests external to media organizations that appear to pose an increasing threat to investigative journalism in Malaysia. In this same period, through the activities of News Corporation, Malaysia provides a stark illustration of the way editorial matters can be compromised by wider internal commercial interests of large media conglomerates.

In 1994, the News Corporation-owned *Sunday Times* had been investigating alleged connections between British aid to Malaysia of £234 million to build the Pergau hydro-electric dam and a £13 billion contract to buy British arms. The paper made claims of high-level corruption involving the Malaysian government, infuriating Prime Minister Mahathir in the process. According to then *Times* editor Andrew Neil, the paper's owner, Rupert Murdoch, became uneasy about the potential threat this posed to the prospects of his Star TV satellite service being granted entry into Malaysia. As Neil put it: 'the whole episode had frightened Rupert: he wanted to placate Mahathir and send a signal to the rest of Asia that *The Sunday Times* was not a loose cannon that would soon be exposing business practices they would rather keep hidden. Murdoch and Mahathir came to an understanding.'[59] No less important is Neil's claim that Murdoch had also come under direct pressure from a range of British business interests who insisted action be taken to silence the editor. As it transpired, Neil was soon offered a lucrative television post with Murdoch's Fox TV in America.[60]

Hong Kong: Business Opposition to a Free Press

Hong Kong stands in sharp contrast with both Singapore and Malaysia as the place in industrializing Asia where both domestic and international press have thrived in recent decades and critical and investigative reporting has been the norm. Some 180 international media organizations have offices in Hong Kong and the city-state houses 59 daily newspapers and 675 periodicals.[61] Hong Kong has served as the regional headquarters for nearly all major international press organizations as well as for electronic media organizations such as CNN (Cable News Network), CNBC (Cable News and Business Channel) and for publishers such as McGraw-Hill. However, with the reversion of Hong Kong to Chinese sovereignty, will Chinese authorities pragmatically resign themselves to a liberal press, seeing this as necessary to secure Hong Kong's continued commercial success?

While it is too early to know the full answer to this question, another scenario is shaping as more likely. Instead of business taking up the cudgels for the retention of a free press in Hong Kong out of commercial self-interest, thus far it has exerted a great deal of pressure on newspapers to reform themselves along lines more acceptable to China's authoritarian leadership. Indications from both Chinese officials and Hong Kong's new chief executive, Tung Chee Hwa, also suggest a new role is expected of the press. The full details of this are yet to be spelt out, but both parties are open admirers of the Singapore model which successfully reconciles market development with political censorship in the media. Moreover, a pattern of self-censorship is already discernible among Hong Kong's domestic press – both in the Chinese and English-language publications. It simply remains to be seen whether the international press follows suit and, if so, to what extent.

In anticipation of concerns about the future of freedom of expression after 1997, Article 27 of the Basic Law – the blueprint for Hong Kong's governance as a Special Administrative Region (SAR) of China – guarantees Hong Kong residents 'freedom of speech, of the press and of publication'. However, Article 23 also instructs the Provisional Legislature of the Hong Kong SAR government to adopt laws prohibiting 'treason, secession, sedition, subversion against the Central People's Government, or theft of state secrets'.[62] Mild reforms by the Provisional Legislature to existing laws in these areas, with the intention of limiting the threat such laws posed for freedom of expression, have been rejected by Tung Chee Hwa. He has pledged his government to abolish them, and something approximating the original treason and sedition laws seem to be in the offing.

Similarly, Xinhua (New China News Agency) vice-director, Zhang Jungsheng, contends on the one hand that press freedom will be increased after 1997, but states on the other hand that 'because of the law, ethics and the social environment, a certain amount of discipline is necessary'.[63] The director of China's Hong Kong and Macao Affairs Office, Lu Ping, has thrown some light on what this discipline involves in a series of interviews in May and June 1997. According to Lu, the media would 'absolutely not' be allowed to 'advocate' controversial political views such as favouring the independence of Hong Kong or Taiwan.[64]

In any case, journalists in Hong Kong can compare their experiences with Chinese authorities in the lead-up to 1997 with protestations about press freedom after handover. These included: a blacklist of Hong Kong reporters compiled by Chinese authorities after the Tiananmen Square massacre; the banning of journalists from going to the mainland who work for Hong Kong's 'irreverent' *Apple Daily;* and the arrest in October 1993 and subsequent imprisonment of Hong Kong reporter Xi Yang of the Chinese-language newspaper *Ming Pao.* Xi was sentenced to 12 years in gaol for publishing 'state secrets', which simply involved the disclosure of bank interest rates.[65]

The knowledge that Hong Kong's new political masters are less appreciative of critical journalism not only exercises reporters' minds. It has also been a matter of concern to business interests in Hong Kong, resulting in pressure on journalists to curb critical reporting. This has taken the form not only of withholding advertising from publications out of favour with Chinese authorities, but of editorial interference from proprietors. Most of Hong Kong's media are owned by corporations with substantial investments in mainland China. In many cases, media activities are not even the main interests of the corporations which own Hong Kong's press, which only increases the apparent reluctance to be associated with criticism of China's leaders or its policies.

The most conspicuous case of business distancing itself from critical publishers involves Jimmy Lai, owner of the tabloid *Apple Daily* – which had a circulation average of 317,332 in 1996 – and magazines *Next* and *Eastweek.*[66] In an open letter in 1992 in *Next* to Li Peng, Lai referred to the Chinese premier as 'a turtle's egg' for his part in the Tiananmen Square massacre. *Apple Daily* has also earned a reputation in the Chinese leadership's eyes for political hostility. The labelling of Jiang Zemin as the world's 'No. 2 enemy of press freedom' by the New York-based Committee to Protect Journalists, for example, was front page news in May 1997. It was the only paper in Hong Kong to publish the last, and very unflattering, known photo of Deng Xiaoping alive. Lai's attempts publicly to list on the Hong Kong Stock Exchange his Next Media, the publishing group that owns *Next* and *Eastweek*, have twice failed. On the last occasion the underwriter, Sun Hung Kai International Ltd., withdrew its support just one week prior to the scheduled float.[67] Yet, in terms of market capitalization, Next Media would be a mid-range company offering investors definite opportunities.

The magnitude of self-censorship in Hong Kong is indicated in the results of a survey of 367 journalists by the University of Hong Kong's Social Science Research Centre in 1994 and 1995. As many as 24 per cent of respondents admitted to frequently practising self-censorship and a further 64 per cent to occasionally doing so.[68] A subsequent survey by the Centre also found that 50 per cent of respondents agreed that 'Nowadays, most journalists hesitate to criticise the Chinese government'.[69] The Hong Kong Journalists' Association has also been detailing individual cases of reported self-censorship within media organizations in its annual reports over recent years, including the withdrawing of opinion columns and the withholding of various articles reporting negatively on China or Chinese officials. Probably the starkest collective case of self-censorship involved the media coverage of Tung Chee Hwa's rise to the position of Hong Kong's chief executive officer. As Willy Wo-Lap Lam, China editor of the *South China Morning Post*, observed: 'Tung's selection was covered by the media just as China would have wanted it – no investigation of his background, no scrutiny of the fact that it was not an "election", as the press called it, but more an appointment'.[70]

To draw out some of the factors behind, and processes involved in, the move towards widespread self censorship, let us look at two of Hong Kong's major newspapers – one a Chinese and the other an English language daily.

Following its launch in 1959, the Chinese daily, *Ming Pao*, earned itself a reputation for informed and critical accounts of Chinese politics, especially for its coverage of the military and developments in the Politburo. It attracted a loyal readership among Hong Kong's Cantonese intellectuals and middle class and also became a valuable source for Western military and diplomatic analysts.[71] Its coverage of the Tienanmen Square massacre greatly irritated the Chinese leadership. However, subsequent to ownership changes, *Ming Pao* has undergone editorial and cultural modifications which have led to a shift in content and style. The transformation can be traced to the purchase by businessman Yu Pun-Hoi of *Ming Pao* in 1993 from its founder Louis Cha, a renowned writer. When financial troubles led to Yu selling his shares, Tiong Hiew King gained control in 1995 and the transformation accelerated. Tiong is a Malaysian

Chinese with extensive timber interests in the region and an expanding media empire. He established *The National Daily* in Papua New Guinea where his company has considerable forestry operations. Oei Hong Leong, a Singaporean Chinese with close business connections in China, has also been a substantial shareholder in *Ming Pao*.[72]

Tiong has aspirations of taking the paper into the enormous mainland market, but access is of course conditional on political acceptability to Chinese authorities. Accordingly, under Tiong, strategic appointments have been designed to broaden the paper's appeal to the mainland, including the hiring of a Taiwanese editor who has presided over a diminished coverage of politics. New editor, Kao, has also brought on board a senior opinion writer from Shanghai who was employed there in a Chinese government propaganda department. When important political issues about the mainland are covered nowadays, not only is reporting uncritical, but the stories get little prominence. When Chinese authorities were preparing to release dissident Wang Dan, for example, this was relegated to latter pages and given only brief account. In keeping with the practice on the mainland, *Ming Pao* now also refers to Taiwan as 'Taiwan Province'. This direction by the paper appears to have earned the appreciation of Chinese authorities, however. *Ming Pao* journalist Xi Yang was released from prison in February 1997, some nine years ahead of the full sentence.[73]

This is not to suggest that *Ming Pao* is uniformly comprised of sycophantic journalists. However, as the newspaper's deputy editor in chief for finance, Ivan Tong, laments: 'What worries us is not whether reporters themselves will be courageous, but whether their news organizations which are now all looking for market share in China itself will support us when we are courageous'.[74]

Hong Kong's leading English-language daily, *The South China Morning Post (SCMP)*, has also undergone ownership change in the 1990s. Rupert Murdoch divested himself of the *SCMP* between 1993 and 1996 to concentrate on his Star (satellite) Television interests. The subsequent owner, Malaysian-based, overseas Chinese business tycoon Robert Kuok, is estimated to be the second largest of all foreign investors in China. Kuok is also an advisor to the Chinese government on Hong Kong affairs. In Kuok's time, the *SCMP* has been uncharitably labelled by Britain's *The Independent* and the *Index on Censorship* as the 'Pro-China Morning Post'. Criticisms of a turnaround may be exaggerated in the *SCMP*'s case, however, since it has always been an establishment paper; but the establishment itself is changing in Hong Kong. There have nevertheless been a number of important developments since Kuok bought the paper and they could lay the basis for more substantive self-censorship or political influence over time.

Questions were first seriously raised about self-censorship in the *SCMP* in 1995, when the satirical strip by cartoonist Larry Feign, 'The World of Lily Wong', which had been running for 12 years, was discontinued immediately following a series about Hong Kong's citizens on death row providing kidneys for illegal organ transplants in China. The explanation from the paper's editor was that Feign had been caught up in a ten per cent staff cutback. The cartoonist saw it differently: 'It's bullshit that the editor wanted to cut costs by cutting out his most popular feature.'[75] Feign pointed to the influence of Robert Kuok, whom he described as 'a friend of Li Peng'. *The Independent* subsequently contracted Feign for the 100 days before handover and syndicated his work world-wide. There were no takers from Hong Kong.

One *SCMP* development which has aroused a great deal of concern is Kuok's appointment of a new editorial adviser, Feng Xiling. At the time of appointment, Feng was a member of the People's Political Consultative Committee, one of the most senior organs of the Chinese government. Feng has also served on the Chinese national propaganda committee. The exact purpose of Feng's appointment is guarded by the *SCMP*, editor Jonathan Fenby maintaining *SCMP* would be surrendering commercial advantage to reveal such.[76] The fear among journalists and others is that this portends a shift towards the Chinese system whereby cadres offer editors political advice.

It is not just a few multi-millionaires who happen to own Hong Kong newspapers who are concerned about the impact of critical press reporting on their interests, however strategically significant this may be. The business community on the whole has been at pains to demonstrate its preparedness to co-operate with new political masters in Beijing. This has taken various forms in the lead-up to and following handover. It includes public denunciations of Governor Patten and his reform agenda, such as through the advertisements of local tycoon James Tien, chairman of the Hong Kong Chamber of Commerce. Rather than a constructive contribution to debate in Hong Kong, these are often merely gestures to the mainland elite.[77] It also includes the extensive attempts by the old establishment companies such as Jardine and Swire, and other Western corporations, to secure mainland business partners as a safeguard against an uncertain future.

If it is the case that global financial players and international businesses require a free press as a defence against corruption and political interference in the market, which is in prospect as Hong Kong becomes more fully integrated into the mainland economy, this has not resulted in strong advocacy of a free press by business. Instead, the only organized public stance taken on the press issue by business has been that of Advance Hong

Kong. Led by Ted Thomas, a public relations and market consultant, and comprising a range of tourist and property-related interests, the campaign condemned the international press in particular for writing negatively about the implications of Hong Kong's reversion to Chinese rule.

Nevertheless, the immediate commitment to Hong Kong from the international press does not seem to have wavered. Since 1995, both *Time* and *Bloomberg Business News,* for example, have established editorial functions in Hong Kong and virtually all existing publishers have retained editorial headquarters there.[78] One exception is the monthly *The Nineties,* which moved to Taiwan for the stated reason of avoiding anticipated political interference.[79] Meanwhile, there are precedents from other sections of international media adopting a commercial strategy from Hong Kong of editorially appeasing Chinese authorities. This is what Rupert Murdoch did in withdrawing BBC World Service from Star TV's satellite service. News Corporation has subsequently secured a $20 million deal to build four TV studios in Tianjin and has also been given approval to supply hotels in China with Star's pay-movie channel.[80]

It could be argued that other international news organizations have a more dedicated commitment to the provision and analysis of news, so that Murdoch's approach will prove unrepresentative. However, the strength of that commitment is yet to be fully tested. The taming of the domestic press is obviously the first priority of the Chinese authorities, as it was for the PAP in Singapore. Whether the same organizations that have accommodated authoritarian rule in Singapore behave differently if similar pressures are applied in Hong Kong remains to be seen. If that sort of pressure is applied, on current indications it certainly would not appear that the business community in Hong Kong will rally to the defence of a free press.

Conclusion

The full implications of economic development for the international press in Singapore, Malaysia and Hong Kong – let alone industrialising East and Southeast Asia more generally – are still far from clear. However, the above account does suggest that the prevailing association of market development with liberalised media is far too simplistic. Such a functionalist and deterministic understanding of the relationship between economic and political development is not borne out by the brief case studies here. Instead, we have seen that the growth of markets can be as much an inducement for constrained reporting as it can for more critical and wide-ranging coverage and information to assist business investment decisions and associated institutional development. In particular, the experience of the international press in Singapore has shown that media organizations have their commercial susceptibilities, so deftly exploited by Lee Kuan Yew in effecting a moderation of critical reporting in that city-state. That experience provides practical inspiration for other authoritarians also seeking to marry advanced market economies with extensive political controls.

The success of Lee Kuan Yew and his government in combining media control with increasing market sophistication invites consideration of precisely what sort of information and analysis is important to the investment needs of business. Is this limited to data about market prices? Can this be separated from questions of politics and power? At the very least, this study has established the urgency of a research agenda examining such questions. This study has also shown that, if a free and investigative press is a functional requirement of a sophisticated market economy, it does not necessarily follow that the private sector is a source of support or advocacy for it. On the contrary, in Malaysia the private sector poses an increasing threat to a stronger and more critical press through its mounting legal actions against journalists. Similarly, in Hong Kong, where a strong and independent press has been in operation for decades, that legacy is under threat with the resumption of Chinese rule and accompanying attacks from the private sector.

The political significance of expanding media and other markets in East and Southeast Asia is certainly much more complex and problematic than has hitherto been recognized. However, this discussion not only cautions against blind liberal optimism about the international press, it also rejects portrayals of the international press's difficulties with authoritarian regimes as a 'values conflict' between 'East' and 'West'. Such a depiction obscures both the dynamics and the nature of conflict involved. Asia's changing position in the global political economy is generating commercial and political alliances across so-called 'East' and 'West'. Not only have external pressures been applied to media organizations from international and domestic-based investors hoping to secure access to growing markets, their sentiments are not infrequently echoed by politicians and others from liberal democratic societies. The further growth of markets in Asia is thus likely to reveal something about the strength of liberal democratic values outside as well as inside industrializing Asia.

NOTES

1. Larry Diamond and Marc F. Plattner, 'Introduction', in Larry Diamond and Marc F. Plattner (eds.), *The Global Resurgance of Democracy* (Baltimore, MD: Johns Hopkins University Press, 1993), pp.ix–xxvi; Samuel P. Huntington, *The Third Wave: Democratization in the Late Twentieth Century* (Norman, OK and London: University of Oklahoma, 1991).

2. Kinichi Ohmae, *The Borderless World* (London: Collins, 1990); Christopher Lingle, *Singapore's Authoritarian Capitalism* (Barcelona: Edicions Sirocco, S.L. and Fairfax, VA: The Locke Institute).

3. International Federation of Newspaper Publishers, *World Press Trends* (Paris: FIEJ, 1996), pp.103–4, 129–30.

4. The regional figure for the *Far Eastern Economic Review (FEER),* for example, has risen from 65,612 in 1987 to 81,443 in 1995, despite being effectively shut out of the Singapore market for much of this time. Circulation for *Asiaweek* has jumped from around 80,000 in 1990 to 100,000 by 1995. The *AWSJ* figure has risen from 35,865 in 1987 to 50,356 in 1995. The *AWSJ* also reported dramatic circulation growth for the second half of 1995 of 83 per cent for Thailand, 44 per cent for China, 18 per cent for Korea and 12 per cent for Indonesia compared with the same period for 1994. This compares with a global average rate of increase of nine per cent for the *AWSJ.* See Janine Stein, 'Asian Media Discover Big Distribution Gains; TV, Print Media Stay Healthy; Local partners Key to Future Roll-Outs', *Crane Communications Inc. Advertising Age,* 12 Feb. 1996, p.112.

5. This has involved the introduction of dedicated Asian or international editions in some cases, and a general bolstering of the number of correspondents based in the region.

6. International Federation of Newspaper Publishers, pp.103–4, 129–30. This figure includes revenue from dailies, weeklies and Sunday papers.

7. In the case of Dow Jones News Service, as recently as 1993, for example, there were only 40 reporters and editors, and 11 bureaux in the Asia-Pacific region. However, by early 1997 this had expanded to 158 staff and 21 bureaux. Bloomberg's total Asian reporting staff comprised of just five editors in the one bureau in Tokyo in 1991, and a few stringers. By early 1997, staff levels escalated to 104 reporters and editors in 16 bureaux in Asia. Reuters has opened 14 new bureaux in Asia and the editorial staff in the region has risen from 282 in 1990 to 401 in 1997.

8. Reuters, for example, has operated in Singapore for decades with just a couple of minor skirmishes with the sensitive Singapore authorities.

9. Francis T. Seow, *The Media Enthralled: Singapore Revisited* (Boulder, CO: Lynne Rienner, 1998).

10. One of the first publications to be subjected to pressure was *Newsweek.* In 1971, various executives and staff of *Newsweek* were imprisoned following a front page photograph of Mao Zedong which Lee seemed to consider unhelpful for his designs to firm up political support amongst Singapore's ethnic Chinese community. See John A. Lent, 'Lee Kuan Yew and the Singapore Media: Protecting the People', *Index on Censorship*, Vol.4, No.3 (1975), pp.7–16. Three years later, another freelance journalist, Pang Cheng Lian, writing this time for *Newsweek,* was convicted of contempt of court for an article alleging that Singapore courts were not independent but biased in the government's favour.

11. In 1971, the government charged that *FEER* freelance journalist Anthony Polski, in assisting Amnesty International compile a report on the treatment of political prisoners in Singapore, was 'acting outside his duties as a journalist' (see 'Singapore Expels American Newsman', *New York Times*, 4 June 1971, p.3). Thereafter there were periodic clashes between *FEER* editor Derek Davies and Lee Kuan Yew and incidents involving journalists Ho Kwon Ping and Arun Senkuttuvan revolving around similar government concerns.

12. One significant incident in this period was the government's refusal to renew the work permit of Patrick Smith of the *FEER* as a result of an article in 1982 about the use of the ISA against political opponents.

13. The action was taken by Lee Kuan Yew who contended that the article implied executive control over the judiciary. The *AWSJ*, charged with criminal contempt, pleaded guilty.

14. Nancy Batterman, 'Singapore's Newspaper and Printing Presses (Amendment) Act 1986: A

Bad News Bear?' *Lawasia* (1987), pp.35–6. Criticism about this from Singapore Law Society President Francis Seow was not tolerated by the government. It earned the Law Society and Seow a stern rebuke and a reminder that organizations in Singapore not registered specifically for political activities are required to abstain from political comment.

15. 'Gazetting' refers to the publication in the government Gazette, by order of the Minister, of a declaration that a newspaper has engaged in the domestic politics of Singapore. Any, or all, sales or distribution in Singapore of a 'gazetted' newspaper can be curtailed.

16. The amendment did not stipulate that reproduction required the publisher's permission.

17. Arising out of this article, Lee Kuan Yew commenced legal action in January 1988 against the journalist, editor, publisher and printer responsible, seeking damages for libel. In Nov. 1989, the Singapore High Court awarded Lee Kuan Yew S$230,000 in damages.

18. The immediate past revealed an exceptional capacity to achieve this too. In 1986 alone, the *AWSJ* 'published 13 letters from Singapore government officials, comprising just under half of all the space devoted to letters from officials of all other governments combined'. Dow Jones and Co., Inc., *Lee Kuan Yew vs The News, A History* (New York: Dow Jones & Co., Inc., 1990), p.14.

19. Quoted in Dow Jones & Co., p.16.

20. Those affected by these actions included John Berthelsen and Raphael Pura of *AWSJ*, Rodney Tasker, Nigel Holloway, N. Balakrishnan, Carl Goldstein and Jonathan Freidland of *FEER*, and AP-Dow Jones correspondents Matthew Geiger and Simon Elegant.

21. Lee sued for libel as a result of the 7 Oct. article in the *FEER,* and was awarded a judgement in 1989. Dow Jones then appealed and Lee, in turn, cross appealed. The President of Dow Jones, Peter Kann, subsequently issued a statement which contended the judgement was unwarranted. Lee interpreted this as an accusation that the Prime Minister had exerted improper influence over the trial judge. He thus filed three more libel suits against Dow Jones in Malaysian and Singaporean courts.

22. This action only resulted in confirmation that the Minister for Communication and Information has the full power to restrict the circulation of any foreign publication the Minister considers to have interfered with Singapore's domestic politics.

23. This provision arose, according to the government, as a consequence of difficulties experienced in serving writs on the *AWSJ* over a contempt of court action and a defamation suit.

24. 'To Our Readers: Keeping Up With the Customers', *Asiaweek* (21 Oct. 1988), p.14.

25. Another such case involved *The Economist*, which in 1988 had closed its Singapore office, even though it continued to occasionally report on the city-state. An article in June 1993 about the prosecution of five people under the Official Secrets Act aroused a protest from the Singapore government, unhappy with what it regarded as a 'mocking tone' to the account. Although a letter by the Singapore High Commissioner to London was published shortly afterwards, the editing out of one sentence precipitated further protests from Singapore authorities. *The Economist* subsequently published the original sentence in full, but it failed to publish another letter by the High Commissioner in response to one published by J.B. Jeyaretnam. This resulted in gazetting and circulation restrictions of 3,500 copies per week in August and the requirement of a US$125,000 bond as well as the appointment of a local representative to accept documents in the event of any future legal actions. *The Economist* published the letter in the next edition and in January of the subsequent year it was de-gazetted and circulation limits were lifted.

26. 'Full Court Press', *New York Times* (31 March 1991), p.9.

27. See 'Sense of Responsibility Must Follow Power of Press: BG Yeo', *Straits Times Weekly Edition* (14 Aug. 1993), p.13.

28. From Sept. 1989, there had been no correspondent based in Singapore following the denial of a visa for the *FEER's* N. Balakrishnan.

29. Chris Merritt, 'Singapore Law in Time Capsule, says Kirby', *Australian Financial Review* (9 Feb. 1995), p.2.

30. Lingle was fined S$10,000, Richardson S$5,000, publisher and IHT chief executive Richard McLean S$2,500, and the local distributor and the printer S$1,500 each. Legal costs totalled S$83,876.

31. 'Lee Kuan Yew Wins $70,972 in Libel Case', *Asian Wall Street Journal* (12–13 April 1996), p.5.
32. Quoted in Colin Climo, 'IHT, Government Forget Their Differences for Trade Conference', *Australian Financial Review* (27 Sept. 1995), p.16.
33. Quoted in Richard Harwood, 'Publish and Be Damned – Who Really Decides?', *The Washington Post* (17 Feb. 1995), p.A25.
34. These observations are based on interviews with reporters conducted in late 1996. At the request of correspondents, the anonymity of interviewees has been maintained throughout this study. In many cases this includes anonymity of organizations. Concern that comments and information supplied in interview could lead to difficulties with authorities was the primary reason for these requests.
35. This interview took place in Kuala Lumpur on 20 Feb. 1997.
36. Based on interview in Dec. 1996.
37. Bloomberg, for example, has increased its Singapore-based reporters from one to six between 1991 and 1996.
38. *Dateline: Hong Kong* (http://www.geocities.com/Athens/Forum/2365/pind.html)
39. The government's opposition to the Megawati visit was first conveyed in a private meeting between the FCA President and a senior official of the Ministry of Information and the Arts. The position was subsequently confirmed in an official meeting with the FCA committee. The committee was given an indication at that meeting that, should the FCA persist with the invitation, the event might not take place.
40. 'Forum with Indonesian Opposition Leader Cancelled at Singapore Request', *Agence France Presse* (3 Sept. 1997).
41. 'Dow Jones Taking Up Stake in Asia's First Business News Satellite', *Business Times*(Singapore) (30 July 1993), p.2.
42. Salil Tripathi, 'If You Can't Beat Them ...', *Asia Inc.*(March 1994), p.26.
43. Prominent international television networks including the US entertainment and video loan giant Home Box Office, the music channel MTV, sports network ESPN and multimedia Walt Disney are now operating from Singapore.
44. Stephanie Langenfeld, 'How Commerce Conquers Censorship in Southeast Asia', *Christian Science Monitor* (24 March 1997), p.19.
45. Jon Vanden Heuvel and Everette E. Dennis, *The Unfolding Lotus: East Asia's Changing Media* (Columbia University, New York: The Freedom Forum Media Studies Center, 1993), pp.152–3; Eric Loo, 'Malaysia: Media Tightly Prescribed', *Nieman Reports,* (1996), p.79.
46. '"All knowing" Asiaweek Raises Mahathir's Ire', *The Star* (Malaysia) (6 March 1997) (http://www.jaring.my/~star).
47. Interview 20 Feb. 1997.
48. 'Ultra-Rich Out to Impoverish Developing Nations, Says Mahathir', *The Straits Times* (25 Sept. 1997), p.45.
49. 'Anwar Reminds Media of its Role to Public', *The Straits Times Interactive* (http://www.asia1.com.sg/straitstimes/pages/stsin1.html), 6 Nov. 1997.
50. Stephen Vines, '"Unscrupulous" Soros Fires a Broadside at Mahathir the "Menace"', *The Independent* (22 Sept. 1997), p.18.
51. Through the Soros Foundation and Open Society Institute, both established by Soros, hundreds of millions of dollars are spent annually in over two dozen counmtries — mainly in Eastern Europe, on philanthropic projects, of which most relate to information and media freedom. For an introduction to Soros's philosophy on business and how this relates to information flows, see George Soros (with Byron Wein and Krisztina Koenen), *Soros on Soros* (New York: John Wiley, 1995).
52. Sheila McNulty, 'Free Speech Suffers as Bourse Plunges', *The Asian Wall Street Journal* (17 Sept. 1997), p.18.
53. 'Panel to Screen Foreign Reports', *The Star* (Malaysia) (19 Nov. 1997) (http://www.thestar.mom.my/current/191sc.html)
54. Ian Stewart, 'Malaysia Threatens to Unplug CNN', *The Australian* (24 Nov.1997), p.5.
55. Ian Stewart, 'Malaysia Muzzles Academics', *The Australian* (7 Nov. 1997), p.10; 'Malaysia Bans Academics from Commenting on Haze', *The Straits Times Interactive* (7 Nov. 1997)

(http://www.asia1.com.sg/straitstimes/pages/stsin1.html).

56. Zailani Ahmad, 'Hamid: Govt aims to keep Muslims united', *The Star* (Malaysia) (9 Nov. 1997) (http://www.jaring.my/~star).

57. Hiebert's bail was 250,000 ringgit.

58. Shaila Kosby, 'Court Jails Journalist for Three Months. Judge: Attacks Have Gone Too Far', *The Star* (Malaysia) (5 Sept. 1997) (http://www.jaring.my/~star).

59. Andrew Neil, *Full Disclosure* (London: Macmillan, 1996), p.432.

60. The Malaysians launched its MeaSat satellite in 1996, which will carry government-approved television, which Murdoch hopes will include Star TV. Only satellite dishes attuned to MeaSat will be permitted in Malaysia. See William Atkins, 'Satellite TV Transforming Broadcasting', *Nieman Reports*, Vol.L, No.3 (1996), p.57.

61. 'Press freedom and Hong Kong's future', *Asia Times*, 7 May 1997, p.8; Alan Knight, 'Hong Kong: The Future Begins', *IPI Report*, Third Quarter, (1997), p.8.

62. Elliot Cohen, 'Hong Kong: The Future of Press Freedom', *Columbia Journalism Review,* May/June (1997), p.48.

63. Quoted in 'World Press Freedom Review', *IPI Report* (Dec.1996/Jan. 1997), p.42.

64. Quoted in John Shidlovsky, 'Grim Prospects for Hong Kong', *Media Studies* (Fall, 1996) (http://www.mediastudies.org/peril/schidlovsky.html).

65. Xi Yang was released early in Feb. 1997.

66. Although many local companies have shied away from this mass publication for advertising purposes, Hong Kong Telecom, international investment banks and travel agents have contributed to *Apple Daily*'s HK$670 million advertising revenue in 1996.

67. Andrew Sherry, 'Core of the Problem: Newspaper's Fate Will Gauge More Than Press Freedom', *Far Eastern Economic Review* (3 July 1997), p.62.

68. *Dateline: Hong Kong* (http://www.geocities.com/Athens/Forum/2365/pind.html)

69. Hong Kong Journalists' Association, *Freedom of Expression in Hong Kong*, 1997 Annual Report (hhht://www.freeway.org.hk/hkja/rept97/).

70. As quoted in John Schidlovsky, 'Hong Kong: As Deadline Nears, Self-Censorship Begins', *IPI Report*, First Quarter 1997, p.8. Conspicuously absent from discussion was the fact that Tung's shipping company had been bailed out of financial trouble in the 1980s through a US$120 million loan from China.

71. Joseph Kahn, 'China Has No Need to Suppress the Press in Hong Kong Now', *Asian Wall Street Journal* (21 April 1997), p.1.

72. Philip Bowring, 'Hong Kong's Diverse Media Watchful, Fearful', *Nieman Reports* (Winter 1995), p.42.

73. Kahn, p.6.

74. As quoted in Orville Schell, 'Self-Censorship in Hong Kong', *Media Studies* (Fall 1996) (http://www.mediastudies.org/peril/schell.html).

75. 'Hong Kong: The Future of Press Freedom', *Columbia Journalism Review* (May/June 1997), p.48.

76. Jonathan Fenby, 'For Britons and Americans, the Hong Kong Storyline is Simple: The Place is Going to Go Down the Tube After 1 July', *The Observer* (20 April 1997), p.30.

77. Jonathan Mirsky, 'The Way We Live Now', *Index on Censorship*, 1 (1997), p.142.

78. Elliot Cohen, 'Hong Kong: The Future of Press Freedom', *Columbia Journal Review,* Vol.36, (May/June 1997), p.48.

79. Reporters Sans Frontiers, *1997 Report,* (http://www.calvacom.fr/rsf/RSF_VA/ Rapp_VA/ Carte_VA/Rapp_VA.html).

80. Jonathan Karp, 'Sleeping with the Enemy', *Far Eastern Economic Review* (22 June 1995), p.93.

Seeking Theory from Experience: Media Regulation in China*

RICHARD CULLEN and HUA LING FU

The progress that has been made in securing greater freedom of expression in China, especially since 1979, is reviewed. The review considers how the factors driving this improvement can be identified, described and understood. The aim in studying such factors is to develop some theoretical insights concerning how to encourage positive, realistic change. This development of theory is not meant to displace mainstream democratic rights theory. Rather it is meant to act in a subsidiary role, although it may also feed back into mainstream theory. The theoretical structure proposed here is not confined in its application to freedom of expression issues, nor is it specific to East Asia, but the origins lie in a study of media regulation in East Asia, notably China.

Introduction

In Western democracies, individual freedoms are not solely or even mostly dependent on legally enforceable Bills of Rights or general law protections of individual liberties. Making the right to govern dependent on securing a majority vote in free and open elections is considered by many to be the key political structure factor protecting individuals. Democratic governance systems deliver rights both directly and indirectly. They deliver them directly by conferring a widely available, meaningful right to vote. They deliver them indirectly by making governments wishing to vary or reduce individual rights (amongst other things) answerable to the electorate. This marriage of democracy and individual freedoms is not a universal experience, however. Hong Kong provides a clear example of a jurisdiction where individual freedoms comparable to most Western democracies have been enjoyed for decades in the absence of democratic governance. Hong Kong demonstrates that democracy is not a necessary pre-condition for the enjoyment of such rights. The Hong Kong experience also reveals, however,

* Parts of this contribution draw significantly on H.L. Fu and Richard Cullen, *Media Law in the PRC* (Asia Law and Practice, Hong Kong, 1996), Chapters 2 and 13. The authors would like to thank everyone who has helped in the preparation of this study, in particular Winnie Tam of the City University of Hong Kong for her assistance and Claire Wong, Sally Yam, Choice Choi, Winnie Yeung, David Hui, Heidi Choy and Pinky Choy for their valuable research work and general assistance. This work is generously supported by a Strategic Research Grant from the City University of Hong Kong. The views expressed are those of the authors.

that without full democracy, the continued enjoyment of those rights will always be less secure.[1]

In the People's Republic of China (PRC), the Constitution sets out an extensive regime for protecting individual rights. Were all these provisions enforceable in independent courts in the way, for example, such rights are enforceable in many Western democracies, the PRC would be a very different place in terms of permissible political activity. These rights are not so enforceable, however. China's democratic development, also, is notoriously limited. Moderately open elections, where it is not mandatory to be a member of the Chinese Communist Party (CCP) to be elected, have yet to advance much beyond the village level. In particular, no such elections are permitted in large towns and cities, still less in selecting Provincial and Central Governments.[2] Most of the current effort to improve individual freedoms in China both from within and externally, tends to be focused on making progress in improving constitutionalism.

China repeatedly decries the excesses of the 'rule of man' today and exhorts the virtues of the rule of law (which still really means rule *by* law).[3] The campaign for greater democracy is not moribund, but it is overshadowed by the battle to secure greater constitutionalism or adherence to legalized modes of regulation of both society and government. This is because of the need to address immediate problems, such as the treatment of peaceful political protest, endemic corruption and the abuse of criminal and related laws by authorities. This approach also dominates as it remains within the margins of acceptable political debate in China. The PRC Government itself speaks often about the crucial importance of legality. Discussion of Western-style democracy for China implies the end of the CCP one-party state[4] which is beyond the margins of open political discussion. The strengthening of the position of the individual *vis-à-vis* government has recently been described as a 'division of powers' in the context of post-1989 political structure development in Eastern Europe.[5] This description also aptly captures an important aspect of how individual freedoms may develop even within a one-party state.

This account, by drawing on research related to China, considers how the quest for securing greater individual freedom can be advanced by looking at achievements to date from a series of new perspectives. Its focus reflects the dominant current concern with constitutionalism in China; there is a concentration on how individual rights have been affected and what factors have been influential. The development of democracy in China (and in other places where it is absent) will be influenced by the same or similar factors in our view. The reality for jurisdictions such as the PRC, however, is that step-by-step progress in enhancing individual freedoms is more likely than any 'big bang' advancement. It is widely accepted that Hong

Kong has acted as a crucial model for China's economic modernization. Hong Kong's influence on China seems set to increase still further now that it is part of the PRC. In terms of political structure development, Hong Kong's successful adoption of rule of law principles in the absence of democratic government shows that this can be done. This article thus focuses on what might be termed a realistic staging point on the road to democracy. We see democracy as the clear ultimate aim but we are principally interested here in trying to understand the detail of some of the many stages in achieving full democracy.

The next part comprises a review of some basic features of the concepts freedom of expression and freedom of the press. That is followed by comments on the development of the systems of media regulation in China, and an explanation of factors related to changes in media regulation in the PRC from a more theoretical standpoint. The analysis argues that it would be sensible to devote increased effort to developing a comprehensive theory on the practical implementation of rights as a component in the quest to enhance democratic development. Finally, there is a brief conclusion.

Freedom of Expression: A Functional Outline

Freedom of individual expression and freedom of expression for the press (freedom of the press) are clearly similar concepts, so much so that some consider no real difference exists between the two. However, that there are differences between these concepts and, indeed, they sometimes find themselves in opposition. This part draws on the development of the theory and practice of maintaining freedom of expression and freedom of the press in the West and particularly in the United States (US). The reason for this focus is well put by R.A. Smolla: 'American thinking on freedom of speech is relevant to the rest of the world because our experience in wrestling with free speech conflicts and communications policy is unusually rich. American society may not have the best answers, but it has thought about the problems more.'[6]

During the twentieth century there has been considerable refinement of what is understood by the terms freedom of expression and freedom of the press in the context of the wider ongoing debate about the need to protect individual rights. Particularly since the Second World War, there has been constant attention paid to what are described as basic or fundamental rights. The appalling abuses of individual rights during that war on a scale never before recorded has energised this search for protection ever since, although much ground work had been done prior to that period. In 1946, at the first meeting of the United Nations (UN) after the Second World War, the concept of freedom of expression was identified as a touchstone of all individual rights. The Universal Declaration of Human Rights (UDHR) stipulates, *inter alia*, that individuals are to enjoy rights to freedom of thought, conscience and religion, opinion and expression.[7] The UDHR was just that, a declaration only, but the early UN debates and the UDHR underline the key importance of protecting freedom of expression. Although the UDHR binds the PRC, the UDHR does not impose obligations on parties so bound. Rather, it urges parties to promote, respect and observe those rights set out in the UDHR.

These rights to free expression are also stipulated in the International Covenant on Civil and Political Rights of 1966 (ICCPR). Although the PRC is not a party to the ICCPR,[8] the Constitution of the People's Republic of China of 1982 (Constitution of the PRC) stipulates, in Article 35, that freedom of expression and freedom of the press are protected. Article 51 of the Constitution of the PRC provides, however, that the exercise by citizens of their constitutional rights must not infringe upon the interests of the state and society. The Chinese view that the content of such rights at an individual level is heavily circumscribed by the interests of society is not a post-1949 (PRC) phenomenon. It is an approach embedded in historical Chinese political practice.[9]

Freedom of Expression

Various commentators have elaborated specific reasons why freedom of expression is both intrinsically and instrumentally important.[10] Pre-eminently, it is argued that freedom of expression is necessary to provide a constant testing of conventional wisdom or accepted truth. Flawed 'truths' are eliminated as better explanations arise in the market place of ideas. This justification has two elements. First, it is argued that there is an intrinsic good in seeking the truth. Secondly, it is argued that seeking the truth is good for teleological or consequential reasons, also. That is, the seeking of truth will produce an improved society.

Next, it is said that freedom of expression promotes political participation. This justification addresses the need for individuals in a society to be well informed in order for them to participate effectively in the public affairs of that society. This informed participation is regarded as necessary for the effective operation of democratic government. Thirdly, it is claimed that freedom of expression helps maintain social stability. This justification relates to the benefits arising from a free exchange of information in ensuring social stability. Through a free exchange of information, society's problems, it is said, will be more quickly and accurately identified and responses can be crafted accordingly. Fourthly, freedom of expression can provide a 'safety valve'. This justification is closely related to the previous justification. Here the argument is that freedom of expression guarantees mean that 'steam' can be let off. Individuals or groups in society are less likely to repress their concerns and, in doing so, possibly develop tendencies towards later violent expression of those concerns.

Fifthly, freedom of expression can enhance self-fulfilment. This justification refers to the natural or ethical right (and desire) which, it is said, individuals have to improve themselves and the key role which self-expression plays in that process of development. Finally, freedom of expression provides a crucial check on government. This justification relates to the way that freedom of expression is often pivotal in ensuring the accountability of government. Free expression guarantees mean that a government's behaviour can be openly and effectively criticized.

Freedom of the Press

The justifications just outlined are powerful arguments in favour of maintaining freedom of expression generally. Some of them apply, in particular, to the justification for protecting freedom of the press. A review of these justifications, bearing freedom of press in mind, helps to differentiate between freedom of expression and freedom of the press.

Protecting freedom of the press is clearly important for maintaining the market place in which ideas are exchanged, thus enhancing the operation of a democratic society. Similarly, it provides a forum in which ideas for improving society generally can be argued. The press also serves as a principal mechanism for providing commentary and criticism of government performance. In fact, it is sometimes referred to as the fourth arm of government after the three principal arms of government, namely the Executive, the Legislature and the Judiciary.

There has been long running dispute about whether there are differences, in principle, between the concepts of freedom of the press and freedom of expression and their significance.[11] As a matter of practice, we can identify differences, however. In the US, for example, the press enjoys special privileges with respect to expression which individuals do not enjoy. These privileges include an immunity from some defamation actions[12] and immunity from having certain requirements imposed on the press, for example being ordered to provide a right of reply. Thus, in certain cases, where a citizen (or a group of citizens) wishes to express a point of view in a given newspaper, freedom of the press, that is the right of the newspaper to decide on its own contents, prevails over the freedom of expression of that citizen or these citizens.[13] As we noted earlier, although they share many characteristics, freedom of expression and freedom of the press can some-times find themselves in conflict. Finally, freedom of expression is necessary to fulfil the 'safety valve' and self-fulfilment functions mentioned above. Freedom of the press can assist in achieving these ends, but it is not necessary in the same way as freedom of expression in this quest.

Synopsis

In the real world, the worthy rationale outlined above for freedom of the press is severely tested. As is shown below, the PRC provides a stark example of the very serious problems which can arise from complete public ownership of the press, particularly where there is a dominant and enforced ideology. A common impulsive, reform-minded response to such a system as that prevailing in the PRC is to urge a rapid change to full private ownership. Private ownership of the press presents its own serious difficulties, however. An unregulated private press is likely to abuse its freedom by excluding points of view, misrepresenting information, avoiding public issues and playing to the fears and biases of the population. These problems are exacerbated when press ownership is concentrated in a few hands.[14] The drive for profits, the demands of advertisers and the weak position of consumers are key factors which distort the role of the privately owned press apart from any considerations of ideological bias amongst proprietors.[15]

Some argue that the market will in due course solve most or all these problems by regulating press performance (and ownership). These market based arguments, in the case of the press (including the electronic media), are quite weak and indeed faulty. In the first place there usually are serious economic barriers to entry of new operators. These include the capital intensive nature of media operations, distribution difficulties and costs and the 'brand-name' advantage of existing participants. Secondly, the consumer often is in a poor position to judge the worthiness of existing products or take action. There frequently is little opportunity to make comparisons and the average consumer is rarely well enough informed (or with the time to become so informed) to recognize other than egregious sub-standard performance, manipulation or editorial abuse by the media.[16]

Some commentators go so far as to say that, functionally, the processes of control in the West of the media are comparable with those which used prevail in the old East European communist world.[17] This overstates the position; the fact that such commentators can freely make such claims establishes this. The general thrust of this comparative observation is sound, however. The 'free press' in the West is free only according to a definition of 'free' shaped by numbers of deforming influences.

Of what relevance, though, are the concepts and practices just discussed in the one-party state? One response is to say that one-party states simply ignore or distort all these arguments and run the media as they wish. This argument drives one to the conclusion that without the overthrow of the one-party state, freedom of expression in such jurisdictions is barely worth talking about. This view is an over simplification, however. It can also serve as a pretext for avoiding the difficult task of trying to understand the complexity of political life in a one-party state. Our research shows that, even in the case of a one-party state like the PRC the reality of media regulation is significantly more complex than one might expect. Some of this complexity and the direction that media regulation appears to be taking in China are outlined below.

Media Regulation in China[18]

The Present Position

The overall picture of media regulation in China is one of a miasma of laws, bureaucratic rules, endless official exhortations and vast discretionary zones. Some headway is being made in bringing greater order and predictability to the regulatory landscape. Thus, defamation, advertising, copyright and obscene and indecent materials are now subject, at least in form, to much more legalized control than was the case even a decade ago, although impartial and effective enforcement of the law in all these areas does not yet exist. In respect of direct regulation of the print and electronic media, even the embryonic order just noted is largely absent. This is especially so in the case of the print media. China has been trying for well over a decade to produce a Media Law. China and the world are still waiting.

One important reason for the lack of clarity and effectiveness in media regulation is lack of resources, both human and material. Alas, even if an army of well resourced and adequately trained regulators were to parachute into the PRC tomorrow their impact would overwhelmingly be restricted by the root cause of the problem: PRC media policy. Once upon a time, before 1979, PRC media policy was quite clear: the media were both the mouth and tongue *and* the eyes and ears of China as embodied in the Chinese Communist Party (CCP). Since 1979, things have grown far more complex. This original principle is still adhered to both as a matter of official ideology and, more importantly, as a practical means of maintaining the one-party state. However, although the media, like so many of the other institutions of civil society and the judiciary too, remain woven into the one-party state, the massive changes in China since 1979 have placed the entire system of media regulation under enormous strain. There is growing need for media outlets to stand on their own feet financially; the government simply cannot pay the cost of all those eyes, ears, mouths and tongues from the central purse. With financial independence has come a breakdown in some of the more stiffling control measures. Moreover, China's huge problems with law enforcement apply, also, to media regulation. The result is increased ignoring of the rules, especially where economic gains are to be made.

China does not, of course, have a free-wheeling media as a result. It is still massively stifled, especially in the reporting of a wide range of sensitive political issues. Herein lies another harbinger of change, however. The single greatest blight arising from the open-door policy is the colossal increase in corruption which it has unleashed, not least within the CCP and government. One of the most useful tools in tackling this curse, which touches virtually all PRC citizens, is the media. Thus far, the authorities have tried to manage the exposure of corruption. This is not working; the problem remains as intractable as ever. The pressures to lengthen the leash on the media to help combat corruption are significant.

Another pressure for change comes from the consumers. In a fully commercial market, the *People's Daily*, China's flagship newspaper would likely vanish without trace, so great are its credibility problems.[19] Nothing like a fully commercial media market is in prospect. Nevertheless, China's leading papers are already struggling under China's hybrid brand of market-authoritarianism.

The mechanisms for maximum media control, including all the draconian ones like the laws on sedition, subversion, national security and state secrets remain in place. Nevertheless, the days of total media management seem to have passed, for various reasons including those outlined above. The state still has all the tools to achieve brutal suppression of the media (and free expression) and it continues to use them. But, as one commentator recently noted: '[The PRC's] totalitarianism has receded into what some call normal Asian authoritarianism.'[20]

The control resources of the state have increasingly been devoted to monitoring political speech. The result is a curious inversion of freedom of the press as practised in the West. There, political speech related to elections and government performance enjoys strong protection. Regulators are more active in controlling commercial speech and pornography and violence in the media. In the PRC, principally due to the resource imbalance between regulators and the regulated, publishers of pornographic and violent materials and commercial advertisers enjoy real freedom from control while the state devotes most of its energies to controlling political discussion of issues such as the legitimacy of the one-party state and its principal leaders. The picture, then, is one of formal, rigid control alongside a degree of substantive freedom bordering on anarchy occasionally. Progress in improving the regulatory structure is being made. The progress is largely at the margins, though. The core issue of regulation of the media itself is still beset by the most fundamental policy tensions.

Future Directions

The most likely future direction of regulatory change is that the current experience of reform through drift and *ad hoc* initiative will continue with spasms of harsh even brutal imposition of controls in response to perceived crises. This assumes that no major political upheaval occurs. But considering the enormous political tensions in the PRC, this assumption seems a touch heroic. However, against the background of where the PRC has been (the Great Leap Forward and the Cultural Revolution) and where it now finds itself (looking at becoming the world's most powerful economy within two decades),[21] the assumption seems more plausible.

Looking beyond the current political reality some new questions arise, however. In the PRC the CCP seeks to preserve and legitimate its hold on power. This aim is being pursued (with more than some success) mainly through the massive program of economic reform launched almost two decades ago, backed up by the apparatus of the one-party state (of which all media outlets are still part). Suppose, as many hope, the PRC were to follow the example, sometime over the coming decade or two, of South Korea and Taiwan. This could conceivably happen if the CCP felt that, having delivered sufficient economic benefits it could (safely) seek re-legitimation through some version of multi-party politics. What are the implications of any such development for media regulation? In answering this question, the issue of context must be revisited.

Clearly, Marxist-Leninist philosophy still remains the main influence on the formal shape of the PRC system of media regulation. Were that influence to pass away the pre-existing context could become more relevant again. Pre-1949 China does not exhibit a Western-style position on freedom of the press or freedom of expression. There are some distinctively Chinese views on the place and the role of the media in society. These views see the media as an instrument for use by those who control it. There is little or no tradition of impartial or objective media, a 'fourth estate' role for the media or, even, professional independence in journalism.[22] Historically, all rights enjoyed by the individual in China have been circumscribed significantly by the interests of society – and the state.[23] Moreover, there remains behind all Chinese political thinking, regardless of epoch, a deep intuitive fear of societal chaos. Chinese political history demonstrates both great hunger for change and a profound dread of disorder. The capacity of the media to influence casts them both as a power for good and bad. This is not to say that these values must (let alone should) determine the shape of media reform in a soft-authoritarian PRC.[24] They are bound to remain influential, however, especially while good mass education (and literacy) remain far from being attained in China.

Elsewhere in East Asia, the message on mass media regulation is somewhat mixed. Professional, objective media traditions do prevail in Hong Kong – alongside a free-wheeling, scandal-trawling tradition. Despite two generations of concentrated exposure to the West, deliberate influence from the US and a highly advanced economy, Japan's media remain, according to some commentators, far from fearless and objective[25] and South Korea's media remain state-influenced.[26] In Taiwan, the last powerful formal controls on the media were lifted in 1991. The results since have been encouraging; the media certainly express a wide range of political views forcefully.[27] However, it is rather too early to say if an objective and professional reporting is now a permanent part of Taiwan's political landscape (see the account of Taiwan's media by Rawnsley and Rawnsley in this volume).

The PRC is, apart from its present political system, vastly different from any other part of East Asia. Its sheer size, both in area and especially in terms of population ensure this. For several millenia China has dominated the region culturally. China, perhaps alone among extant nations of the world, can lay claim to being unique. Despite this uniqueness, or perhaps because of it, China has proved remarkably adaptable. Yet it seems always to leave its own clear stamp on practices it has absorbed from the West and elsewhere. This has resulted less from explicit nationalism than the momentum of Chinese history.

An Ancillary Theory of Democratic Rights

Factors Effecting Change in the Regulation of Expression in China

The copiously documented liberal legacy of thinking on freedom of expression has been a critical influence on the debate on the regulation of expression in China. The political arguments on freedom of expression in China all pivot on this accumulated thinking. Even Chinese attempts to debunk this thinking acknowledge its central influence. Precisely what the effect of this paradigm has been in concrete terms is hard to establish, but it has kept the theoretical debate anchored to a significant degree.[28]

Moving beyond the theoretical battlefield, there are other, often inter-related, factors that appear to have influenced developments in media regulation in the PRC. These factors include: the impact of technological developments; the impact of global economic change; the impact of international politics; the activities of professional journalists and others; resources issues; competency issues; and the influence of widespread corruption.

Technological developments in communications have been

instrumental, it seems, in liberalising the mass media in Taiwan.[29] This is also happening in China (though to a significantly lesser extent). Overseas short wave broadcasts are readily available in China. Stations such as the Voice of America and the BBC (British Broadcasting Corporation) are important information sources for the Chinese public. Telephone, fax, and more recently Internet communications have improved both the quality and quantity of information-exchange between the Chinese public and the outside world. Economic growth has put the financial means of gaining access to such sources in increasing numbers of hands. Despite much official nervousness, the growth of the Internet in China has been quite significant.[30] Indeed, access to the Internet is more widely available in authoritarian China than in democratic India. The principal reasons appear to be the greater (and growing) sophistication of China's telecom systems and the healthier competitive environment. One of the consequences is that it has become much more difficult for the government to disinform the public. These pressures also place the credibility of government under further challenge.

It is quite wrong to overstate the impact of technology to date. So far its impact in China is less than in Eastern Europe during the 1980s. The PRC authorities have moved quickly both to control 'polluting' influences and to provide effective competition. China is currently building the World's largest cable television network at a remarkably swift pace. The rapid development of technology and its tendency to offer ever increasing sophistication at ever decreasing prices shows that the authorities face an immense task if they wish to hold the line long-term, however. The demands arising from international competition also are pushing China towards embracing new technologies as quickly as possible.[31]

The moves to a socialist market economy in the PRC have changed China profoundly. Forces have been unleashed which have drastically loosened controls on free expression, albeit, mostly indirectly. Thus, advertising in the PRC breaks (often recklessly) all manner of old taboos, and salacious reporting and writing are rife. These changes are hardly to be wildly applauded. But they clearly indicate the power of the market to effect change. The market also has exposed the costs of running a non-credible media; the established press[32] in China is beset by all kinds of financial difficulties. The market economy has resulted in slashed subsidies and fading readership for the mainstream established press.[33]

As the Chinese economy has expanded, one apparently odd result is that government revenues have shrunk drastically. In fact, this shrinkage is not so odd as it seems at first. Prior to market reforms, the Chinese economy was largely centrally controlled. This control has slipped to a very significant extent. Moreover, those parts of the economy still under direct government control are, for the most part, a huge fiscal burden on government.[34] Government expenditure as a share of Gross Domestic Product (GDP) is estimated to have dropped from 39 per cent in 1978 to 14 per cent in 1994.[35] At the same time the numbers of media outlets has soared. The number of newspapers, for example has risen from 186 in 1976 to 2040 in 1993.[36] This shift of resources helps explain why government finds it increasingly difficult to fund measures to control expression. The results include a concentration on trying to control certain sorts of political expression whilst control of other forms of expression is neglected. Official encouragement of private enforcement of China's new defamation laws is also, likely, a response to this resourcing problem. Encouraging citizens to sue the media shifts some of the economic burden of control to where resources have flowed under market reforms.[37]

The GDP figures just given do not include a variety of 'off budget' expenditures. The trend is still very clear, however. There has been an extraordinary loosening of the grip of government on the economy compared to 20 years ago. It is also true that much of the wealth transfer has been into the pockets of a limited numbers of individuals and enterprises who often are closely allied to government or to the CCP. These beneficiaries, nevertheless, clearly now take a proprietorial view with respect to this wealth transfer, so it is not correct to suggest that things remain much as before. The political dynamics of the socialist market economy could hardly be more different from those applying to the political economy which emerged from the Cultural Revolution. We need also to remember that in the West, wealth and power are very narrowly held and nowhere more so than in the case of the media. Yet there is no doubting the extent of relative media freedom prevailing in, say, the US compared to the PRC.

As it happens, China's decision to adopt the 'open door' policy in the late 1970s coincided with a major shift in world trading relations commonly referred to as 'globalization'. Globalization in this economic sense refers to the rapid movement away from national and regional markets towards global (or near-global) markets in an ever increasing spectrum of goods and services ranging from cars and televisions to entertainment and news to legal services. The technology revolution, which has freed capital to move at astonishing speed and in astonishing amounts, has been instrumental in creating this phenomenon. The end of the cold war has provided significant extra momentum. Many other developments have followed in its wake including 'globalized' public policy-making by governments and even the drafting of national constitutions based on global standards. That is, even such fundamentally national activities as these are being affected. The 1996 Constitution of South Africa provides a prime example.[38] One outcome of this process appears to be a serious erosion of the ability of national governments to pursue any sort of agenda frowned upon by international capitalism.[39] This weakening of the power of national governments has taken its toll also, though, on the power of ruling elites in one-party states to micro-manage the lives of their citizens in the manner hitherto common. It also has contributed to the collapse of one-party states across Eastern Europe.

In the case of the PRC, the interaction of the open door policy and the process of globalization help explain both the remarkable rates of economic growth in China over the last two decades and the equally remarkable shift in resources in China out of state hands. The role of private property in fostering and securing individual rights is widely acknowledged, although its influence remains a matter of controversy, nowhere more so, perhaps, than in the PRC.[40] The fact remains, however, that the loosening of controls over the lives of ordinary people in China, the real improvement in the scope for expression and the greater access to external commentary all have been facilitated by the shrinkage of the state. It is, thus, difficult to imagine another Cultural Revolution on the previous scale ever being launched again in China. The dispersal of economic power has often been far from fair in China but it has produced a new balance of economic (and thereby political) forces which has had beneficial effects for the majority of citizens.[41]

International politics has had an impact on media regulation in the PRC in a variety of ways. The closure of the cold war phase in history has created an atmosphere of ideological uncertainty; who is 'good' or 'bad' is far less a matter of labels today than it was. For repressive regimes, the consequence is increased confusion about what must be repressed. In the case of China, the removal of old 'certainties', means that the highlighting of individual rights abuses has greater impact nowadays. Since 1989 the individual rights discourse has enjoyed significant revaluation as a factor in international politics. The cause and effect matrix can be quite complex, however. The Chinese reaction to pressures with respect to individual rights can be yet more repression, especially when discussions about rights are linked to considerations of the need for 'containment' policies. Rightly or wrongly, China sees many hostile forces, both economic and political, ranged against it. Talk of the need for the PRC to be contained confirms the worst of these fears which, in turn, exacerbates the intolerance of domestic dissenting views.[42]

The track record of attempts by individual and groups to push the boundaries of acceptable reporting in China is both proud and depressing. Notable steps forward have been wiped out almost overnight, such as in the case of newspapers caught in the post-June 1989 crackdown on expression. Yet the 'information-market' constantly applies pressure for 'product improvement' and with information now having such a powerful economic (as well as political) edge the pressures are only increasing.[43]

One product of the Chinese government's resourcing difficulties has been an exacerbation of competency problems in the bureaucracy. Diminishing resources means less funds for adequately competitive salaries and training. In terms of media regulation, this factor is double-edged. Lack of highly trained and attentive regulators has played a significant part in allowing many media operators and personnel to ignore rules and guidelines they find inconvenient or oppressive.[44] The same lack of competence leads, however, to capricious, arbitrary and sometimes extremely harsh 'crackdowns' in reaction, in part, to frustrations felt by regulators.

Corruption is widely regarded as the single most significant blight on life in the PRC, at every single level of society. There is no question that it has grown much worse since 1979. Problems of corruption exacerbate the impact of resource and competency problems in media regulation. On the other hand, corruption can provide a means by which harsh rules and regulations can be circumvented. Media reform has successfully converted many of China's media outlets into businesses. That is, although they remain in the ownership of government or the CCP, they have, more than ever, to be self-financing. They have to be run as businesses. Rigid media rules have to be circumvented if these businesses are to be successful. Corruption has, in a perverse way, facilitated positive change within the PRC media. Given the increasingly businesslike outlook of the media and the rigid controls (over, for example, the purchase of government-subsided newsprint; the allocation and distribution of government-controlled permits which are necessary for the publication of books or magazines; and the selection of printers and distribution systems for publication), the regulators are provided with both opportunities and incentives to make 'exceptions'. Harsh regulations can, paradoxically, lead, indirectly, to greater freedom of expression in a socialist market economy.

Developing the Theory

The one-party state remains very much intact in the PRC but it is a markedly different one-party state to that which existed 20 years ago in many respects. In the case of media regulation, there have been significant improvements under the influence of vectors such as those just discussed. This suggests there is a case for developing an ancillary theory on the implementation of democratic rights. This would not be a substitute for a theory of democratic rights, but, rather, a subsidiary theory. It would be concerned with the serious practical implications of mainstream theory. It may 'feed back' into the primary framework.

The purpose of developing an ancillary theory on the practical implementation of rights would be to consider, in a scholarly way, factors (such as those listed above) which clearly influence rights development, in the medium to long term, from a rights-development perspective. The effects of economic, technological and political change on rights have often been discussed, it is true, but largely in a descriptive way, and after the event. The impact of personal and group initiatives on developing freedom of expression, especially in the media, also are studied, but mostly from political-analytical perspectives rather than as a component of a more sophisticated rights achievement strategy. The same comment is largely true of academic treatment of resourcing, competency and corruption issues. Moreover, in all these cases, the commentary tends to take a short-term perspective.

The proposed theory (with its emphasis on a longer-term perspective) can be represented diagramatically (see Figure 1):

FIGURE 1

THEORY ON THE IMPLEMENTATION OF DEMOCRATIC RIGHTS

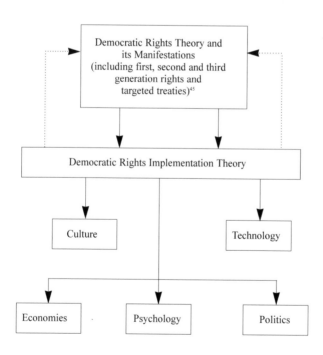

The commentary that follows considers, briefly, what an ancillary implementation theory could achieve, and refers back to the fields set out in Figure 1.

Culture

Placing emphasis on practical implementation theorizing allows context to be discussed without causing a head on clash between the 'universal nature of rights' and 'cultural relativism'. It is appropriate, here, to consider a practical example. Property rights enjoy an uneasy place in the Western lexicon of individual rights. Some (including, famously, Karl Marx) have argued that individual property rights are a conspiracy against the non-wealthy.[46] Other Western political philosophers, such as Nozick, see individual property rights as central to any theory of societal organization.[47] On balance, especially since the retreat of Marxist communism as a serious theory of the state, it is fair to say that property rights are considered to be of great importance in the West and well beyond. In a hierarchy of rights they may not rank with freedom of the press, still less, freedom of expression or the right to vote in free elections but they remain a crucial component in all liberal schemes stressing the protection of individual rights.

One important property right is copyright. Copyright is a typical intellectual property right; intangible but, if protected, often of immense value. Yet, in China, the tradition over a long period of history has been hostile to the development of the concept of copyright as a private right. Various factors appear to explain this. First, in Confucian society, intangible creations of the individual mind were regarded as the product and property of society. Secondly, Chinese aesthetics have placed the highest value on reverent and highly skilled imitating of classical works of art. Thirdly, the famed professional bureaucracy of dynastic China was accessible only to those who could master, *inter alia*, the memorization and written reproduction of classical written works. Fourthly, dynastic China was the World's most sophisticated agrarian society by far. This society rated commercial trading enterprises as a regretable necessity requiring stringent controls lest they empower their owners and thus corrupt the established political and social order.[48] This attitude towards trade and commerce was hardly encouraging for the growth of complex private property rights.

The reality of the Chinese cultural perspective on intellectual property rights is readily accepted by commentators. To talk of having to take this context into account when considering, for example, mechanisms to protect the individual right of copyright in China is not controversial. In fact, to ignore this context risks the failure of any protecting initiative. As it happens, the problems related to property copyright in China, both for

Chinese and foreigners, remain immense. Understanding the context in this case provides no easy answers but it does inform the search for solutions.

There is an element in this debate about the validity of intellectual property rights *per se*, but most of the discussion is more practically focused; what mechanisms will work to protect copyright best in a Chinese context? The argument put forward here is that the approach of considering context in practical implementation terms has a wider application.. Such an approach also creates a space in which to discuss rights implementation strategies more generally within authoritarian states. Clearly some authoritarian states generally treat their citizens less odiously than others. The question arises whether this is simply: a matter of economics; or lack of advanced technology; or whether a range of other factors also apply. Few aspects of life are black and white. Even within the one-party state there is a difference between something and nothing or, if you like, bad and worse. Moreover, many such states show few signs of disappearing. And in some cases, the lack of any alternative political governing group suggests that any abrupt change may well give rise to a period of political chaos and perhaps worse. China is a case in point. Some sort of step-by-step approach to tackling rights issues is thus worthy of consideration on both pragmatic and principled grounds.

The term 'Asian values' lacks a clearly agreed definition. It is a term increasingly in common usage, however, as a convenient shorthand for the broad position that there exists some sort of Asian-related alternative to the Western-liberal political paradigm, particularly with respect to the theory and practice of individual rights protection and the role of democracy. The political-geographic basis for this alternative position is more accurately stated as East Asian rather than Asian. That is, the traditions which are said to underpin Asian values are, typically, East-Asian traditions. These traditions, in turn, are especially heavily influenced by Confucianism and, hence, Chinese political culture.[49] When authoritarian elites emphasize the fundamental importance of 'Asian values', others are right to be sceptical. When they do so to justify repressive political measures, the self-serving nature of such arguments is transparent. But when arguments about such values are raised as serious commentary in debating future political policies for East Asia they deserve to be treated on their merits; the message needs to be considered separately from the messenger. A discriminating approach to the Asian values debate allows for the abusive proseletyzing to be identified and dealt with without need for recourse to more polarizing denunciations. By making the debate a matter of implementation theory, the risks of polarization can be reduced even further.

Technology

There is currently much discussion about standards for a variety of important developments in the electronic media. These include digital television standards and future development of the Internet. These standards appear largely to be debated by technical and commercial parties.[50] The process of settling these standards would benefit from perspectives on their function in improving free expression, *inter alia*. In particular, a technically informed, democratic rights perspective on setting such standards might well argue for standards that maximized the openness of communications and encourage the widest possible competition in order to lower costs. There is little discernible such input, for example, in the battle being waged over control of the Internet. The purpose of this desire to dominate the Internet, fairly clearly, is to maximize profits. Moreover, many commercial parties involved with the Internet are working with all haste to find ways in which to increase revenue flows from its use. The liberalizing potential of the Internet is the focus for slogans and exhortations far more than it is for careful research.

Compared to even a decade ago, technology today is far more rapidly available throughout the World after any new innovation. The days when the West prospered due to its special access to new technological developments have faded. Generally, this improved accessibility is a positive development. A rights implementation perspective could help develop policies and strategies to encourage this largely market-driven process further, for example by stressing accessibility for those most in need.

Economics

A much better understanding of the liberating effects of certain sorts of macroeconomic decision-making might also flow from development of a theory on the practical implementation of rights, and thereby improve the standard of discussions in such organizations as the World Trade Organization (WTO) and the Asia Pacific Economic Cooperation forum. Little, if any, such input was evident at a major conference of the WTO held in Singapore in December 1996, apart from unsuccessful attempts to get the WTO to examine certain employment rights issues.[51] Regrettably, much of the contribution from activists (and some theorists) to macroeconomic debates also tends towards denunciation of 'exploiting multinationals' or harangues against free trade, even now. Neither free trade theories nor multinationals dine with the angels but their impact on rights issues almost certainly is significantly more complex than is often portrayed. Moreover, concerned but poorly informed arguments on rights can be quite counter-productive.

Psychology

Parallels are drawn by some of commentators between Western religious evangelism in East Asia and more modern rights advocacy. The argument proceeds along the following lines: Western religious evangelism has a far from blemish-free record due to its association with political and economic imperialism; individual rights doctrines are the West's latest 'religious' product; and they are suspect for similar reasons. Moreover, these doctrines make the same sort of supremacy claims as Western monotheistic religions: that is, what is being advocated is not really Western but universal. Attacks on modern rights advocates are often launched disingenuously by those intent on retaining existing power structures. Yet they touch a responsive nerve. It is clear that the effectiveness of traditional, originally Western-conceived, rights protection mechanisms and the detail of implementing democratic reform are matters of academic debate, especially in East Asia. The debate is concerned with the practical relevance of these systems for East Asian societies and how they mesh with East Asian cultural traditions, *inter alia*. A by-product provides some commentary on the way in which rights protection systems in particular have affected some Western societies. The proselytizing of 'Asian values' often is done by members of East Asian power-elites. This often leads Western commentaries on rights to reduce the Asian values debate to a stereotyped dichotomy: self-serving Asian political leaders are juxtaposed with their rights-deprived citizens.[52] Strategically, in some cases this deliberate polarizing may serve a useful purpose because it can be a fairly accurate representation of reality and it is a powerful counter to dissembling. But in other cases it is a poor strategy, alienating and sometimes offending researchers who do not share identical views. Natural allies then find themselves less allied than they could be. And, especially the more zealous may find themselves less well informed than they ought be. An ancillary theory of rights could serve to remind all serious participants in the rights debate (from East and West) of the influence of personal psychological factors on scholarship in an area of ongoing, real controversy.

Politics

A subsidiary theory on rights would help foster a rights implementation perspective on global political developments. There has been scant attention paid in the West, for example, to the rights implications of any China-containment policy. There is no question that the siege mentality of the McCarthy era in the US played havoc with the rights of communists and others on the left, during the 1950s. There is hardly any reason to believe that Chinese xenophobia is any less virulent than that of the US. Any development of a containment policy or even a quasi-containment policy should be informed by a discourse on possible domestic rights consequences in China.[53]

The end of the cold war has unfrozen many ideological views. An open-minded perspective on rights implementation would enhance the likelihood of spotting opportunities to have a positive influence in the post-cold war ideological debate. In this regard, seeking common ground with serious scholars of Asian values suggests itself as a sensible starting point. In the world of commerce, it is now well recognized that failure to undertake adequate 'cultural due diligence' studies frequently leads to a clash of corporate cultures in the case of mergers – often with disastrous consequences for a merged company's personnel and for its profitability.[54]

Conclusion

In the quest to expand democratic government throughout the world, the twentieth century has seen many disappointments as well as some significant successes. What is becoming more clear, is that progress towards democratic governance proceeds in different ways in different jurisdictions. What is also becoming clear is that there can be 'staging points' in this process. In Hong Kong, for example, the British oversaw the creation of a highly developed form of constitutionalism which delivered the widest range of freedoms to the citizens of Hong Kong, in the absence of democracy. The lack of democracy means that the foundations of this structure are weaker than they should be, but the achievement itself remains significant and largely intact. There are also signs in the PRC that this model has *some* attractions. Legalism, if not the rule of law, is making steady inroads in China; it is becoming an accepted part of the political structure, as the world's most unwieldy one-party state struggles to modernize still further.

A wide range of factors are affecting, often positively, the process of political change in the PRC. These factors appear to be of general importance – that is, they are not specific to the case of China. The changes occurring fall far short of significant democratic reform. But they deserve to be recognised for what they are as much as for what they are not. One important vector for change has been economic reform. Macroeconomic theory and practice have moved on from where they were 50 years ago. It is now widely accepted that 'giant strides' simply do not work economically whether in the form of Stalinist industrialization, Chairman Mao's 'Great Leap Forward' or African experiments in taxing agriculture to promote rapid industrialization. This is apart from the appalling humanitarian consequences of such experiments. Economic development in the late twentieth century is far from fair in its outcomes but lessons have been learned (and applied) from the past with good effect. In particular there is now more of a step-by-step mentality. China's economic reforms of the last two decades are in this mould. For ordinary citizens, this means they are far less likely today to be subjected to idiosyncratic or maniacal authoritarian economic experiments. And the development of the global economy, whilst it has brought vast profits for a few, has also brought some benefits to millions in poorer nations through trade.

Politics has seen some progress too. Over 50 years ago, V.M. Molotov, Foreign Minister of the world's then leading one-party state, the Union of Soviet Socialist Republics, observed that: 'The disadvantage of free elections is that you can never be sure who is going to win them.'[55] Today, the leading one-party state, the PRC, is at least experimenting with democracy at the grass-roots level. Since 1988 some 80 per cent of villages and rural communities (comprising perhaps 800 million people) have elected, by universal suffrage and secret ballot, their own leaders and committees who serve for three years. The number of participating communities has grown since then. The majority of elected persons are not CCP members.[56]

Perhaps the most important new factor in effecting positive change has been the extraordinary growth in communications technology. One day, Guglielmo Marconi may be recognized as having made as great a contribution to the progress of rights as John Locke. As it happens, Marconi often explained that he was especially motivated in his remarkable, pioneering work on the development of radio by a desire to improve the human condition, through facilitating what he saw as a key aspect of any such improvement – expansive and open communication.

These and other factors are, collectively, having a marked effect on political structure development in China. The effects are incremental, however. Steps backward are commonplace, of course, but the direction, overall, is forward. The wide variety of ancillary processes effecting change have been relatively neglected by scholars concerned with the closely linked issues of democratization and individual rights. Hence the importance of studying the media and in particular the regulation of the media in China, and the significance of identifying the evolutionary changes that are taking place. Hence also the utility of devoting increased scholarly effort to developing a theory of practically implementing rights.

Democracy is the ultimate aim of an ancillary theory of rights. For some jurisdictions, constitutionalism as discussed in this study offers a possible preliminary goal and, more importantly, a base from which to move forward. Few would disagree that we need to understand more about that goal and the ultimate aim. We need to understand more about their imperfections, their vulnerabilities and their possibilities. A stronger theoretical perspective on secondary factors shaping political change would assist this understanding.

NOTES

1. Carol Jones, *Politics Postponed: Law as a Substitute for Politics in Hong Kong and China,*
   in *Rule of Law in Eastern Asia* (London: Routledge, 1998).
2. 'Out of the shadow of Deng', *The Economist* (20 Sept. 1997).
3. Jones, op. cit.
4. By one-party state is meant a nation state controlled by a single political party or ideology
   which allows no other significant competing ideology in the political arena; real political
   pluralism is excluded. Some states where competing political parties are allowed to
   participate in law making bodies nevertheless control the extent of that participation closely.
   Examples in this category include Mexico and Singapore where a single party has dominated
   the multi-party landscape and has always formed the government. Other one-party states
   simply bar or suppress all political opposition with violence if necessary. Myanmar provides
   a good example. Yet other one-party states allow 'approved' alternative political parties but
   confine them to the most minor role. China provides a good example. The relationship
   between the CCP and the democratic parties allowed in the PRC looks like nothing so much
   as an elephant shepherding a family of field mice. See further Albert Hung-yee Chen, *An
   Introduction to the Legal System of the People's Republic of China* (Singapore: Butterworths,
   1992), pp.63–5.
5. Wojciech Sadurski, 'The Tension between the Division of Power and Constitutional Rights
   (with Special Emphasis on Socio-Economic Rights)' (unpublished conference paper on file
   with the authors).
6. Quoted in Eric Barendt, *Importing United States Free Speech Jurisprudence?* in Tom
   Campbell and Wojciech Sadurski (eds.), *Freedom of Communication* (Aldershot: Dartmouth,
   1994), p.57.
7. See Articles 18 and 19 of the UDHR. See also Asbjorn Eide; Gudmunder Alfredsson, Goran
   Melander, Lars Adam Rehof, Allan Rosas and Theresa Swinehart (eds.), *The Universal
   Declaration of Human Rights: A Commentary* (Oslo: Scandinavian University Press,1992).
8. The ICCPR does, however, apply in Hong Kong, See further Yash Ghai, *Hong Kong's New
   Constitutional Order* (Hong Kong : Hong Kong University Press, 1997),pp.376–80.
9. See: Stanley Lubman, 'Studying Contemporary Chinese Law: Limits, Possibilities and
   Strategy', *American Journal of Comparative Law*, Vol.39 (1991), pp.293, 324–8; and W.F.J.
   Jenner, *The Tyranny of History* (London: Penguin, 1994), Ch.7.
10. This Section draws on a number of sources including: the judgment of J. Brandeis in *Whitney
    v California* (1927) 274 US 357, 372; John Zelezny, *Communications Law: Liberties,
    Restraints and the Modern Media* (Belmont: Wadsworth, 1993); Thomas I. Emerson,
    'Towards a General Theory of the First Amendment', *Yale Law Journal*, Vol.72 (1963),
    p.877; Alexander Meiklejohn, 'The First Amendment is an Absolute', *Supreme Court
    Review*, (1961), p.245; Lucas A. Powe, 'Or of the (Broadcast) Press', *Texas Law Review*,
    Vol.55 (1976), p.39; Owen Fiss, 'Building a Free Press', *Yale Journal of International Law*,
    Vol.20 (1995), p.188; and Kevin, Boyle, 'The Right to Freedom of Expression', paper
    presented at Hong Kong's Bill of Rights Conference, Faculty of Law, University of Hong
    Kong, 20–22 June, 1991.
11. For discussion of this issue see, for example, Melville B.Nimmer, 'Is Freedom of the Press
    a Redundancy – What Does it Add to Freedom of Speech?', *Hastings Law Journal*, Vol. 26
    (1975), p. 639.
12. Frederick Schauer, 'Social Foundations of the Law of Defamation: A Comparative
    Analysis', in Eric Barendt (ed.), *Media Law* (Aldershot: Dartmouth, 1993).
13. See, for example, *Columbia Broadcasting System v Democratic National Committee* (1973)
    412 US 94 where the Supreme Court denied the public interest supported any right to have
    paid political announcements broadcast.
14. Lee C. Bollinger, 'Freedom of the Press and Public Access: Toward a Theory of Partial
    Regulation of the Mass Media', *Michigan Law Review*, Vol. 75 (1976), p.1.
15. Fiss, op. cit., p.190.
16. These difficulties are discussed in detail in Lee C. Bollinger, Lee C., *Images of a Free Press*
    (Chicago, IL: University of Chicago Press, 1991); and Thomas Gibbons, *Regulating the*

Media (London: Sweet & Maxwell,1991). See, also Fiss, op. cit.

17. See, for example, John Pilger, *Distant Voices* (London: Vintage, 1992), pp.11–12.
18. For a detailed exposition (with examples) of the issues raised in this Part, see H.L. Fu and Richard Cullen, *Media Law in the PRC* (Hong Kong: Asia Law and Practice, 1996), Chs.2–4 and 6–11.
19. Nicholas Kristof and Sheryl Wudunn, *China Wakes* (New York: Vintage Books,1995), p.287.
20. William H. Overholt, 'Chinas After Deng', *Foreign Affairs*, Vol.75 (1996), p.63.
21. 'China looming', *The Economist* (17 Aug. 1996), p.11.
22. Kuldip P. Rampal, 'Press and Political Liberalization in Taiwan', *Journalism Quarterly*, Vol.71 (1994), p.637. See also Allison Liu Jernow, *Don't Force Us to Lie: The Struggle of Chinese Journalists in the Reform Era* (Baltimore, MD: School of Law, University of Maryland, 1994), Ch.1.
23. Lubman, op.cit. See also Albert, Hung-yee Chen, 'Developing Theories of Rights and Human Rights in China', in Raymond Wacks (ed.), *Hong Kong, China and 1997: Essays in Legal Theory* (Hong Kong: Hong Kong University Press, 1993), pp.125, 146ff.
24. The term soft-authoritarian is used to describe the sort of regime that could possibly emerge in the PRC by following the Taiwan model (or even the Japanese model). Multi-party politics exists, but widely shared values permit and even encourage powerful, poorly accountable bureaucracies to regulate and run society in a manner not acceptable in the West.
25. R.J. Guthrie, 'Speak no Evil', *Window* (13 Sept. 1996), p.15.
26. 'Burning Desires', *The Economist* (21 Sept. 1996), p.33.
27. Rampal, op. cit.
28. Chen, op. cit.
29. Daniel K. Berman, *Words like Colored Glass* (Boulder, CO: Westview Press, 1992).
30. Fu and Cullen, op. cit., Ch.4.
31. Ibid.
32. The term, the 'established press', is used to indicate those newspapers and periodicals produced under official auspices (and close official control) sometimes referred to as the 'party papers'. See further ibid., Ch.2.
33. Some 'minor' papers such as *Beijing Youth* have flourished, however, through watchful market-oriented reporting. They also enjoy considerable financial independence. Ibid.
34. Donald J.S. Brean, 'Financial Perspectives on Fiscal Reform', Paper presented to Eleventh Annual Conference of Chinese Economists' Society, 9–11 August 1996, University of Western Ontario, London, Ontorio, Canada.
35. Ibid. Even in free market Hong Kong, the share is closer to 20 per cent.
36. Fu and Cullen, op.cit., Ch.2.
37. Ibid., Ch.9.
38. Yash Ghai, 'The End of Constitutionalism', paper presented at Conference on Trends in Contemporary Constitutional Law, University of Hong Kong, 13–14 Dec. 1996.
39. Ibid.
40. Chen, op. cit., 149.
41. Antoine Kernan, 'The Erosion of the State in China and Hungary', *China Perspectives*, Vol.8 (Nov. 1996), p.64.
42. H.L.Fu,, 'Sedition and Political Dissidence: Towards Legitimate Dissent in China', *Hong Kong Law Journal*, Vol.26 (1996) p. 210.
43. Fu and Cullen, op. cit., Chs.2 and 3.
44. Ibid., pp.89–90.
45. First generation rights include typical civil and political rights (often referred to as negative rights because of the restrictions they place on the state or authorities). Second generation rights include positive social and economic rights such as the right to work or the right to education. Third generation rights include those broader rights involving complex interactions of multiple rights and duties holders such as the right to a clean environment. The term, targeted treaties, refers to the various instruments, usually emanating from the UN, building on the UDHR such as the ICCPR.
46. Marx's views on the topic of property rights are well explained in, Peter Singer, *Marx* (New York: Oxford University Press, 1980) Chs.4 and 5.

47. Robert Nozick, *Anarchy, State and Utopia* (New York: Basic Books, 1974).
48. Gungwu Wang, *China and the Chinese Overseas* (Singapore: Times Academic Press, Singapore, 1991), Ch.4. On the historical Chinese view on copyright, see also William P. Alford, *To Steal a Book is an Elegant Offence: Intellectual Property Law in Chinese Civilization* (Stanford, CA: Stanford University Press), Ch.2.
49. There is no space here to do more than note these dimensions of the meaning of the term Asian Values. For, further commentary see, for example, Julia Tao and Ho Mun Chan, 'Which Human Rights' and Joseph Chan, 'Asian Values Confucianism and Human Rights', papers presented at Conference on Human Rights: Culture, Philosophy and Law, held at the University of Hong Kong, 16–19 December 1996.
50. See 'Copy Wrongs', *The Economist* (14 Dec. 1996), p.79.
51. 'Cheers for beer and BMW', *The Economist* (14 Dec. 1996), p.90.
52. Some serious Asian commentators have not unreasonably likened basing the interpretation of Asian values on the pronouncements of certain Asian political leaders as akin to relying principally on the views of Ronald Reagan, Margaret Thatcher, John Major and Tony Blair in studying liberalism.
53. Fu, op. cit..
54. See 'Why too many mergers miss the mark', *The Economist* (4 Jan. 1997), p.59.
55. Quoted in 'How to run a referendum', *The Economist* (23 Nov. 1996), p.74.
56. 'China's grassroots democracy', *The Economist* (2 Nov. 1996), p.27. It is said many successful non-CCP members later joined the party.

The Media and Democratization
in the Middle East:
The Strange Case of Television

ANNABELLE SREBERNY-MOHAMMADI

One of the major changes within the Middle Eastern cultural landscape is the burgeoning of national, regional and international television providers. There is an increasing public access to the medium. This study maps out the changes in the context of a changing global political economy and explores the possible consequences for political and cultural democratization. One key issue is changing gender dynamics, as more women are brought into the national public sphere. Other important issues involve the tensions between political attempts to strengthen national political and cultural identities, the potential cultural discount of the Arab language and culture in the furtherance of a regional identity, and the impact of an increasing circulation of western cultural and political images and information in the complex process of transformation to modernity.

'If you stop football being freely distributed over the airwaves today, you'll have a revolution in the Middle East.'[1]

While the Middle East remains a politically volatile area, it is usually thought that the pressures are clashes of ideology or religious-secular tensions: televized football is not often thought of as a major cause of political upheaval. Yet in a milieu where people are most often addressed as consumers or as audiences, rather than as citizens or political participants, mediated culture may play a more significant role than the typical instruments of formal politics. This examination focuses on the television environment in the Middle East and its implications for democratization, for a number of reasons. First, because it has changed so rapidly and is continuing to do so, both bringing externally-produced materials to the region but also allowing trans-regional programme flows and audience groupings. As Callard has argued, 'over the last seven years the Middle East has moved from a situation of very limited access to television which was

The author thanks Lena Jayyusi of Al-Quods University, Jerusalem and Stephen Barraclough of the Australian National University, Canberra for their thoughtful critical comments; she alone is responsible for the final product.

virtually all government controlled, to a market where there is a vast number of channels to choose between, often more than that of many European countries'.[2] Second, in contexts of considerable illiteracy, audio-visual media can reach larger audiences than print and thus potentially serve to construct a national audience and create a shared cultural-political space for the first time. Third, in contexts where patriarchal culture remains dominant, supported by religious values and social tradition, and there is an often intense masculinization of public space, the penetrative reach of television into the family home could have profound consequences. Fourth, while national and international radio broadcasting is well-established and popular, its audience is being challenged by television, as Boyd[3] has recently argued.

Some Notes on the Middle East

The very term 'the Middle East' is a geo-political label given to a region by western powers after the First World War; that it has stuck as a name and is used as a way of clustering certain countries should not lead to assumptions about similarities between these countries. The histories of Ottoman and colonial rule may have left some shared legacy across the region, while the political boundaries of the region are the result of various 'lines in the sand' drawn by Western powers, arrived at through international conflict and colonial settlements. The enduring struggles of the Palestinians, not yet fully a state, the Kurds, perhaps further than ever from statehood, and the Armenians, a global diaspora, are part of the cruel historical legacies of the region.

Yet the region reveals remarkable differentiation along almost any indicator one cares to chose. It includes countries that have some of the highest per capita Gross National Product (GNP) in the world (United Arab Emirates (UAE); Kuwait, Israel) and the lowest (Yemen) (see Table 2). While Arabic is a key linguistic unifier, it is neither singular nor universal, since Turkish, Persian and Hebrew are also important regional languages. Similarly, while Islam is the dominant religion, there are significant and varied communities of Christians and Jews, and confessionalism dominates the politics of some states, such as Lebanon. There is also differentiation within Islam, perhaps most crucially the Sunni/Shiite division, and divergent interpretations of the appropriate role of religion in politics.

The Middle East is also a region that has experienced considerable population mobility. There is significant internal and inward migration: Iran has the largest refugee population of any country in the world, made up of Afghani war refugees who have not returned, and Kurdish and Iraqi Shiite refugees on its western border; guest-workers play an important economic role in many countries, bringing different cultural values with them. Some countries have sizeable proportions of non-nationals; in Kuwait, for example, approximately 70 per cent of the population in 1990 were non-nationals, with long and complex procedures for claiming citizenship; where citizenship remains an issue, participation and democratization are stalled. It is also a region that has exported people: Turkish 'guest-workers' to Germany and elsewhere; the global Lebanese, Palestinian and Armenian and most recent Iranian diasporas; Saudi, Iraqi and Algerian dissidents and so on.

It is a region that has flirted with periods of constitutional reform, often based upon western models, as in the Iranian Constitutional Revolution of 1905 and the period of Turkish modernization under Ataturk; while a number of states are long-standing republics, many of those are highly centralized mobilizing regimes, and the area still boasts many of the last autocratic monarchies in the world (see Table 1). One of the enduring problems for many states in the region is how to build a modern state infrastructure and administrative capacity, establishing modern political and civic institutions.

While crude neo-Orientalist argument has focused on Islam as an impediment to democracy, that argument has been subjected to heavy criticism and there are far more significant structuring factors including foreign intervention in the region and the political economy of oil.[4] Many, but not all, of the states in the region owe their high GNP and economic development to oil extraction, and have been labelled 'rentier states'.[5] Under this peculiar mode of production, the state does not need to engage its workforce and raise revenue; hence there is less pressure for democratization. From the outside, Western concerns about the oil resources of the region have led to persistent military and political intervention in the region, with support for clientelist and un-democratic regimes against movements of self-determination. It has even been suggested that there exists 'an historic incompatibility of oil and democracy'.[6]

The Middle East is thus a highly complex region, and any attempt to describe processes of political change and democratization within it has to be mindful of the real historical and contingent differences and particular political economies that exist – no essentialist or culturalist models will suffice. Further, the region's insertion into the global political economy, indeed the differential roles of particular states within the global order and the varying impacts of markets, migration and media, have to be considered. Hence, the pressures toward and dynamics of political change need to be examined both from outside and from inside the region.

TABLE 1

MEDIA SYSTEMS IN THE MIDDLE EAST AND NORTH AFRICA*

Country	Population	Literacy (15+ can read and write) MALE (%)	Literacy FEMALE (%)	Type of Government	Suffrage	GDP Per Capita ($)	Radio Number of Receivers (000s) (1994)	Radio Number of Receivers per 1000 Inhabitants (1994)	TV Number of Receivers and/or Licences Issued (000s) (1994)	TV Number of Receivers in used and/or Licences Issued per 1000 Inhabitants (1994)	Daily News-papers (000s) (Titles) (1994)	Daily News-papers per 1000 inhabitants (1995)	No. Cinemas (1994)	Cinemas per Cap. Annual Attend (1994)
ALGERIA	29,183,000	73.9	49.0	Republic	18 yrs universal	3,800	6450	236	2150	79	6	46	249	0.9
BAHRAIN	590,042,000	89.1	79.4	Trad. Monarchy	none	12,000	305	556	236	430	70	128	149	0.3
EGYPT	66,094,000	63.6	38.8	Republic	18 yrs universal and compulsory	2,760	18950	307	6700	109	17	64		
IRAN	66,094,200	78.4	65.8	Theocratic Rep.	15 yrs universa	14,700	15550	237	4076	62	12	18	277	0.5
IRAQ	21,422,300	70.7	45.0	Republic	18 yrs universal	2,000	4335	218	1500	75	4	27	266	1.8
ISRAEL	5,422,000	97.0	93.0	Republic	18 yrs universal	15,500	2610	478	1500	275	1534	281	35	0.0
JORDAN	4,212,100	93.4	79.4	Constitutional Mon.	20 yrs universal	4,700	1265	243	395	76	4	48		
KUWAIT	1,950,000	82.2	74.9	Monarchy	adult males	17,000	726	445	620	380	9	401	14	0.3
LEBANON	3,776,300	94.7	90.3	Republic	21 yrs	4,900	2590	889	1050	360	16	172	79	35.3
LIBYA	5,445,400	87.9	63.0	Republic	18 yrs universal and compulsory	6,510	1180	226	525	100	4	13		
MOROCCO	29,779,100	56.6	31.0	Constitutional Mon.	21 yrs universal	3,000	5800	219	2100	79	13	13	203	0.8
OMAN	2,186,500	N/A	N/A	Monarchy	none	10,800	1210	583	1375	662	4	30		
QATAR	547,761,000	79.2	79.9	Traditional Mon.	none	20,820	231	428	215	3984	148	4		
SAUDI ARABIA	19,409,000	71.5	50.2	Monarchy	none	10,100	5125	294	4455	255	19	54		0.6
SUDAN	31,547,500	57.7	34.6	Transitional Rep. under	NA years, universal military regime	800	7050	258	2180	80	5	23	55	0.3
SYRIA	15,608,600	85.7	55.8	Republic	18 yrs universa	15,900	3640	257	880	62	8	18		
TUNISIA	9,019,600	78.6	54.6	Republic	20 yrs universal	4,250	1740	199	710	81	7	46		
TURKEY	62,484,400	91.7	72.4	Republican Parl. Dem.	18 yrs universal	5,500	9850	162	11000	181	57	44	341	0.3
UAE	3,057,300	78.9	79.8	Federation w. special powers Republic	none	24,000	580	312	200	107	8	161	33	
YEMEN	13,483,100	53.0	26.0	Republic	18 yrs universal	2,520	450	32	390	28	3	17		

Source: * This table was compiled from data in the UNESCO *Statistical Yearbook 1996* and from the CIA Factbook (http://www.odci.gov/cia/publications/nsolo/factbook/sa.htm).

Notes: 1. Naturalized 30 years+ prior to 1920+ male descendants at 21 yrs.
2. Males compulsory; females 21 with elementary education.

Global Pressures toward Democratization

While the past decade has witnessed growing concern about the institutionalization of democracy and processes of democratization in the Third World it is worth asking why there is such a strong focus on democracy in the South? Leftwich[7] suggests four main reasons, all political: one is the legitimacy of conditionality as an instrument of policy, whereby international institutions, but especially the International Monetary Fund (IMF) and the World Bank, have developed 'structural adjustment' packages which aimed to curtail the power of the state and support deregulation, privatization and the growth of market economies. Democratic electoral politics were seen as a way of controlling vested interests and limiting the power of states. A second is the ascendancy of neo-conservative or neo-liberal theories and ideologies of political economy in the West, which not only extol the virtues of individual personal freedom, rights and liberties, but also hold that political liberalization compels a government to be more accountable, less corrupt and more efficient in terms of development. Third is that the collapse of communism provided evidential support for this general orientation, and led to the massive movement post-1991 to rebuild Eastern European economies as both market economies but also as politically liberal and pluralist democracies. Last is the growth of real and popular democratic pressures inside many developing countries including South Africa, Haiti and Thailand, from the 1980s onwards. This emerging orientation has had the effect of reversing the predominant argument of modernization theory: that socio-economic development was a prior necessity for democracy. Now the logic is reversed: democracy can help development, a position increasingly articulated by the United Nations Development Programme (UNDP) and the World Bank.

Sklair[8] tries to propose a less totalizing notion of 'developmental democracy' that steers between 'the cruel choice of laissez-faire liberalism without social justice ... and dictatorial forms of state-centered development', and argues that elements can already be found in all regions of the world, contrary to common assumptions that cultural, religious or social barriers obstruct the progress of democracy in 'non-western' countries. 'Democracy is a means to effectuate improvement in the overall quality of human life' and in all countries 'democracy is manifested in diverse forms, or fragments, which reinforce one another in the production of developmental effects'. Among these 'fragments' might be included freedom of the press and the autonomy of professional organizations as well as juridical independence; guaranteed health services and welfare benefits as well as equal protection of the laws; elements of industrial democracy as well as electoral democracy. Deegan also, referring specifically to the

TABLE 2

HUMAN DEVELOPMENT INDEX AND GENDER-RELATED DEVELOPMENT
RANKINGS FOR MIDDLE EAST AND NORTH AFRICA*

COUNTRY	HDI RANK	REAL GDP RANK	GDP MINUS HDI (1)	GDI RANK (2)	HDI MINUS GDI (3)	HDI/ GDI/ GEM (4)
ALGERIA	69	56	-13	81	-22	50/59/79
BAHRAIN	39	27	-12	52	-17	N/A
EGYPT	106	76	-30	87	-5	64/62/80
IRAN	66	59	-7	75	-18	48/54/90
IRAQ	109	155	-24	96	-11	67/69/55
ISRAEL	24	28	4	N/A	N/A	N/A
JORDAN	70	69	-1	N/A	N/A	N/A
KUWAIT	51	5	-46	55	-10	40/42/74
LEBANON	97	106	10	77	-1	N/A
LIBYA	50	38	-9	73	-20	N/A
MOROCCO	123	88	-34	97	-2	76/70/76
OMAN	82	37	-45	N/A	N/A	N/A
QATAR	50	3	-47	58	-14	N/A
SAUDI ARABIA	63	32	-31	85	-30	N/A
SUDAN	146	138	-7	118	-3	93/85/82
SYRIA	92	73	-19	82	-10	N/A
TUNISIA	78	63	-14	68	-5	53/49/84
TURKEY	84	72	-12	61	5	55/45/92
UAE	42	8	-34	56	-19	33/43/88
YEMEN	142	133	-8	122	-11	N/A

Source: * compiled from UNDP, *Human Development Report,* 1996

Notes: (1) A positive figure indicates that the HDI rank is better than the real GDP per capita
rank; a negative the opposite

(2) The gender-related development index (GDI) reveals gender inequality in basic
capabilities. Rankings recalculated for a universe of 137 countries. The lower the
number the more favourable to women.

(3) A positive difference between a country's HDI and GDI ranks indicates that it
performs relatively better on gender equality than on average achievements alone.

(4) GEM is the gender empowerment measure, which concentrates on participation,
measuring gender inequality in key areas of economic and political participation and
decision-making, recalculated for a universe of 104 countries. GEM is based on flow
variables, and thus subject to considerable short-term fluctuation. The creation of
opportunities for women does not necessarily depend on a country's income level or
economic growth rate. Hence a GEM rank significantly lower than the GDI rank
indicates that a country has not translated basic capabilities into real economic and
political opportunities for women.

Middle East, rejects any simplistic notions of political homogeneity or singular models of democracy:

> Distinct differences exist between the nation-states to the extent that a move toward democratization in one country may be symbolized by the removal of a ban on the formation of political parties, whilst in another, it might be characterized by the establishment of a more equitable parliamentary system.[9]

While there is clearly much debate about definitions of democracy, there is increasing agreement about the need for greater participation, growth of civil society and development of human resources as part of the development process. The growing acceptance of measures of 'human development' instead of simply economic development, and the importance of women's participation and activity in new measures of development, all imply a more inclusive and holistic notion of development with implications for political and cultural participation. As the UNDP's *Human Development Report 1996* argues:

> active democracy can aid economic growth in several ways. More open and transparent forms of governnance can reduce corruption and arbitrary rule ... the real issue is whether growth helps democracy. Democracy, participation and empowerment are valued in themselves – whether they enhance growth or not[10]

The Middle East does not score well on such new indices (see Table 2). Of 20 countries taken to comprise the emerging political-cultural region of the Middle East and North Africa (MENA), all but two score lower in their Human Development ranking than in their GDP, with the largest discrepancies to be found in the oil-rich principalities of Qatar, Kuwait and Oman. Nor do the oil states fare much better in indices of gender development or gender empowerment. The significance of these indices, which are increasingly used as an indicative currency of social development, is that they separate pure economic power from state policy; the poor scores found in many of the richer Arab states suggest a considerable policy lag, an outcome of the democracy deficit.

The World Bank's most recent (1997) *World Development Report* also focuses on the state and argues that states and markets need to work together and that states need to build capability, inform and respond to citizen needs, allow greater transparency in decision-making, foster executive recruitment and so forth. It argues that while in 1974, only 39 countries were democratic, by 1994 117 countries used elections to choose their national leadership, and suggests that of all world regions, the Middle East and North Africa is the most resistant to formal democracy.[11] While the region does possess some of the most unreconstructed autocratic monarchies and weak state institutionalization, there are clearly significant moves to democracy in some countries in the region and dissenting voices arguing for greater openness and political diversity in yet others.

Emerging Democracy in the Region

The end of the cold war, increased developments – as yet still tenuous – in an Arab–Israeli peace process with a Palestinian state as its outcome, and the changing global order have all weakened autocratic justifications for 'national security states' and could result in considerable political and social pressures within Arab countries for a share of the 'peace dividend'.[12] It could however be argued that this is far from being translated into actual practices, since recent evidence suggests that the Middle East accounts for 40 per cent of a £25 billion global arms trade, with Saudi Arabia alone buying £5.5 billion's worth.[13]

Democratization takes a crab-like configuration in the region, with some steps forward and many steps of set-back. More and more states have experienced multi-party electoral competitions (for example, Algeria, Tunisia, Egypt, Morocco, Jordan, and Yemen). Elections were held in the unified Yemen for the first time in 1993, although civil war from 1994 has undone much. Algeria, which nullified the 1992 election, has tried again in late 1997, although proscribing participation of the Islamic Front and some other political groupings. But Iran convincingly elected a more liberal President who took office in August 1997. And in the most politically traditional regimes such as Bahrain, Oman and Saudi Arabia, often under pressure from dissident groups, experiments in consultative councils are being tried. Global concern about human rights has been specifically recognized through Islamic Declarations on Human Rights, promulgated in 1981 through UNESCO (United Nations Educational, Scientific and Cultural Organization) by the Islamic Council; and in 1986 at Syracuse by the League of Arab States.

Norton has neatly summed up the process:

> there has long been little doubt that the regimes in the region are under increasing pressure from their citizens. Repression at the hands of the state has become a topic of public discussion, and human rights activists, though relatively few in number, have become increasingly vocal. In short, the regime's governments, especially the Arab ones, are facing persistent crises of governance ... the pressures for change are general and growing, although they are obviously not equally intense in all states.[14]

Thus concerns for greater participation, freedom and democracy press in from the outside and well up from inside. In a global environment where talk of democratization, human rights and participation have become staples of political rhetoric, the authoritarian regimes in the region are increasingly under pressure to democratize, from within and without. Population movements in and out of and across the region, whether of labour migrants, business and professional peoples or students, spread images of other lives and rhetorics of change. And so do the media. Appadurai has presciently argued that media and migration are the two most powerful forces for modernity at work in the world (but he downplays markets, an omission that needs to be rectified).[15]

There is as yet little theoretical focus on media in the region, and what research exists is predominantly descriptive and devoid of analytic framing.[16] At the same time, a major project of comparative analysis of civil society in the Middle East paid almost no attention to any forms of media or the changing media-scape in the region, although it aimed to examine 'society in juxtaposition explicitly to the state, and implicitly to the fate of authoritarianism' and identified a host of social spaces as constituting civil society, such as 'co-operatives, unions, professional syndicates, women's movements, and a panoply of sporting clubs and informal circles'.[17] But a focus on political institutions and the development of civil society can no longer afford to ignore the media as potential instruments of civil society, particularly in a global context.[18] It is clear that there has been rapid and dramatic change in the media environment in the Middle East, the effects of which are only now beginning to make themselves felt.

The Changing Televisual Landscape

While similar pressures and dynamics can be seen across the region, the bulk of the following comments focus mainly on the Arab states of MENA (Turkey, Iran and Israel – for linguistic, cultural and religious reasons – share some but not all of these configurations and need separate analytic attention). The focus here is on the televisual landscape because that is undergoing the most dramatic change, with possibly profound impacts on the region. Also the various issues around the press and censorship are not only extremely complex to try to cover and are well reported by *Index on Censorship* but they also speak to a more traditional kind of political democratization, while examination of the dynamics of broadcasting raises some very new as well as fundamental questions.

Up until the 1990s the development of broadcasting in the region has been somewhat limited. From the 1950s, television was introduced into the region by the United States military and the big oil companies such as

ARAMCO, and many countries had a state-controlled broadcasting system by the late 1960s.[19] Regional co-operation supported the development of ARABSAT in the late 1970s with the launch of ARABSAT 1-A and 1-B in 1985. Because of the limitations of state-supported broadcasting provision, by the 1990s the region demonstrated remarkable video penetration, estimated at over 80 per cent in the Gulf States, and the growing circulation of non-regional produced material. But the big push to a new stage of televisual development was prompted by the Gulf War.

The Gulf War of January–February 1991 brought 24-hour American news coverage to the region, found eager audiences and created pressure for change in the regional media industries. The sudden significance of Cable News Network (CNN), the Pentagon's role in constructing the news agenda and the lack of alternative, distinctively Arab, voices provided impetus for media development, especially in electronic media. These changes, supported by a post-war economic boom which has aided increased access to media, have radically altered the government broadcasting monopolies and produced a far more open media environment in the region. Ayish recently summed up these changes:[20]

> greater political liberalization, the expansion of national privatization programmes and the diffusion of new communications technologies … seem to have had a significant effect on the Arab broadcasting scene. They have contributed to the relaxation of government controls over broadcasting; to the creation of more autonomous radio and television corporations; to the abolition of some ministries of information; to the granting more air-time access to diverse political views; and to permitting broadcasters to solicit commercial advertising to supplement dwindling government financing

Much change has been provoked by intense national competition. The Egyptian Space Channel (Space NET) produced by the Egyptian Radio-Television Union (ERTU) was one of the first to launch an international television service, having just negotiated a deal with ARABSAT at the start of the Gulf War. It provided military and public information broadcasts to Egyptian and other allied Arab forces, countering strong Iraqi propaganda, although its post-war programming is far more varied fare.

SpaceNet was followed closely in 1991 with the launch of MEBC, latterly MBC, television from London, supported by a range of Arab investors, but most centrally by Walid Ibrahim, a brother-in-law of King Fahd and Shah Kemal, a prominent Saudi businessman. Its London headquarters reinforced the stations's physical and political detachment from Arab governments, although it identifies as 'the world through Arabian eyes'.[21] Since it broadcasts from outside the region, it enjoys a far greater political licence than domestic channels, including the establishment of a correspondent's office in Jerusalem.

The mad rush into broadcasting saw the launch in 1994 of no less than 20 pan-regional satellite-delivered television channels. Orbit, a satellite television and radio network carries 16 television channels and four radio networks in Arabic and English. Headed by yet another Saudi Prince, Orbit, based in Rome, provides an encrypted system which requires a decoder to view the programming. Initially very expensive, there was widespread belief that such a process of delivery would not take off in the region. However, decoders have come down in price (pressured by an active black-market) and Orbit has built a subscription base. Its 'bouquet', as the package of channels is fragrantly called, includes US news channels, CNN, the Hollywood Channel, Discovery and the Music Channel. Initially, it also included the BBC World Arabic channel, one of the first commercially self-supporting channels of the new BBC WORLD organization. However, increasing pressure from the Saudis, who objected particularly to the BBC showing programmes on human rights issues such as *Death of a Principle* (the title echoing the much earlier documentary *Death of a Princess)*, meant that the BBC channel was pulled off the air in 1996.

Arab Radio and Television (ART), headed by yet another Saudi entrepreneur, broadcasts from Rome, with major production centres in Cairo and Jeddah. It carries four specialised television channels, three of which broadcast 24 hours a day. In 1996, Showtime, supported by Viacom Inc. and Kuwaiti partners, was launched in competition with Orbit, and closely aligned with 1st Net, the region's other satellite package from Arab Radio and Television. Gulf DTH which is the parent company of Showtime is half-owned by Viacom, and half by Kuwaiti Investment Properties Co., KIPCO, a public company of which 8.5 per cent is owned in turn by the Kuwait government through its investment arm, the Kuwait Investment Authority.

Some of the experience of the long-standing and highly productive Egyptian film industry has been harnessed into television production, and the state Egypt Radio and Television Union, (ERTU) is massively investing in building a new media production city, dubbed 'Hollywood on the Nile', in order to maintain Egypt's historic position as provider of entertainment to the Arab World.[22]

These brief examples show the complex and rapidly changing broadcast media environment in the region. There are national channels, regional distribution systems, transnational co-production and distribution arrangements, and strategies to locate corporate headquarters outside the region to maximize autonomy and evasion of local political and regulatory controls. The number of satellite-delivered channels in the Middle East and North Africa has nearly doubled just over the past year. Indeed, it is such a dynamic environment that any descriptive material is guaranteed to be out of date before publication.[23]

Doing the Dishes: The Return of Paternalistic Policies

The public uptake of such new provision was dramatic, but then so too has been state reaction. The satellite dishes that mushroomed in 1990–91 were slowly banned in many countries. Saudi Arabia banned dishes in June 1994, since they constituted a 'threat to traditional values' (nor does it allow public cinemas) and proscribed any subscription offering of television packages, thus limiting the money to be made in the television market. Increasingly worried about the inroads made by satellite television channels in their audiences, Jordan and Qatar, which had allowed dishes, have both moved to MMDS (multi-channel multi-point distribution system), a relatively cheap delivery system which covers large areas of desert as easily as densely populated urban areas, allows a central (state) authority the power to filter out any programming that it disapproves of, and also means that revenue is not lost to foreign conglomerates. Arab states have also attempted to block terrestrial re-transmission of foreign programming at prime time, a measure especially applied against MBC.

In 1996 the region had around 50 million television homes, a figure which is expected to grow to 60 million by 2000 and 70 million by 2005.[24] Satellite penetration is still limited: around 3.7 million homes in 1996, about seven per cent, but this is expected to triple to ten million by 2005. Algeria, Kuwait, Israel, Oman and the UAE have satellite penetration of more than 20 per cent and Saudi Arabia is not far behind with 17 per cent, despite dishes being legally banned. Forrester claims that Cairo's skyline has probably altered more over the past year than in the last 50, not because of high-rise building but because of the tens of thousands of satellite dishes that crowd the roof tops.[25] On my own trip to Palestine in Spring 1997 I was struck by the extent to which the flat roofs of poor housing in the old Qalandiya refugee camp on the outskirts of Jerusalem appeared to groan under the weight of the huge dishes perched on them, while the personnel of the Palestinian Authority in their newly-built housing in Ramallah sport antennae that resemble miniature Eiffel Towers.

The focus of market attention is slowly moving into North Africa. Although it is recognised to be less wealthy a market, it is currently more liberally disposed toward satellite reception. In the spring of 1997 there were estimated to be 1.2 million dishes in Morocco. The Tunisian government has lifted its ban against dishes, estimated to be already 50,000 and growing. Zilo of Orbit already thinks Algeria is the next big market:

Algeria is a tremendous dormant market at the moment. The political events are such that nobody wants to travel to Algeria, but that will change with time. And when the situation appeases, that market will be as important as Morocco, and it could be the number one marketplace in North Africa. But like comedy, it's about timing. In Algeria there is something between 900,000–1,000,000 dishes. But you have to be sensitive; you can't carpet bomb the whole region, you have to work with the local resources.[26]

Much of the initial concern about satellite television had to do with the large amounts of foreign, especially American, programming coming into the region; yet much of this was in English and reached only a small elite, many of whom are foreign-educated. Slowly, however, television providers, concerned about potential restraint but still more about reaching a broader audience, are increasingly working with local producers to make Arab-language programming suitable for the value system of the region. Zilo, again, says:

The Middle East has two unifying elements: whether you go from Casablanca to Kuwait the great majority of the population is Muslim so there's a common culture, and although there is variation with spoken Arabic, you can put a Moroccan together with a Kuwaiti and they will understand each other so the language and religion are common and given that religion plays a tremendous role in culture and the family structure, you have two tremendous unifying factors.[27]

Orbit has local production centres in Kuwait, Egypt and Lebanon, producing a variety of genres. Yet Zilo might be too sanguine. The region is far from homogeneous, and programming appropriate in one national context might well not merely raise eyebrows but give offence in another. For example, Orbit is proud of a live discussion programme called Al Oula, made in Lebanon:

we deal with sexuality, and issues such as why married men have affairs. These subjects have not been addressed before in the region. There is no censor in this building. The approach we have taken is that we've put the responsibility on everybody to ensure that what we're putting out is acceptable and morally sensitive. And that has nothing to do with whether you are a Muslim or a Christian. If you have a family and you have values for your children, the values are very similar if you are a Muslim or a Christian. What we try to put out is appropriate family programming.[28]

Yet this has included showing an uncut version of *Basic Instinct*, on the grounds that with direct-to-home transmission, the censorship should lie in the hands of the viewers. Orbit argues that as long as such material has been clearly scheduled so that the recipient knows what is to be broadcast, no further restraint is needed.

> Governments around the world have historically played the role of the governing body who controls what's in the best interests of the home. But with the passage of time that has changed. And in our particular region, given the respect the population has for its own culture and in fact lives its religion, we can trust the individual to make his [sic] own call ... in the growing concept of the global village where people can pick up signals from everywhere, government entities have to realise it is going to be impossible to control and censor. So therefore they do business with responsible broadcasters and as a responsible broadcaster, we proceed in such a way that we can be responsible of our product [sic] [29]

Indeed, Orbit has significantly expanded its package with its Star TV alliance, adding Fox Kids, NBC, Sky News and Disney; Ist Net and Showtime now offer 22 services between them, including MTV Europe, Movie Channel and Lifestyle. Advertising is also growing on satellite channels, including cosmetics and perfume companies which have been banned from some of the terrestrial channels.

But it appears that simply to make programmes in the region will not be sufficient to satisfy some states, who are responding by producing more of their own programming for their national audience. Bahraini television production is consciously aimed at Bahrain nationals, says its chief executive officer, with a 'focus on local areas of interest and the cultural values of the society'.[30] Emirates Television is also expanding output, concerned, as its director Al Gaoud says, that 'leaving the societies under the control of foreign TV stations alone means that we are leaving the job to those stations which may not have the maintenance of our cultures as a priority. This may lead to a negative development of the new generations'.[31]

It is not only popular culture that is a cause for concern. Lebanon, which had one of the most open and dynamic media environments in the region, also fears internal instability and fragmentation, as confessional groupings become consolidated into divided audiences. Al-Umran, once a member of the Ministry of Radio and Television in Bahrain but now Director of MBC in London has argued that political content no longer provokes much concern in the region, since from the advent of short-wave radio, new technologies have made that battle impossible to wage; the current strategy is to provide competitive alternative news provision to the biases of western content.[32] Yet even cursory evidence suggests that is not quite the case. For example, the Lebanese Ministry of Information, known as one of the most progressive in the region, instituted a new broadcasting law in January 1997 that introduced pre-censorship of news bulletins and political programmes intended for satellite transmission and is authorized to stop the transmission of any news or political item affecting state security, fomenting sectarian sedition or undermining public order. Evidence of the banning of printed materials such as newspapers and journals is plentiful across the region, most recently during the elections in Jordan in November 1997, and can be readily gathered from the monitoring efforts of *Index on Censorship*.

But the wider issue that Al-Umran also mentions, is the growing concern with 'culturally sensitive programming', an issue which it is claimed enjoys government and public agreement, at least in the conservative states of the Gulf: 'the biggest concern from open access to highly attractive and superior quality programming from the outside world is fear of its effect on the national language and the values and traditions of the society'.[33] It is this concern which has justified the development of MMDS systems: in Bahrain, the system allows encryption of entire undesired channels; in Qatar they use delayed programming while the new Saudi venture *Saravision* will provide 'cleaned up'[34] tailor-made programming for most channels.

At work within such approaches, yet often very weakly elaborated, are deeply embedded understandings of cultural propriety, of the nature of childhood and the dynamics of family life, and particular assumptions about the role of women, in Gulf and wider society. Yet there is evidence from within the region of women's growing unease concerning not only their most basic of economic and political rights such as access to formal education, employment and political franchise. The concern extends also to possibly less important yet still significant cultural limitations, including most famously, the Saudi women's drive-in to gain the right to drive, and most recently, Iranian womens' invasion of a Tehran football pitch to welcome home their World Cup standard team, penetrating a space that had been rendered male since the Revolution. Increasingly, Islamic women are reinterpreting the Koran and putting forward their own culturally-sensitive yet feminist arguments. Thus a simple paternalism in national policy-making that does not take on-board the internal pressures for change from many women in the region could backfire.

The gender politics needs to be addressed. It is recognized that without women there can be no development, and the corollary must also be acknowledged: that there can be no democracy without women. Televisual media may have some of their strongest effects in the area of gender, but this is also an area of the least research. All that can be done here is sketch some of the possible consequences, in the absence of detailed empirical evidence to support the argument.

Public space in the region has been, and in many places remains, male space. Women enter it veiled, covered by the rubrics of religious decency and appropriate relations between the sexes, they work and shop under a male ethos and return to the female arena of the interior. In such a cultural context, the very fact that broadcast media recognize no boundaries and can pass through borders, means that within private space women can increasingly access a range of images and information, to be viewed together or alone, to be reacted to or acted upon.[35] Sketchy indications of these dynamics come from the work of Abu-Lughod and Davies, women anthropologists who have each conducted ethnographic work in the region. Abu-Lughod locates television within 'a complex jumble of life' in which modernizing pressures have already been encountered through state intervention in such areas as agricultural production, the military, tourists, and migrant labour. She does however raise three possible 'effects' of television (which need research to clarify further). One is shifting patterns of social life with less visiting as people stay home and watch, so that 'television may have increased the number of "experiences" shared across generation and gender', although conflicts also arise by generation and gender as to which programmes to watch. Second, television may alter the nature of experience itself, and third, and most relevant for this discussion, television may facilitate 'new identifications and affiliations' as 'imagined communities of citizens or consumers'.[36]

Yet in the Middle East, as many places elsewhere, citizenship has traditionally been defined as male and women are often used as symbolic markers of cultural purity and national honour.[37] Correspondingly, women's associations and involvements in local activities are often ignored in a gender-biased understanding of civil society.[38] As patriarchy itself modernizes, shifting from patriarchal structures rooted in everyday, private, life to forms of neo-patriarchy, the state's role in 'defending' female honour becomes both more contradictory and overt.[39]

Consumption versus Citizenship?

What does all of this development have to do with democracy? The statistical evidence alone suggests that it is the new television broadcasting which is binding populations into 'national' audiences in a way that no medium has truly done before. Enduring illiteracy, especially among women, and urban concentration have meant that in many states the press has not reached beyond an already highly politicized, heavily male, educated readership (see Table 1). Television is constructing a national public space that addresses men and women, old and young, urban and rural.

At the same time, as already indicated, regional programming and alternative newscasts are available as well as English-language news and programming. Thus audiences are increasingly able to compare 'lifestyles' across the region, which do differ markedly, and with images from the US, the UK and elsewhere. Civil society is usually seen as that space between state and market where public discussion can develop. While much television in the region is imbued with both commercial and statist concerns, it may nonetheless bring new images into the family home and address ordinary people in a way they have never previously experienced. If democratization is to be understood in its widest form, as increasing participation in public life and public debate and encouraging cultural pluralism, it is here that the potential role of the media becomes so important.

A political-economic analysis of the current television environment in the region suggests a growing tendency toward privatization and commercialization; indeed, the evidence of low expenditure on advertising combined with youthful and often wealthy audiences, only suggests that a significant increase in advertising content and further commercialization will occur in the media sector.[40] Yet it would be utterly naive to see television as the vanguard of materialism or consumption in the region, with its deep mercantilism and trades in land and gold and weaponry. Television will undoubtedly diffuse more modern, capitalist forms of profit-making and consumerism. Western industrial societies are now concerned about tabloidization, 'dumbing down' of content and the demise of civil society, and commercialized media dynamics are thought to work against the political traditions of the public sphere and an active citizenry. In the Middle East, we should be interested in whether new political ideas can actually be provoked/promoted by the same dynamic. Ironically, in a region where the dynamics of civil society have been somewhat weak, commercial media might bring more news, information and debate than many state systems have previously allowed. Ayish also stresses that the likely impact of commercial broadcasting operating alongside the state sector will be as a catalyst for the latter to improve its performance, and provide the public with alternative outlets of expression, making a contribution to critical debates on the issues facing Arab societies[41]

Similarly, a concern about western cultural domination would focus on the considerable amounts of US and UK programming shown on local channels as well as on the English-language channels aimed at the varied expatriate communities in the region. Yet colonialism has left its imprint here, not only in territorial boundaries but in languages, cultural orientations, religious affiliations. That is to say, the West is not a new arrival here; nor do flows of students, businessmen, scientific and other experts suggest total cultural incompatibility. While such concerns still raise provocative issues, they also miss much of the particularities and evocative dynamics of television development in the region. Almost for the first time, men, women and children are being drawn into a national socio-cultural space that offers news, entertainment and discussion. On the same dial are also available channels from other Arab countries as well as 'newsfeeds' from Western news media; that is to say, comparisons are readily available, and the lack of coverage of a certain story on one channel can be easily revealed by tuning to another. This is not to suggest that Middle Eastern audiences are going to be particularly active viewers, or less channel-loyal than most audiences. It is to suggest, however, that the possible range of news imagery as well as cultural content is already quite large, making both political and cultural censorship harder and harder both to legitimate and to achieve.

The inter-regional competition for audiences, markets and even political hegemony undermines any too-easy assertion of an Arab 'cultural discount'[42] or the simple emergence of a geo-regional media zone;[43] such developments are clearly not without considerable internal conflict and rivalry. Indeed, there remains a significant tension between narrow, competitive, geo-political nationalisms configured by existing state-formations and a regional pan-Arab nationalism which still exists as a politico-cultural project for some; only detailed empirical research could begin to identify which of these tendencies the expansion of television serves to reinforce. The increasingly wide variety of imagery being produced within the region also erodes a simple traditionalist, often religious critique about the negative impact of western material; the distinction between 'us' and 'them' is harder to make if producers in the region are themselves testing the boundaries of cultural taste.

Arguments about the nature of late modernity focus increasingly on self-reflexivity and the chosen life, as compared with life lived within the remit of unchallenged tradition.[44] Television, especially with significant doses of foreign programming, displays the variety of lives in the world, including the far greater individualism, freedom and emancipation of women in Western societies (as well as in some Arab societies in comparison to others). These images flow more easily from outside than do the dissident voices of Middle Eastern exiles, who are often based in Paris or London and actively press for political change from outside their nation-state. The Saudi dissident Al-Masari and his famous fax-line is but one example; others range across Algerian, Kurdish, Iraqi and Iranian dissidents in London and their print, audio and visual media. Such exile activity also points up the limits of a model bounded by territory, and the importance of examining the external as well as internal contexts in which national politics are enacted. There are also limits to a model bounded by traditional forms of media; many dissident groups are using the Internet to great effect, posting critiques of government policy, information about political activities both inside and outside the country and again articulate the parts to each other. There is no room here to develop this line of argument, but merely to point to yet another factor that erodes the sovereignty of the territorial border and its functioning as a limiting factor on political imagination and action.

Gender must again be highlighted as a key marker of potential cultural instability and democratization. In contexts where women's lives are still heavily bounded by religious culture, patriarchal values and sheer habit, the force of mediated culture, especially images, which travel through public space into private living-rooms may be far greater than elsewhere. It is precisely the family-orientation of Arab/Middle Eastern life, with parents and children viewing and discussing together, that makes the family a potential cauldron of conflict between generations and between genders with pressures for greater individuation, autonomy and self-determination. The limited research on these matters suggest a playful and creative appropriation by women of images and styles that appeal to them, and their use in challenging some aspects of the privatised patriarchal culture.[45] The impact of external, western and other cultural production, is only minimally constrained by a 'Cinema Paradiso' approach of cutting out the (mainly sexualised) 'naughty bits' because the entire programming is suffused with assumptions and values about individual choice, freedom of action, gender equality, attitudes toward parenting and the nature of childhood. We know that media effects are not direct or uni-directional; it does, however, seem likely that a more open and diverse media environment will spur greater debate in Middle East societies, with further pressures for both cultural and political democratization. There might be limits to the extent to which a population can be addressed solely as consumers without encouraging any other forms of participation in public life or decision-making processes.

Lerner's famous book *The Passing of Traditional Society*, based on the Middle East, was published in 1958.[46] It was 40 years too early in its analysis of the impact of media which are only just beginning to construct national audiences, although prescient about some of the dilemmas the region would face. The triumphalist or capitalist motifs of the modernization paradigm do not have to be endorsed in order to recognise democratization as one of the universally progressive ideas to have taken global root. A more recent volume, attempting an Islamist vision, was bizarrely premised on 'the passing of modernity' particularly in the region.[47] Clearly, both arguments are wrong. The tensions between local and global definitions of tradition and modernity are being played out in each and every country. These struggles are complex in the Middle East, for the reasons spelled out here, and certainly the media can be used both to redefine and maintain tradition as well as to destabilize it. The combination of external and internal pressures toward greater openness and participation in the region suggests that a strategy of diversity and tolerance has to be the preferred solution. And it is reasonable to assume that the region will evolve its own forms of political institutionalization and democratization, with gender as a catalyst for change, while the outcomes may still function within an Islamic frame.

NOTES

1. Alex Zilo (of the media organization Orbit), cited in Rebecca Hawkes, 'The Zilo Interview', *Middle East Broadcast and Satellite*, Vol.5, No.3 (1997), p.28.
2. Sarah Callard, 'Cross-Cultural Broadcasting', *Middle East Broadcast and Satellite*, Vol.5, No.2 (1997), p.18.
3. Douglas Boyd, 'International Radio Broadcasting in Arabic', *Gazette*, Vol.59, No.6 (1997), pp.445–72.
4. Douglas Boyd, 'The Democracy Agenda in the Arab World', in 'Democracy in the Arab World', *Middle East Report*, Vol.174, No.22 .1 (Jan.–Feb. 1992).
5. Hossein Mahdavy, 'Patterns and Problems of Economic Development in Rentier States', in M.A.Cook, (ed.), *Studies in the Economic History of the Middle East* (Oxford:Oxford University Press, 1970); see also the discussion in Heather Deegan, *The Middle East and Problems of Democracy* (Buckingham: Open University Press, 1993).
6. Boyd, 'The Democracy Agenda in the Arab World', p.47.
7. Adrian Leftwich (ed.), *Democracy and Development* (Oxford: Polity Press, 1996).
8. Richard L. Sklair, 'Toward a Theory of Developmental Democracy', in Leftwich, op. cit., p.39–40.
9. Deegan, *The Middle East*, p.9.
10. UNDP, *Human Development Report 1996*, p.59.
11. World Bank, 'The State in a Changing World', *World Development Report 1997* (Oxford:Oxford University Press, 1997), p.112, based on work of Jaggers and Gurr.
12. Augustus Richard Norton, 'Introduction', *Civil Society in the Middle East*, Volume One (Leiden: E.J.Brill, 1994), p.2.
13. Ian Black and David Fairhall, 'The Profits of Doom', *The Guardian* (16 Oct. 1997), p.17.
14. Norton, 'Introduction', p.3.
15. Arjun Appadurai, *Modernity at Large* (Minneapolis, MN: University of Minnesota Press, 1996).
16. Y. Kamalipour and H. Mowlana (eds.), *Mass Media in the Middle East* (London: Greenwood Press, 1996); a useful overview is provided in Hossein Amin, 'Egypt and the Arab World in the Satellite Age', in John Sinclair, Elizabeth Jacka and Stuart Cunningham (eds.), *New Patterns in Global Television: Peripheral Vision* (Oxford: Oxford University Press, 1996).
17. Alexander Richard Norton, 'The Future of Civil Society in the Middle East', in Jillian Schwedler (ed.), *Toward Civil Society in the Middle East? A Primer* (Boulder, CO: Lynne Rienner Publishers, 1995), p.viii.
18. As clearly recognized in the important work by John Esposito, *Islam and Democracy* (Oxford: Oxford University Press, 1996).
19. This section draws on the work of Amin, op. cit.
20. Muhammad I. Ayish, 'Arab Television Goes Commercial: A Case Study of the Middle East Broadcasting Centre', *Gazette*, Vol. 59, No. 6 (Dec. 1970), pp.473–94.

21. Ibid.
22. Chris Forrester, 'Regional Broadcasting Update', *Middle East Broadcasting and Satellite* (Oct. 1995), p.370.
23. 'Global Resource Guide', *Multichannel News International* (March 1997), p.5A. It is noteworthy that at least three commercial publications, *Middle East Broadcasting and Satellite*, *Middle East Communications*, and *Middle East Satellite Today*, focus solely on tracking the developments in media regulation, delivery systems and new players in the region, in itself a powerful indicator of the strength of this regional market.
24. *Multichannel News International* (March 1997).
25. Chris Forrester, 'Regional Broadcasting'.
26. Rebecca Hawkes, 'Gathering Pace-Broadcasting in the UAE', *Middle East Broadcast and Satellite* (March 1997), p.27.
27. Ibid., p 24–5.
28. Ibid.
29. Ibid., p.28.
30. Quoted in Sarah Callard, 'Broadcasting in Bahrain: an interview with Khalil Ebrahim al-Thawasi', *Middle East Broadcast and Satellite* (March 1997), p.7.
31. Quoted in Rebecca Hawkes, 'Gathering pace', p.24.
32. Hala Al-Umran, 'MMDS-the Cultural Alternative to DTH', *Middle East Broadcast and Satellite* (Sept. 1996), p.19.
33. Al-Umran, *Middle East Broadcast and Satellite* (Sept. 1996), p.22.
34. Ibid., p. 24.
35. Arguments about media undermining social boundaries were best and originally made by Joshua Meyrowitz, *No Sense of Place* (Oxford: Oxford University Press, 1985).
36. Abu-Lughod, "The Objects of Soap Opera", in Daniel Miller (ed.), *Worlds Apart* (London: Routledge, 1995), p.206.
37. Nira Yuval-Davis, *Gender and Nation* (London: Routledge, 1997).
38. For arguments regarding the Middle East, see both Jenny White, 'Civic Culture and Islam in Turkey' and Annika Rabo, 'Gender, state and civil society in Jordan and Syria', both in Chris Hann and Elizabeth Dunn, *Civil Society – Challenging Western Models* (London: Routledge, 1996).
39. Hisham Sharabi, *Neo-Patriarchy: A Theory of Distorted Change in Arab Society* (Oxford: Oxford University Press, 1988).
40. 'The Key to the Kingdom', *Media International* (Nov. 1997).
41. Ayish, 'Arab Television', p.491.
42. Colin Hoskins and Roger Mirus, 'Reasons for the US Dominance of International Trade in Television Programming', *Media, Culture and Society*, Vol.10, No.4 (1988), pp.499–515.
43. Joseph Straubhaar, 'Beyond Media Imperialism: Asymmetrical Interdependence and Cultural Proximity', *Critical Studies in Mass Communication*, Vol.8 (1991), pp.39–59.
44. See for example Ulrich Beck, Anthony Giddens and Scott Lash, *Reflexive Modernization*, (Cambridge: Polity, 1994).
45. See the work of Abu-Lughod cited above and Hannah Davies, 'American Logic in a Moroccan Town', *Middle East Report*, No.159, Vol.19, No.4 (1989), pp.12–18. This is of course not to argue that Western media representation is free of patriarchal values; they are however more subtle, more varied and do allow women greater range of movement.
46. Daniel Lerner, *The Passing of Traditional Society* (Harvard: Belknap Press, 1958).
47. Hamid Mowlana and Laurie Wilson, *The Passing of Modernity* (London: Longman, 1990).

The Promotion of Democracy at the Grass-roots: The Example of Radio in Mali

MARY MYERS

With the advent of multi-partyism, the West African state of Mali has seen the liberalization of the airwaves and a dramatic expansion in the numbers of privately owned radio stations. A background to the development of both urban and rural stations is given and a discussion follows as to radio's actual and potential role in defining and defending a democratic culture. The overt political stance of the urban stations is compared and contrasted with the more subtle forms of democratic education used by rural studios. Problems relating to funding, sustainability, bias, regulation and popular access are discussed. The examination concludes that despite facing many problems radio is an important force for the promotion of civil society and a democratic culture in Mali.

Introduction

The 'free press' in the sense of independent radio broadcasting is the subject of this examination of the actual and potential role of radio in defining and defending a democratic culture at the grass-roots level in the West African state of Mali.

Since 1991 Mali has officially been a multi-party democracy. Having ousted the military dictatorship of General Moussa Traoré after 23 years, this former French colony is regarded – notably by the United States – as something of a flagship democracy in an otherwise uncertain region. After winning the country's first elections in 1992 President Alpha Oumar Konaré has remained popular. His party, ADEMA (*Alliance pour la Démocratie au Mali*), managed to consolidate its base in the most recent round of elections early in 1997.

However, these latest legislative and presidential polls were not a smooth affair. The first round 'produced chaos at polling stations, an opposition boycott ... and streetfighting in the capital, Bamako.'[1] The legislative round was annulled and had to be re-run, while the procedure by which Konaré was re-elected President was condemned as flawed by both the Malian opposition and by international observers. The opposition mood has remained hostile and the West looks on anxiously, noting a number of human rights violations such as the arrest of journalists.[2]

Recent events show that Mali's democracy, though real, is extremely fragile. The very existence of opposition parties is the proof that it is real. But the recent curbing of the press is partly what makes observers uneasy. The question is, to what extent are the popular mass media (which in Mali takes the form primarily of radio) helping to strengthen this fragile democracy at the grass-roots and what chance does independent radio have to survive?

Why Radio?

Radio is perhaps the most natural 'press' for a largely non-literate country such as Mali (average literacy rates are among the lowest in the world at only 29.3 per cent).[3] In many ways radio is the tangible modern extension of oral tradition. Since the end of one-party rule radio stations have burgeoned. With over 60 independent studios, Mali now boasts the highest number of radio stations of any country in the region. Although individual ownership of transistors is not particularly high by African standards (officially 44 radios per 1,000 people in Mali compared to an average of 149 for sub-Saharan Africa)[4] radio is acknowledged as the most effective way to reach the majority of Malians. For instance, UNICEF and other health agencies have chosen to concentrate on radio broadcasts as a means of public education about AIDS, after surveys showed that 76 per cent of men and 50 per cent of women in Mali cited the radio as their primary source of information about the disease.[5]

Radio is the most powerful mass medium in Mali. Furthermore, independent radio stations see themselves quite explicitly as integral to the democratic process. Born out of popular socio-political changes, they are perceived as both a product of the Malian 'revolution' and a motor behind the gains made by that revolution. Just as Mali's new-found democracy is viewed by the international community as a 'promising experiment'[6] so its new popular radio network presents an interesting case study of the potentials – and problems – of grass-roots democracy.

Background to the New Radio Pluralism

The first urban community-type radio station to break the monopoly of the state-run broadcasting corporation (ORTM) was *Radio Bamakan* in 1991 (though a rural community radio had been run by an Italian Non-Governmental Organization (NGO) in Kayes since 1987). Five others (*Liberté, Kayira, Klédu, Tabale* and *Fréquence 3*) followed in quick succession, as the Transitional Government (1991–92) enshrined the liberalization of the press in law.[7] Broadcasting in local languages, where state radio had always broadcast in the colonial language of French, these *Radios Libres* (free radios) saw themselves essentially as the mouthpiece of the population in direct contrast to ORTM – the mouthpiece of the government. Free speech over the airwaves followed the lead taken initially by radical newspapers. Lansana Traoré, the founder of *Radio Fréquence* 3, a teacher and union leader says: 'The creation of *Les Echos* [newspaper] in 1989 helped awaken people's consciousness. *Les Echos* was laying bare everything that was corrupt and fascist about the old regime. I asked myself: couldn't the same thing be done with radio? Because the written word only touches the intelligentsia.'[8]

Radios like *Fréquence 3* began with a great self-awareness of their role in promoting a democracy based on the common person. For them, democracy meant *'transparence, participation du citoyen, civisme'* (transparency, audience participation and civic responsibility), not just elections or party politics (though for some – notably *Radio Kayira* which identified itself strongly with one of the opposition parties – this was also an option). Political debates, interviews with the opposition, students and intellectuals, round-table discussion, educational programmes about rights, health, civic issues: all these mixed with local music and a fresh style of live presentation in local languages combined to attract large audiences and to establishment of a reputation as 'platforms for the defence of democracy'.[9]

In September 1993 President Konaré signed the Bamako Declaration on Radio Pluralism[10] which declared 'Radio pluralism is an essential component in the deepening of the democratic process now underway: it allows people greater access to a diversity of information, and guarantees increased popular participation in sustainable human development'. In so doing, Konaré not only committed his government to encouraging plural and multiple radio stations, but also placed Mali firmly at the symbolic forefront of media liberalization in Africa: 'African states must speed up the ending of the monopoly over the air waves, and give priority to national proponents of independent radio when allocating broadcasting frequencies ...'.[11]

This significant official backing gave strength to diverse groups such as religious organizations, women's groups, NGOs and rural associations to start up their own small FM stations all over the country. Though less overtly political than the first urban *Radios Libres*, these stations were – and still are – no less committed to the fundamental principles of democracy: transparency, participation, civic rights and responsibilities. Rural radios, especially, started with a mission to 'give a voice to the voiceless' – the vast rural majority. For rural stations, the democratic imperative was less a call to arms than a quiet but firm assertion of rural people's priorities, languages and culture in order to counteract years of centralism.

Though some may be privately owned, some funded by NGOs and others run on a more commercial basis, whether urban or rural, all these independent radios have become known collectively as *radios de proximité* – literally radios which are 'close-by', but figuratively radios which are part of the landscape of everyday life.

Urban Free Radios

The proportion of radio ownership in Malian towns is far higher than in rural areas (96 per cent of the population of Bamako have at least one radio set at home[12] whereas the national average is 44 sets per 1,000 people). These figures reflect the huge disparities between the rural and urban milieu which is so typical of much of the Sahel: only 26 per cent of the Malian population is urban[13] yet it has a disproportionately large influence over social, political and economic affairs. In Mali the way radio stations have established themselves has largely followed this urban bias, with the majority of the 63 new stations concentrated in urban centres such as Bamako, Ségou, Koulikoro and Koutiala.

The majority of local urban stations are small outfits, based on music and local news, broadcasting on FM (frequency modulation). Typically, they are housed in basic premises, with relatively weak (one kilowatt) transmitters, reaching a radius of up to 50 kilometres. Often they are set up with a grant from a local NGO or community association, and sustain themselves financially from advertising revenue and receipts from record requests and personal announcements. In some cases sponsors are Malian businessmen or well-known figures such as film director, Cheik Omar Sissoko, who is president of the association which runs *Radio Kayira*. The better established studios often negotiate sponsorship from international bodies like United Nations agencies for specific public service programmes. Capital investment is relatively low and is seen by backers as a cost-effective way to reach thousands of listeners. For the young men of Bamako's suburban shanties, where unemployment is a major scourge, there is the opportunity of a job and to become something of a local celebrity as a disc jockey.

Costs at Radio Bamakan are illustrative: the recording and transmitting equipment cost approximately 8 million CFA Francs in 1992 (roughly £15,000 sterling), while its monthly revenue is 300,000 CFA which almost covers its total expenses. Salaries for technicians and presenters are not fixed but are derived from the station's daily takings and are typically about 30,000 CFA per month each – about four times the Malian minimum wage.[14]

While the new urban radios deliberately sought to establish themselves at the physical heart of their local communities, their popularity among the population rose steadily and is still unchallenged. After liberalization of the airwaves the incidence of radio sets in Bamako equipped with FM bands increased from 77 per cent in 1988 to 89 per cent in 1993, and Malian national radio was forced to establish a new FM channel – called O'FM – in order to compete with the popular independents. In a survey of spontaneous awareness of FM stations in Bamako carried out by the BBC in 1993, the four key independent stations (*Bamakan, Kayira, Liberté* and *Klédu*) were the clear favourites.[15]

In the months following the popular 'revolution' of March 1991 the new FM stations offered listeners in Bamako a level of debate which had been unknown hitherto, and news which was no longer biased in favour of the ruling elite. On *Radio Liberté* programmes such as '*L'Heure de Vérité*' (The Moment of Truth) and '*Expliquez-vous sur Liberté*' (Explain yourself on Radio Liberty) invited politicians from all parties to defend themselves in turn. On *Radio Kayira* a programme entitled '*La Parole aux Maires*' (The Mayors Have the Floor) attempted to find solutions to citizens' real problems, such as unemployment and lack of health facilities. The new-found euphoria of free expression is summed up thus:

> Most of them [independent radios] ... spark wild enthusiasm among listeners ... The switchboards are deluged with phone calls. For lack of a phone, listeners show up at the studios, in the corridor or the courtyard, to continue – in the flesh – debates begun on-air. Others ... stay glued to their transistors to follow their favourite programmes. Press summaries are translated from French (which no one understood) into local languages. At last! Adversarial political debate and discussions about social issues that were once taboo ... .[16]

At the same time programmes of an educational nature were begun, covering practical 'life skills' such as nutrition, health and hygiene – often sponsored by international bodies such as UNICEF and the United Nations Food and Agriculture Organization. Other programmes began which were more overtly persuasive in tone such as those aimed at women. A case in point is *Radio Bamakan*'s weekly magazine entitled *Pour Votre Eveil, Madame* (roughly translated as Women Wake Up!), which aims to 'inform, awaken opinion and educate'. On *Fréquence* 3 a programme called *Travaillons en musique* (Music while you work) aims to 'remind the population of their duty, to magnify the spirit of enterprise and to fight against idleness'.[17]

Added to these were a whole section of programmes aimed at informing and educating urban dwellers specifically of their democratic and civic rights – and duties. According to Programme Director Mohamodou Cissé of *Radio Bamakan:*

The role of Radio Bamakan is to struggle positively in favour of the democratic process; to defend democracy and serve the population. There are a lot of aspects of democracy that the people don't know about, and we are obliged to raise awareness, to explain that democracy is not anarchy; that democracy involves rights and obligations. We have the right to demand, but we also have obligations to the state.[18]

Programmes such as *Les Institutions de la 3ième République* (The Public Institutions of the 3rd Republic) on *Radio Kayira* exemplify this kind of public education aimed at fostering a civic spirit.

Democratic Impact of Urban Radios

Inevitably, there is a corollary to high-minded talk of rights and responsibilities. Not all presenters were entirely impartial and not all have succeeded in staying as dispassionately detached as the authorities would like. Whether it is a matter of energetic investigative reporting or making potentially explosive allegations, the forthright character of some urban free radios has provoked harassment from the Malian government on several occasions. That the authorities should fear these radios' influence is itself an indicator of their power and impact.

In the immediate years following the revolution the most famous cases have involved the repeated closure of *Radio Kayira* by the Konaré government. The station, which is openly opposed to the ruling ADEMA party, was primarily accused of inciting armed revolt against a young and fragile democracy. As groups of students occupied the state radio station in March 1993 and massive demonstrations were held against the government's economic policy in April, there is some anecdotal evidence that the allegations about *Radio Kayira*'s involvement are true. *Kayira*'s broadcasts were jammed in 1995 and again on the occasion of a student strike in January 1996.[19] In September 1997 international alerts were issued in defence of two of *Kayira*'s employees, arrested as members of the opposition Solidarité Africaine Pour la Democratie Indépendante (SADI) party.[20] Staff of other radios stations such as *Klédu* and the relatively new *Guintan* have also been the subject of police harassment, interrogations, even beatings on occasion.[21]

There is a legitimate question of quality of output. Because of the veritable mushrooming of small FM stations and a lack of trained technicians and journalists, it is possible that the reputations of the more responsible stations could be tarnished by amateur outfits, which are little more than music and 'chat' stations. Rumours and misinformation are known to have been spread via radio in Bamako; for example, staff of the NGO Plan International have noticed with disquiet that some young listeners believe that condoms (which are distributed free as protection against HIV/AIDS) are actually infected with the AIDS virus and are being donated by Northern agencies as part of a conspiracy to control the Malian population.[22]

There is also the problem of defining what is meant by what *Radio Bamakan* calls 'a positive struggle in favour of the democratic process'. A look at voter turn-out provides a pertinent case in point. During the most recent elections (which were re-run in July 1997, after the initial legislative poll of April was cancelled), there was a low turn-out by voters,[23] which was disappointing for the ruling ADEMA party who would have wished to see its mandate strengthened by consensus at the polls. But opposition parties had called for a boycott, accusing ADEMA of manipulating the election timetable. The boycott appeal was publicized by opposition newspapers and by a number of urban radios. This may partly explain the low turnout. But the question arises: were radios infringing their democratic responsibilities by advocating a voter's boycott? Or were they, on the other hand, defending the rights of all political players – opposition parties in particular – to articulate their views by any means – including, in this case, a boycott?

In order to arbitrate in such questions and to advise the government on the granting of broadcast licences, the need for a regulatory body is accepted by all concerned. The *Conseil Supérieur de la Communication* (CSC) is meant to fulfil this function at present, and is closely monitored from the journalists' side by URTEL, the Union of Free Radio and Television. However, there is some dissatisfaction about the CSC's supposed neutrality. Instead of allowing its Secretary General to be elected by CSC members, the government have appointed a civil servant in his place, thus opening the CSC to charges of partiality.[24] Moreover, as abuses against journalists continue, neither the CSC nor URTEL seem at present to have any real power.

Such issues of responsibility, impartiality and accuracy on the part of broadcasters, and of neutrality on the part of regulatory bodies, are germane to the ongoing discourse on the role of the free press in a democracy – in whatever region or continent it may take place. In Mali, like anywhere else, a free press can be a double-edged sword. On the one hand it has the potential to promote dangerous divisions and to incite violence; on the other, it can promote respect for the rule of law and foster healthy and informed debate. As far as the future is concerned, the Malian government's threshold of tolerance *vis-à-vis* its chattering urban classes will continue to be monitored with interest.

'Radios Rurales'

While the urban *Radio Libres* were causing a political stir in the early 1990s in the Bambara-speaking heartland, a number of rural radios were quietly establishing themselves and redefining what mass media means to ordinary Malians. The majority of the population are rural peasants, cattle herders and traders; they live for the most part in semi-arid zones of subsistence agriculture, in some of the harshest and poorest habitats in the world.

Radio Kayes was the first alternative rural radio and it began in 1987, even before the end of Traoré's dictatorship, under a special agreement between an Italian NGO (Gao International Co-operation) which sponsored it, and the government. (This special arrangement may have been partly due to Kayes being President Traoré's home area).[25] Following *Radio Kayes'* lead in providing a public service for the Soninké-speakers of the Kayes area, other radios like those of Douentza and Bankass followed in 1993 and 1994. These provided a voice for Peulh/Fulani-speakers and Dogon-speakers respectively. For the first time Dogon-speakers on the dry eastern plains, hundreds of kilometres away from the capital, were able to tune into programmes in their own languages. Furthermore, they could listen for the first time to subjects and music which not only interested them but which, in some cases, they had recorded themselves: subjects such as cereal and livestock prices, rural taxation, literacy, environmental issues and local conflicts over land and water.

Like Kayes, both Douentza and Bankass radios began life by virtue of their links with long-term integrated rural development projects sponsored by international NGOs. They also received enthusiastic backing from local people in the provision of land, labour and materials to build the studios. All three radios – Kayes, Bankass and Douentza – share a distinctive vision of what rural broadcasting means. Though supported by international NGOs, they are all run by local associations made up of members of the local community: peasants, traders, teachers, housewives, traditional leaders and youth groups. These associations maintain the organizational and editorial control and therefore ensure that local issues, culture and music receive priority. Essentially, these radios are developmental tools, designed and run to foster a spirit of local identity and empowerment; to 'bring knowledge to the rural communities and to give them a say'.[26]

Although the proportion of families owning radio sets in rural areas is low in comparison with the towns, there is evidence of much communal listening and sharing of sets. In one survey in the Douentza area, it was found that ownership of FM receivers in the local vicinity jumped by 140 per cent after the new community station went on air.[27] This indicates that radio listening may be as much a function of people's interest in what is offered over the airwaves as their ability to afford radio sets. For many young men and women in this impoverished area, it suddenly became worthwhile to spend hard-earned cash on a transistor because, for the first time, there was something worth listening to.

As far as their minimal budgets will permit, the programme content of such community radios is based on recordings made in villages where discussions, debates and interviews are organized, then edited and broadcast. Broadly, the themes covered are health, agricultural work, the environment, social issues, local and international news, local announcements; all mixed with plenty of local and national music. More specifically – at *Radio Douentza*, for example – themes include:

> Women's programmes: excision, abortion, young unmarried mothers, being single, divorce, rape, polygamy – the problems of children, old age, contraception, infidelity, sexual equality, AIDS etc. Men's programmes: a programme around the theme 'there is no such thing as a useless job', the generation gap, crime, rape, traditional justice, credit, the cost of marriage, forced marriage, cheating, ignorance, etc. On technology and society: breastfeeding, latrines, the fight against prostitution, public works, the problem of loose livestock, taxation, unemployed graduates, etc.[28]

Education for Democracy On Air

Like their urban counterparts, rural radios take their educational role very seriously, particularly education about Mali's new-found democracy. For example, in the case of *Radio Douentza* the rationale for the station's establishment was based on the promotion of grass-roots democracy through education:

> Politics had opened up in a big way, the [radio's strategy-] document made clear 'that these changes (and their implications) are not known by the rural majority within the population ... the rural communities must, as far as possible, be the instigators of their own development.' Whence the idea to provide farmers and herders with a flow of news which would allow them to take part in the democratic process that was in progress.[29]

Likewise, democratic education was the original *raison d'être* of *Radio Seno* in Bankass:

> Rural radios broadcasting in local languages and dialects can efficiently reach the whole population who are at present ignorant of

their rights under an '*état de droit*' and who have only a vague idea of democratic rules. Programmes explaining citizens' rights and obligations are of utmost importance; politicians and decision-makers will be asked to explain their political platforms and justify their decisions.[30]

Accordingly, long-term education campaigns were instigated at a number of rural radio stations. At Bankass, programme titles include: *Droits et Devoirs des Citoyens* (Rights and Duties of Citizens), *Les Jeunes et la Société* (Youth and Society) and at *Radio Douentza* a two year series was started under the title PDD (*Programme d'Appui à la Democratie et à la Décentralisation),* funded by international NGOs. This latter programme provides us with an interesting case, particularly because it has been the subject of a relatively thorough impact assessment, unlike the majority of other radio initiatives – notably, and regrettably, the urban programmes.

The aim of Douentza's PDD programme was to 'contribute to the consolidation of democratic gains, promote the emergence of a civil society and of citizens' consciousness of their rights and duties and make them capable of resisting infringements and injustices'.[31] Conceived and run by the local NGO, the Near East Foundation (NEF), the radio was used in conjunction with other media, including popular theatre, booklets in local languages and newspaper articles. Mini-dramas, 'spots', interviews, 'game-shows' and translations of key texts were recorded by the radio presenters and systematically broadcast to *Radio Douentza*'s catchment of an estimated audience of about 120,000 listeners. By NEF's estimate the PDD programme has 'directly influenced' a total of about 52,000 people in the Douentza area.[32]

Key texts such as the new constitution, the electoral code and new laws concerning land rights, rural taxes, marriage and women's rights were all translated from French (the official language) and broadcast – with explanation – in Fulani, in a dialect of Dogon, and in Bambara. Mini dramas brought fictional characters together in scenes such as feuds between neighbours, which emphasised respect for modern justice instead of resorting to traditional 'tit for tat' violence. Another drama portrayed farmers and forestry guards in conflict over pruning of trees; this drama reinforced the message that farmers should claim their legitimate rights rather than submit to the illegal, but all too common, fines by corrupt officials.

Short 'spots' of about two minutes each were used in order to repeat simple pieces of information about voting procedures and facts such as the length of the presidential mandate. Interviews were organized with local members of parliament, judges, council officials and women's groups to

discuss the implications of decentralisation at the *commune* level.
Recordings were broadcast of public 'game-shows' (*jeux publics*) in which
whole villages would participate in solving a riddle designed to make some
deeper point about, for instance, the problem of domestic violence or the
importance of women's literacy. These shows, with their musical interval
and displays of traditional eloquence are meant not only to make a serious
point but to offer a high degree of entertainment.

In 1996, after two years of the campaign, an impact study was done by
NEF, the agency responsible. This gathered interviews with villagers to
assess in a qualitative manner the effectiveness of the democracy campaign.
In many cases radio was the favoured medium: 'In Boumbam [village] the
chief declared "we really learned a lot from the radio – about taxes and
women, about the law to do with trees, about decentralisation, but what
others were saying was not so clear to me as what was said on the radio."'[33]
Other testimonies bore witness to how the programme was understood at the
grass roots level:

> 'You opened our eyes' was the reaction from Mondoro. In Gono a
> newly literate man said 'the booklets, the plays, the radio programmes
> helped us a lot to understand the law on decentralisation; we
> understood that those villages that wish can join together to form a
> *commune.*' In Tieécouraré, Prye, Dansa, the inhabitants declared they
> were no longer frightened to speak up [against persons in authority].
> 'Even in the *Commandant*'s office we say what we think; that's
> democracy too!'… Seydou [a man from Boumbam village] said,
> 'before we didn't know much about laws and we were made to do a
> lot of things by force, but now if it's not the law we don't agree and
> we say so clearly and freely'.[34]

Overall, the PDD programme was evaluated by comparing villages which
had been covered by the campaign with those that had not – including
those communities which, for reason of topography, could not receive the
FM signal of *Radio Douentza*. The report concluded: 'It appeared clearly
in all the villages … that the population knew little or nothing about the
[decentralisation] legislation before the programme, but they had learned a
lot thanks to the campaign. In fact, this project is the first and only one of
its kind in Douentza Cercle where women as well as men have expressed
their great appreciation.'[35] The radio station itself served in a sense as a
focal point for those seeking information: 'In concrete terms the interest of
the local youth was shown by the letter they sent to [Radio] *Daande
Duwansa* to ask for repeats, for clarifications and by their visits [to the
studio] to obtain copies of recordings or to discuss issues with the radio
personnel'.[36]

Small but significant events are indicators of the population's heightened awareness of their rights, for example:

> A citizen of the village of Banai claimed his right to an identity card that the *chef d'arrondissment* had refused to issue [in the hope of a bribe] and protested publicly at this official's abuse of his position … Elsewhere, in N'Gorodia, for example, the women who are claiming their right to own their own plot of land for vegetable gardening have seized the chief of the village in protest against another claimant for the land … In Bagui they managed to get their own land. In Dari the youth of the village protested in the Village Association meeting against the mismanagement of the village cereal bank and demanded that the situation be clarified.[37]

Democratic Impact

Small events such as those recorded in Douentza are telling testimonies that the democratic process has found its expression in remote rural areas with the help of radio. Democratic expression lies not only in the direct exercise of, for example, the right to vote, but also in the challenging of age-old exploitative patterns: of corrupt officials over uneducated farmers; of men over women; and of the village elders over the young.

There is, therefore, some evidence that radio is making a difference to people's lives in terms of strengthening a democratic culture: it is helping to create a citizenry which is better informed of its rights and obligations; and is going some way to eliminate corruption and to foster a more accountable civil service and local authority. However, this is only one documented case. More research needs to be done as to the impact of *Radio Douentza* and of the handful of other community radios in Mali which are running similar projects. It is probable that a number of positive results would be found.

Meanwhile, most, if not all, radios are labouring under a number of constraints. The main problem is one of funding. Rural radios have a much smaller potential for attracting advertising revenue than their urban counterparts, and therefore have to rely on grants or sponsorship, in-kind contributions from the local population and revenue from announcements and disk requests. The poverty of the stations limits journalists' ability to travel out to far-flung villages to meet and record their audience's views, news, music and discussions. Since grass-roots reporting and direct access by ordinary villagers is meant to be the *raison d'être* of rural radios, these limitations are a serious block to the stations being truly representative of their constituents.

This problem is linked to the question of who has access to the radio station. Situated, as most studios are, in main towns, it is invariably the male, literate, able-bodied young or middle-aged population who find their way to the studio to air their views or deliver letters or pre-recorded cassettes. Children, women and the elderly are far less well represented, simply because they are less likely to travel beyond their home villages. Significantly, the NEF evaluation[38] in Douentza found that popular theatre was more effective than radio for reaching women. Indeed it is generally observed that women are far less likely than men to listen to the radio for reasons of time and lack of access: radio sets are generally owned by men and are carried with them to their places of work and women's workloads are so heavy that most say they have little time to relax and listen.

The gender problem is also linked to one of language. Rural women, being less educated and less mobile, tend only to speak their mother-tongue. This means that 'minority' dialects – Dogon, for example, has more than 50 – are virtually ignored by radio stations in favour of more universal 'market' languages like Fulani; but this means, again, it is mostly men who benefit. The symbolism of language is important: simply by insisting on languages like Fulani rather than Bambara or French, the rural radios believe they are making a statement of independence from the urban elite, the French-speaking civil servants and the old order. However, if, as Mody[39] puts it, part of the task of popular media is to 'convey the community's consensus upwards', a problem arises if those in power at the top do not understand – and possibly even disdain – the language in which that message is framed.

Moreover, there is the ever-present threat that those in power may act to close or jam rural radios. Although this has not happened to any serious degree to date, there is no doubt in rural journalists' minds that it is a possibility. They look towards Bamako and are all too aware of the difficulties faced by outfits such as *Radio Kayira*.[40] This is a compelling reason for journalists to avoid embroiling themselves in controversial political issues, since it could mean closure of the station and loss of their jobs. Unlike urban journalists who have other job opportunities (or for whom being a disc-jockey may be a part-time job among others) staff on rural radios are far from being investigative journalists, they are not rewarded for probing scandals, nor are they promoted for 'scooping' the latest story about corrupt officials. Thus, simply through a sense of self-preservation, rural radios have had to stop short of pursuing some of the ideals that were initially set for them – for instance, by international agencies such as SOS Sahel: 'The worst evils of Malian society, corruption, nepotism, incompetence and mismanagement of public funds, will recede within a system of transparency and critical journalism'.[41]

Such hopes have not yet been fully realized, although the signs are that the spirit of investigation will grow slowly. But this will not happen as long as radio staff do not feel secure in their jobs. This is as much a matter of sound finance as it is an issue crucial to healthy civil society.

Finally, and most importantly, there is the question of popular expression. *Radios de proximité* have been hailed as the mouthpiece of the people. Trainers and theorists like Querre and Havelange see rural radio as a tool for 'liberating the peasant voice'; Querre writes: that rural radio producers 'will preserve the cultural identity of their audience and hand back to them their right to be heard.'[42] But, as we have seen, problems of access to the radio station, particularly for some social and language groups are serious. Furthermore, lack of funding limits the radios' ability to achieve effective outreach to the socially, physically and linguistically marginalised. Moreover, until recently the particular security problems posed by a civil war with Tuareg rebels in the north were a very real brake on radio's direct contact with rural communities. Even once these problems are permanently solved, the question still remains: given a tape recorder and a blank cassette, what would ordinary Malian peasants actually say?

The fact that 'pirate' radio stations were being spontaneously initiated in villages before the airwaves were liberalized is one indicator that ordinary peasants have something to say and were finding the ways and means to express themselves before being helped by officially-sanctioned radio stations. An example comes from Bankass in the east, where:

> Several pirate radio stations started broadcasting in 1993 ... with extremely simple installations, based on FM microphones and ... antenna wire suspended between trees ... The local school headmaster as well as the village headman confirmed the usefulness of village radio for education and communication. Nobody had to go from house to house anymore to inform citizens on local developments, venues of meetings or dates and places for communal labour.[43]

Legal radios have now extended this very practical use of radio as a message-delivery network to a much wider geographical and linguistic area; a service which is undoubtedly of great value in such a vast and non-literate country. In the Douentza area, for example, notices on-air are proving extremely positive in conflict prevention: farmers give notice to cattle herders as to the dates at which their harvests will be completed, so that the herders may bring their cattle in to browse on the stubble-fields without causing damage to crops. Thus what may seem like simple communiqués are in many cases significant acts of horizontal communication between communities which were previously antagonistic. Radio thus becomes a type of social cement.

But what of vertical communication, as well as horizontal? What of popular media's supposed power to 'convey the community's consensus upwards'?[44] The problem here is that rural Malians have lived in silence and isolation for so long that it may take a long time before they feel safe to speak out against authority. Few do so at present on-air, though journalists may find ways of coaxing them to become more articulate. But ordinary people's in-built conservatism and journalists' own fear of censure combine to make rural radio less politically outspoken than its urban counterparts. Popular expression – for example, of the kind heard on opinionated commercial radio in the West – is limited by a strong traditional respect for authority. The 'liberation of the peasant voice' will be a slow evolution, but at least, with local and community radios, the means and mechanisms for it now exist in most rural areas.

Conclusion

The speed with which community radio stations have grown in Mali since the advent of multi-partyism surely indicates that the medium of radio broadcasting is fulfilling a need for self-expression which hitherto had been suppressed. If democracy is partly about 'the man/woman in the street' expressing their views, then radio has certainly helped promote democratization in Mali. If democracy is also about opposition politics, urban radios have, again, provided a relevant forum.

The question of how far *Radios Libres* actually helped bring about multi-partyism is arguable. A handful of urban radios certainly played a crucial role in the transition period between the fall of the dictator, Moussa Traoré, and the first elections of 1992 by keeping debate alive and helping to define democracy in its broadest sense as *transparence, participation du citoyen, civisme*. However, it was largely thanks to decisions taken by the Konaré government itself (once it was elected in 1992), that radio pluralism was finally allowed to blossom.

The difference between the urban and the rural definitions of democracy are interesting. Although it cannot be said that rural radio is completely unconcerned with party politics, it is still far less engaged in this kind of debate than urban studios. Democracy has perhaps been defined in a much wider sense in the rural context being about the power of the 'little person' in the face of corrupt authority, and even about the new-found power of women and youth in the face of traditional gerontocracy at village level.

That radio has helped to defend as well as to define democracy is also true. To a great extent it has helped simply by being there. The old scenario of a military coup in which the state radio was one of the first and most strategic points to control is now far less likely. The existence of over 60 independent transmitters reaching millions of people – in particular influential urban dwellers – is, perhaps, the guarantee. The type of democratic education by radio shown to be successful in the Douentza case is also an illustration of how powerful radio can be in reinforcing and embedding responsible citizenship and an informed electorate. Possibly, this is promotion of democracy at the grass-roots in its truest form. The problems that radio stations face – lack of funds, lack of trained personnel and problems of popular access – all have their roots in the extreme economic poverty of the country. But in theory these problems are solvable, though probably only over the long-term. The problem of censorship and government control, is, on the other hand, more immediate and more easily solved – given the political will. Both democracy and the free press are fragile in Mali, but the sheer numbers of independent radios and the thirst for popular expression that they have unleashed make them an incontrovertible force.

NOTES

(Note: All translations are the author's.)

1. *Africa Confidential* Vol.38, No.9 (25 April 1997).
2. See 'Committee to Protect Journalists Condemns Arrests of 15 Malian Journalists', *Africa News On-line* (20 Aug. 1997).
3. See United Nations Development Programme (UNDP*) Human Development Report* (New York : UNDP, 1997).
4. Ibid.
5. See United States Agency for International Development (USAID) *EDSM-II Demographic Health Survey, Mali* (Calverton, MD : USAID, 1995/6).
6. Editorial, *New York Times* (29 April 1996).
7. See J. Louarn, 'Radio Fréquence 3 (Mali)', in PANOS Institute, *Et Pourtant Elles Vivent! 4 Portraits de Radios Locales en Afrique de l'Ouest* (Dakar: Panos, 1994).
8. Ibid., p.61.
9. Personal communication from Many Camara, Radio Kayira, 1997.
10. The Colloquium on Radio Pluralism in West Africa was co-organized in Bamako by the West African Journalists' Association and the Panos Institute, 14–18 Sept. 1993.
11. Louarn, op cit.
12. See British Broadcasting Corporation (BBC*) Survey in Bamako District, Mali, Main Findings* (Internal Report, London : BBC/IBAR, 1993).
13. 1995 World Bank figures.
14. See PANOS Institute *Radio Pluralism in West Africa* (Paris : l'Harmattan, 1993).
15. See BBC, 1993.
16. See D. Senghor, 'Introduction' in Panos (1994), pp.7–8.
17. Louarn, op cit., p.62.
18. *InterRadio Newsletter*, AMARC Vol.5. No.2 (July 1993).
19. See *Reporters sans Frontières*, Report 1997.
20. International Freedom of Expression Exchange Clearing House (IFEX) (Toronto 2 Sept. 1997).
21. *Reporters sans Frontières*, Report 1997.
22. Personal communication 1997.
23. Panafrican News Agency, 20 July 1997.
24. See *Radio-Actions*, No.10 (Dakar : Panos Institute, Dec. 1996).
25. Panos (1993).

26. See J. Louarn in 'Daande Duwansa', Panos (1994), p.73.
27. See Francis Rolt, 'Evaluation Report Radio Daande Douentza', Internal report for OXFAM (Oxford : OXFAM, 1995).
28. J. Louarn, 'Daande Duwansa', p.79.
29. Ibid., p.74.
30. See Peter Sturmheit, 'The Priority of Prioritiés : A Free Press for Bankass' (unpublished article, SOS Sahel UK: London, 1993), p.1.
31. Near East Foundation (NEF), 'Rapport Narratif des Activités du Programme d'Appui a la Démocratie et a la Décentralisation' (Internal report NEF – Mail, April 1996), p.1.
32. Ibid., p.1.
33. Ibid., p.16.
34. Ibid., pp.16–18 passim.
35. Ibid., p.16.
36. Ibid., p.17.
37. Ibid., pp.18–19.
38. Ibid.
39. Bella Mody, Designing Messages for Development Communication – An Audience Participation-Based Approach (Newbury Park/London: Sage, 1991).
40. 'We're not like Radio Kayira which spends its whole time criticising people to left and right – they've been closed down five times!' Ernest Damango, Radio Seno, Bankass 1995, personal communication.
41. Sturmheit (1993), p.1. SOS Sahel UK, a registered charity, runs several natural resource management projects in Mali and elsewhere in the Sahel. In 1994 this NGO provided the initial funding for the establishment of Radio Seno in Bankass.
42. François Querre, A Thousand and One Worlds – A Rural Radio Handbook (Food and Agriculture Organization of the UN, Rome 1992), p.20. See also Françoise Havelange, Libérer la Parole Paysanne au Sahel (IRED/Institut Panos, Paris: Harmattan, 1991).
43. Sturmheit, p.2.
44. Mody (1991).

Democracy and the Information Superhighway

MARK WHEELER

Contemporary reports suggest that national and industrial forms of economic and political organization are in decline. In their wake, it is maintained that there has been a global expansion of trade and innovation in communication technology. It is predicted that the Information Communication Technologies (ICTs) will radically alter and decentralize local, national, international and global socio-economic-political institutions. Such reforms provide governments with significant challenges regarding policy. More profoundly, they bring into question how citizens' democratic rights may be advanced with regard to working practices and methods of political participation. The need to activate ICTs for social welfare stands at the core of many of the current debates concerning globalization, the public sphere and the role of the state in the next century. This review will critically address the issues within these key debates. Further, it will provide the reader with a blueprint for an alternative public service model of communication transfer.

Introduction

This study considers the relationship between the Information Communication Technologies (ICTs) and democratic reform. In the near future, American technophiles, such as Alvin and Heidi Toffler, have predicted that individuals will achieve greater autonomy and enjoy significant privileges concerning life-style, working practices and political association. This will be achieved through an epoch-making revolution which will the mark the passing of the industrial order to the information age. As John Frow comments (with apologies to Gareth Locksley):

> The current phase of capitalist development is one characterized by the elevation of information and its associated technology into the first division of key resources and commodities. Information is a new form of capital, and as such it undergoes a change of form; rather than being deposited primarily in an interlocking ensemble of open 'library' systems with minimal entry requirements, it is increasingly managed within a system of private ownership where access is regulated by the payment of rent.[1]

As information is commodified, ICTs are seen radically to alter local, national, international and global socio-economic and political institutions.

It is contended that through the wider dissemination of information provided by the new communications links (Computer Mediated Communication (CMC)) the structures of power within society, the economy and the political sphere will be decentralized.

These arguments will be tested here against the available evidence to provide a critical account of these perceived reforms. To this end, the focus will be on two significant areas of pluralistic practice: economic governance and political participation.[2] With regard to economic governance, it has been suggested that local and national markets will emerge through the alliances that have grown from the financial transaction of information. Moreover, technological reform will lead to an inevitable globalization of communication sources. In this manner, there will be significant changes to the orchestration of the labour market and peoples' working practices. In Britain, Charles Leadbetter of the centre-left think-tank *Demos* argues that a meritocratic working environment will emerge in which the protection of individual rights will subsume the previous collective methods of organization.[3]

The argument for individual empowerment in the information age extends to the grass-root reforms of political structures. The digital environment has been advocated as the means for new or alternative forms of political participation and association. It is maintained that there will be extensions to citizenship as the emerging 'Electronic Democracy' challenges political norms. The Information Superhighway provides an electronic landscape for a re-invented civil society. Through the unregulated *cyberspace* of the internet, information could by-pass state intervention and produce greater citizen empowerment.

This public choice model for information dissemination is being offered as a means of economic prosperity and democratic participation. However, we need to differentiate between the rhetoric and the reality. In particular, it is necessary to address the possibility that people are becoming units for consumption in a corporate world, rather than attaining their rights as citizens through appropriate democratic structures within the workplace and the political sphere. Thus, can these individualistic arguments distinguish between information, knowledge and empowerment? Invariably, the market distribution of communication has been built on closure and the inequitable distribution of resources to produce surplus profit. Therefore, as information, in itself, cannot bestow people with participatory rights, how can it be appropriately disseminated within the public domain so that citizens can attain greater knowledge and empowerment?

The Technological Revolution and the Dissemination of Communications

The technological revolution has produced major transformations within communications for business and domestic use. Interactive fibre-optic cable systems are developing alongside the widespread use of personal computers and video-conferencing. A new generation of networks can promote low-cost broad-band communication. These developments provide access to greater numbers of communications links, permit the distribution of commercial and entertainment material, and advance telephony along the same highways. Moreover, new electronic services located around telecoms, computers and satellites have created a global electronic mail service. Integrated computer networks from universities, companies and the American military, generically entitled the internet, have grown at a staggering rate connecting 1.3 million computers, 8,000 networks and millions of users.[4]

ICTs may enhance the distribution of information in several ways. First, computers increase the amount of data to be stored, retrieved and transmitted. Secondly, mass participation technologies, such as broadcasting, which distribute information from a central source to millions can be enhanced. Finally, they provide interactive communications flows among individuals and organized groups.[5] For instance, there are thousands of on-line Bulletin Board Systems (BBS) and news groups. Thus, ICTs may have the following effects: they explode the limits on the volume of information that can be exchanged; they make it possible to exchange information without regard, for all practical purposes, to real time and space; they increase the control the consumers have over what messages are received; they increase the control the senders have over specific audiences who receive the messages; they decentralize control over mass communication and they bring interactive capacities to television.[6]

The advocates of the internet argue that new methods of communication flow can challenge traditional political structures, institutions and methods of association. First, as the physical limits of time, space and geography are overcome, the constraints over the volume of information available to the public have evaporated. Previously, as direct citizen participation was undermined by time, size, knowledge and access, elitist or representative models of democracy emerged. Alternatively, a wired world would stem the difficulties of *time* because communication and participation become instantaneous. Similarly, problems of *size* are solved because people do not have to be gathered in a single place. Concurrently, the distribution of *knowledge* is widely available through networks, which in turn removes the difficulty of *access*.[7] Whilst the capacity of different interactive services to enhance participation varies, they are distinguished from the previous mass media as the information recipients are no longer passive.

Further, futurists such as George Gilder, Nicholas Negroponte and Alvin Toffler maintain that a *digital revolution* or 'Third Wave' will increase individual citizen participation. Negroponte argues that the hardware is already available to effect significant change. Thus, letters and printed forms ought to be digitalized, virtual reality conferencing must replace business travel, and television should be transmitted by a digital signal (over cable, not the ether). There will be no choice but to switch from dealing with atoms to dealing with 'the DNA of information': binary digits or bits.[8] Digitalization will lead to *decentralization, globalization, harmonization* and *empowerment*. Technology is an agency for change which cannot be denied.

These claims build on the arguments of Marshall McLuhan. McLuhan considered how technologies are an extension of the human body and restructure social relations. In the past, the press was a continuation of eye, thereby stemming the oral flow of information and advancing individualism over communal effort. As Nick Stevenson comments:

> Print supplies the cultural resource for national forms of uniformity, while simultaneously giving birth to notions of individuality. In achieving this, the Gutenberg press converted space and time into the calculable, the rational and the predictable. The linear and logical emphasis of writing was mirrored in the uniform regimentation of clock time. The rationalising impact of the printing press paved the way for geographical maps, railway timetables, and notions of perspectives in painting. According to McLuhan, the advent of print culture had both developed certain human senses (sight) rather than others, and shaped a particular form of human rationality. This, however, was all to change with the arrival of electric forms of communication.[9]

In this context, McLuhan developed the concept of hot and cool medias. Traditional, hot media (print) stem participation as they are high on informational content, thereby setting the agenda and filtering arguments. Alternatively, cool media (telecommunications, television) provide more spaces for audience participation as they provide a lower intensity of information. Consequently, people must fill in the gaps and become active. Thus, the new media decentralize the production of knowledge and democratize opinion formation through interactivity. Through such decentralization, technologies check dominant authorities from managing the flow of information.

McLuhan argued that the new technologies allow for the globalization of the media and multi-media economy, compress time, make spatial relations horizontal, relocate information and undermine the role of nation states. As the co-ordinates of time and space have evaporated, communication systems become constant and immediate providing a diversity of opinions. Individualistic print cultures have been disrupted as many-to-many communications become possible. Thus, the globe's citizens may engage in a shared culture, a global village, which undermines the previously hierarchical or uniform methods of ideological control. McLuhan's words remain the gospel of the internet and the net-user's magazine *Wired* quoted him in their original editorial: 'The medium or process of our time – electronic technology – is reshaping and restructuring patterns of social interdependence and every aspect of our personal life. It's forcing us to reconsider and re-evaluate practically every thought, every action and every institution formerly taken for granted.'[10]

Techno-Populism (1): The Virtual Economy and the Knowledge Entrepreneurs

From McLuhan's vision, the advocates of ICTs suggest that new understandings and cognitive approaches to technology will become apparent. This will mean that the new communication technologies will revolutionize contemporary understandings of the concept of public space and the notion of citizenship. Within the economic sphere, knowledge workers will no longer have to leave their homes to carry out their jobs and this will encourage an increasingly private understanding of rights in which '[there will be a] dissolving (of) the communities that ground a notion of a common good/general will.'[11]

Though drawing inspiration from McLuhan, rather than adopting his vision of a global village or community, many current arguments suggest that instrumental self interest will define the political economy of the Information Superhighway.[12] In particular, it is maintained that the globalization of communication technology has led to novel and severe constraints being placed on traditional political and social institutions which can no longer refract and assimilate the pressures of commodification. Technological reform has circumvented territorial sovereignty, allowing transnational institutions to sever their relationship with home markets and pursue global returns on their investment. Therefore, the deregulation of labour markets is seen as vital in generating increased efficiency and prosperity.

With regard to these technological and economic imperatives, individual enterprise is regarded as the principal source of wealth and social welfare. In turn, private preferences will be facilitated by competitive policies and minimal public regulation. Therefore individual economic liberalization is equated with societal benefit. The notion that political or societal elites can act for the greater good is rejected, as they qualify such freedom. By extension, state powers have to be limited and social communication should satisfy individual choice, rather than be an unprovable public service good.

In particular, *Wired* magazine has maintained that the 'virtual economy' will foster a libertarian view of communications in which no 'fixed' societal order exists. It has drawn on Alvin Toffler's view that there has been a transformation from an industrial to a service-based economy, arguing that there has been an even more inevitable movement to an information-based economy: 'The new economy becomes a sort of a manifest destiny for *laissez-faire*, in which government's role is to 'encourage the new economy to flourish while ensuring [that everyone has] an opportunity to partake of its benefits.'[13] According to the technophiles, this will have a number of beneficial consequences. As the technology flourishes there will be a removal of price controls and entry costs so that everybody can have their own web page independent of income. In common with the eighteenth century concepts of a press market, it is argued that a free trade of ideas will emerge through an open market of producers and consumers using the internet. This means that information is decentralized and that electronic democracy may defy the traditionally centralized power of political and mass media institutions. Moreover, through their sustained ability to consume, these knowledge workers can be more productive. They are both producers and consumers of private rather than public goods. In turn, the distinction between the practices of communications production and consumption have dissolved. For instance, advocates of information technology invoke Toffler's concept of the 'Third Wave Prosumer': '... the 'productivity' of the consumer is [currently] seen ... only as a contribution to the production for exchange. There is no recognition as yet that actual production also takes place [in] ... [the] goods and services produced for oneself ... [which] may displace or substitute ... goods and services turned out [conventionally].'[14]

Invariably, it has been posited that collective forms of economic co-operation and organization become irrelevant. In particular, bodies such as trade unions who have previously protected labour rights are seen as extraneous in a more fluid environment in which the labour force may no longer need to be physically located on one site. Indeed, the very concept of the 'firm' as the key form of economic governance is called into question when individuals can enter the information market-place at a minimal cost and can make profits through direct transactions of information with consumers; the internet may serve a market of 'one'. Further, Leadbetter argues that the economic growth associated with ICTs has been developed through freedom of movement, thereby encouraging a meritocratic working culture, and by the collaborative networks of small companies who transfer information between each other: 'The unit of competitiveness is not the company, nor the sector, but the network.'[15]

The Hollywood film production system has been advocated as a model for such a fluid labour supply. In Hollywood, self-employed producers enjoy greater creative power through their independence so that they can move scripts, stars and directors from studio to studio. Further, they retain control over the project before, during and post-production. For instance, George Lucas demonstrated how massive profits could be made not only by controlling the filming of his *Star Wars* trilogy, but also through the licensing of the products associated with the films. Therefore, old style studio hierarchies have been dispensed with and there has been the contracting out of productions from the technicians to the stars. Moreover, through their mobility, independent producers can move from firm to firm, thereby carrying ideas which are cross-fertilized.[16]

Thus, it is argued that the new technologies have exploded the controls of the nation state such as labour legislation, regulation, contractual obligation and the protection of employment rights. Indeed, to encourage the creative individualism which has driven the new knowledge-based industries states should draw up liberal laws favouring openness and outsiders. In such a manner, flexible workforces can transcend the previously discrete forms of training which encourage sectoral craft-bases and skills. Increasingly, a new unit of prosperity is emerging – the knowledge entrepreneur.

It is predicted that these actors will pursue different forms of industrial democracy in which they will enjoy alternative rights. Previously, in exchange for a wage, people have worked in clearly defined jobs. This notion of wage-labour is seen to be part of a passing industrial order. In contrast, the knowledge entrepreneurs are flexible, multi-skilled, and can negotiate their position in this meritocratic working environment. They will no longer be employees but will be encouraged to engage in a compensation culture in which wage labour is replaced by share ownership and equity pay.[17]

Such ideas have found favour amongst western governments and supra-national organizations. The 1995 US Telecommunications Act removed existing price controls to allow local telephone and cable companies to offer different services. The European Commissioner Martin Bangemann, head of the EC's Directorate General XIII (which has jurisdiction over the telecommunications and information technology policy), argues that a more efficient and less expensive information infra-structure can only be achieved by the deregulation of the European telecommunications market.[18]

In Britain, the new (1997) Labour government is attempting a compromise between limited state regulation and market provision. In opposition, the Labour Party proposed a competitive framework which would encourage private sector initiatives in exchange for the societal provision of hardware.[19] For instance, Tony Blair has struck a deal with British Telecom (BT) to furnish every college, school, hospital and library in Britain with free high-band networks in return for BT's monopolistic control of the cable market (although this is problematical in terms of competition policy). Thus, the libertarian values which have underpinned the thinking of futurologists, think tanks and policy advisors are being realized through public policies designed to establish a private information market-place, thereby ensuring new forms of economic growth.

Techno-Populism (2): Political Libertarianism, Participation and Electronic Democracy

Simultaneously, it is argued that the Information Superhighway will provide the electronic landscape, or cyberspace, for a reinvented civil society so that citizens may participate in their civil, political and social rights. Previously, the Greek agora, town hall, local church, coffee shop, village square and street corner have been the forums for public debate. However, as centralized mass communications institutions, transmitting one-way flows of information, have replaced these public spaces, citizens have been isolated. ICTs make possible the reform of the flow of communication distribution since they make one-to-one, one-to-many and many-to-many interactivity achievable.[20] Ultimately, they will facilitate a truly interactive discourse through an electronic agora which allows alternative ideas to enter the mainstream. As ICTs will serve local, national and global markets, they may establish a series of multiple and overlapping public spheres through which groups can 'seek to build ideological bridges based on common preoccupations and practical measures.'[21] In such a manner, it is argued that political organizations can emerge from the grass-roots and the agenda will reflect the electorate, rather than the political elite's concerns.[22]

As a consequence, they will challenge the perceived clientelistic relations between media organizations and governments. A common argument has been made, by commentators ranging from the anarchistic left to the market-libertarian right, that the political and mass media institutions have undermined citizens' participatory rights. According to this view, the present media organizations have failed to provide free information and have been incorporated into the interests of the powerful. Electronic 'billboards' will circumvent the centralized, conglomerate and outmoded media structures.

Whether representational, direct or communitarian forms of democracy are preferred, electronic technologies appear to guarantee success.[23] For Howard Rheingold,

> Access to alternate forms of information and, most important, the power to reach others with your own alternatives to the official view of events, are, by their nature, political phenomena. Changes in forms and degrees of access to information are indicators of changes in forms and degrees of power among different groups. The reach of the net, like the reach of television, extends to the urbanized parts of the entire world (and, increasingly, to far-flung but telecom linked rural outposts). Not only can each node rebroadcast or originate content to the rest of the net, but even the puniest computers can process that content in a variety of ways after it comes in to the home node from net and before it goes out again. Inexpensive computers can copy and process and communicate information, and when you make PCs independent processing nodes in the already existing telecommunications network, a new kind of system emerges.[24]

Thus, *Teledemocracy* becomes a realistic possibility creating plebiscitary democratic structures and decentralizing political power.[25] Within this technological context, the current norms of political decision-making and information distribution are seen as archaic and resistant to more modulated flows of communication from the grass-roots level. Specifically in Britain, Andrew Adonis and Geoff Mulgan ironically point out:

> On election days, modern citizens come home from offices and factories crammed full of computers, faxes and digital phone systems, to homes almost equally cluttered with telephones and videos, and on the way vote by scribbling a cross on pieces of paper which are then to be put into wooden boxes, to be counted by volunteers in a method that has scarcely changed since the introduction of the secret ballot in 1872.[26]

Moreover, even as a chamber or physical space, the Westminster bi-cameral parliamentary system has become irrelevant, harking back to a pre-industrial form of decision-making. Whilst most people are familiar with PIN numbers, MPs continue to pass into the lobbies so that the tellers can record their votes.[27] To this end, Graham Allen, a former Labour Party spokesman on the media, has argued that the multi-media may establish a new political culture by removing the 'middle-man' of representational assemblies to allow the electorate to input their views within national, regional and local parliaments.[28]

ICTs may significantly alter the future of democratic politics. Geoff

Mulgan, founder of the *Demos* think tank, argues that political decision-making exists within a different multi-media universe:

> ... what makes our time so complex is that these shifts in media forms are now accelerating far ahead of the ability of political institutions to keep up, as new generations are brought up on computer games [and soon virtual reality] each of which carries with it quite distinct cognitive structures. It is not that they will displace the old media, or that linear logics of print culture will disappear altogether. It is rather that new generations will make much stronger demands on politics to deliver what they get elsewhere: not just monologues of 20th-century politics, but rather a politics that is much more personal, confessional and interrogative.[29]

This development has been welcomed by *Demos* and incorporated in its goal of 'Lean Democracy'. The current arrangements of democratic behaviour have failed the citizenry as the political system is bureaucratic and unaccountable to the public. In order to transform this process, it will be necessary to make the democratic system more transparent, responsive, effective and accountable. Therefore, the governed will have greater control over the governors. Thus, *Demos* argues that there should be wholesale redefinitions of politicians' performances; a combination of representative and direct democracy; the creation of 'reflective' bodies such as voter juries and deliberative polling groups; the establishment of an independent election regulator, Ofelect, to scrutinize elections; a raft of reforms to ensure better training for politicians; and a constituent charter. Most specifically, ICTs will allow for '... a more participative, responsible democracy which will use the new technologies of push button democracy.'[30]

Mulgan further contends that political parties are irrelevant and stresses that new forms of political decision-making will offset partisan decline. He has argued that with the loss of ideological certainties and class identities, the democratic process is fragmenting. The significant decline in party attachments has been accompanied by a reduction in party membership. These imperatives challenge the viability of representative democracy which is suffering from an irreversible decay. In the future, 'party-free' politics will reflect the changing nature of political activism and incorporate communications technologies to facilitate plebiscites, agoras, referenda and electronic town hall meetings.

Therefore, there has been an implosion of virtual and real forms of political activism and institutions. In particular, proponents of 'Lean Democracy' and 'Anti-Partyism' place their core emphasis on individual rights over the promotion of collective forms of action. As membership parties decline, technological reform has become the panacea for post-steam-age democracy. With the expansion of global communications links, individuals may be able to contact an infinite series of on-line correspondents and enjoy access to information which had been reserved for political, social or economic elites. In turn, citizen participation can be measured through teledemocracy, deliberative opinion polls and referenda. As Arthur Lipow and Patrick Seyd comment: 'The age of the individual citizen, at last unshackled from the constraints of organizations, has dawned. He or she is able to participate in politics without the mediation of now outmoded institutions such as political parties.'[31]

The Limitations of Techno-Populist Libertarianism

These visions of individualistic economic and political democratization, have been founded on a particular understanding of technological change. Technology is seen as a rational agent which, since it is independent of the centres of economic or political power, can orchestrate reform. John Street has noted that the advocates of ICTs perceive technology as a 'neutral' form which will 'fix' democratic behaviour. However, as Street further comments, the relationship between technological reform, the distribution of information, the production of knowledge and citizen empowerment is far more problematic:

> technical fixes are only 'fixes' because of the way the problem is defined. They do not constitute 'the' answer but 'an' answer. Technical fixes are less about fixing a problem, rather they are *imposing a particular definition* of what the problem is (and to which the technology represents a happy solution). If democracy's problems are practical, then technology may solve them, but if they are not, then technology merely reproduces them in a different form. The technical fix is, in fact, a 'political' solution, in the sense that it seeks to propagate a particular view of the world and of the methods appropriate to ordering it.[32]

We have to consider the economic, political and social forces which have shaped the utilization of technology. This realization has led to significant critiques of electronic democracy. As technology is not an agency but is conditional on those who govern and orchestrate its usage, our attention returns to a fundamental problem – that the new electronic technologies promote the interests of the powerful. For some, the arguments and practices that have been attached to electronic democracy reflect the power of dominant groups, who intend to depoliticize and deskill citizens.[33] For instance, John Gray argues that technological reforms have not created new societies, solved intractable difficulties or redistributed wealth. Instead, they alter the terms for economic or political organization as the uses 'to which new technologies are put depend on the distribution of power and access to resources, and on the level of cultural and moral development in society.'[34] Gray's criticisms suggests that a quick, technological fix will not empower citizens. Rather, the public's attention is falsely distracted from state and capitalist power.

Although ICTs have been represented as a largely anarchic, dirt-cheap, uncensored forum, dominated by amateurs and enthusiasts, in reality governments have allowed media monopolies, computer and cable companies to structure the market. The political economy of the Information Superhighway has been characterized by deal-making between multi-national telecommunications organizations, mass media corporations, and hard and soft-ware computer manufacturers. In turn, this may mean that ICTs replicate many of the flaws which have appeared in traditional media economies. These monopolistic organizations are using the new communication outlets to disseminate more of the same to a wider audience, with interactivity limited to channel selection. Robert W. McChesney compares the evolution of the internet with the development of the now marginalized American public service broadcasting system:

> ... it was the educational broadcasters who played an enormous role in developing AM broadcasting in the 1920s, and then FM radio and even UHF television in the 1940s and the 1950s. In each case, once it became clear that money could be made, the educators were displaced and the capitalists seized the reins. Arguably, too, this looks like the fate of the internet, which has been pioneered as a public service by the non-profit sector, with government subsidies, until the point when capital decides to take over and relegate the pioneers to the margins.[35]

The individualistic or libertarian view of economic reform is built on the fallacy that the market will act as a perfect distributor of information and communication resources. This ignores market closure and substitutes consumerism for citizens' rights. The assumptions which have underpinned the futurists' discourse about democratic reforms to working practices, concerning the more efficient utilization of information to create wealth and sustain labour flexibility, are founded upon an inequitable distribution of communication resources. For instance, the very construct of a 'knowledge entrepreneur' would suggest that *control* over the distribution of information must be held by the producers of the communications market. (How else could surplus profit be extracted?) Instead of 'Prosumerism', the division between producers and consumers will broaden as the distribution of information will be centralized and access commodified.

In this context, Graham Murdock distinguishes between citizenship and consumerism.[36] The former presupposes collective endeavour in the quest for equality and fraternity as well as individual liberty. Alternatively, consumerism forces the individuals to use private solutions to public problems through the purchasing of commodities. It urges people to spend their way out of trouble rather than demand social change and improve provision. It redefines the nature of citizenship so that it 'becomes less a collective, political activity than an individual, economic activity – the right to pursue one's interests, without hindrance, in the marketplace.'[37] Markets provide the consumer with a variety of rival commodities, but can not bestow rights. The citizen is excluded from the market's redistribution of wealth and from the income which allows entrance to the market. An *information rich and poor* may be created as universality of service is no longer guaranteed. Therefore, as material inequalities stem the individual's access to goods and services which are required measures for citizenship, political rights are sacrificed.

As a consequence, the reliance on libertarian individualism is problematic. For labour, whether at work or at politics, power can only be drawn from organization. If aggregated power is dismantled in favour of 'Third Wave' market-liberalism, individual expression is undermined as people become powerless and atomized. Concurrently, elite control is consolidated. With regard to labour practices, we should remain aware of the restrictions which face the workforce rather than the mooted freedoms. For example, Bill Gates' Microsoft campuses in Seattle have been noted for their Orwellian use of ID cards, excessive bureaucracy, differentiation between official staff and 'perma-lancer' employees, jealously guarded hierarchies, non-recognition of trade unions and corporate working cultures.[38]

Similarly, the disaggregation of popular forms of collective political behaviour, which are resistant to elite control, may undermine individual empowerment, despite the current discourses concerning direct democracy. The substitution for legislatures, political parties and representational systems of individualistic and deliberative forms of decision-making, including polls and juries, may appear to close the democratic deficit between the governed and the governors. Undoubtedly, the present systems contain elitist closure and hierarchical control, most especially in the structures of many contemporary political parties. However, another form of elite manipulation may be instigated as appropriate democratic organizations, designed within the workplace to defend employees' interests and to establish grassroot forms of politicization, are dismantled and give way to individualistic and atomized responses to the new communications medium.[39]

In particular, these approaches fail to recognize the issue of class. While it is correct to perceive that class divisions have altered, this does not mean that they have disappeared. The utilization of technology by elites has shaped the organization of power relations in society and, currently and in the future, will encourage global exploitation of communication and information technologies. Thus, the libertarian view of information technology does not distinguish between cultural differences, political antagonisms, and opposing interests based on immense economic inequalities. If information and knowledge resources are not equally distributed, due to the concentration of production and limited citizen access, the divide between information 'haves' and 'have nots' will deepen. Thus, any notion of global citizenship (founded on freedom of speech, complete access, the comprehension of relevant information to create knowledge rights, and fair representation) is undermined. In effect, a technocratic-elite *virtual* ruling class will hold the reins over the multimedia.

Collective Approaches to the Information Superhighway and ICT Policy-Making

Whilst accepting many of these criticisms, we should refrain from becoming too deterministic in our response to technology. John Street suggests that technological change is not simply a product of economic or political choice. Technology has its own momentum which will create many unanticipated consequences:

> Though we can identify the interests and choices around a technology, they do not automatically become the authors of that technology. The technology is not something that exists as a simple object for our use. It acts to structure our choices and preferences, but not in a wholly deterministic way. The relationship is in constant flux: political processes shape technology; and it then shapes politics.[40]

Therefore, it would be incorrect to perceive ICTs as being inherently monolithic or anti-democratic. Although it is necessary to address the economic, political and ideological forces which have 'pushed' technological reform in a particular direction, we should recognize that these imperatives are not fixed or insurmountable.

The changes within the distribution of information can be positively activated if they are tied to 'organized publics' who will provide a meaningful economic, social and political context for reform. Thus, rather than the individualistic notions of political activity, which have dominated the current development of the internet, new ways should be sought out to utilize the information technologies so that they can allow for collective forms of democratic behaviour. To this end, it may be suggested that reforms within working practices and political participation will be successfully negotiated if they are incorporated into appropriate forms of democratic organization such as trade unions, political parties or workers' councils. Moreover, local or city-level initiatives, rooted in communal traditions, may also successfully advance on-line activism. Instead of the top-down plebiscitarian democracy advanced by the techno-populists, ICTs could be employed to advance collective democratic organization by generalizing information and creating an informed citizenship. In turn, the collective usages of technologies may provide us with previously unforeseen concepts and practices of electronic democracy which will encourage greater communal linkages and broader methods for political expression.

For instance, Anne-Marie Gingras has identified several phenomena that have emerged from the entanglement of social and technical logics with on-line activism. First, social movements can be successfully modified as the collective usage of new technologies may promote alliances or joint actions with allies. In such a manner, strategic reforms in resource allocation should facilitate greater collective activity. Secondly, collective on-line activism can enhance public discussion by setting the political agenda and producing reactions amongst social and political actors. Thirdly, this use of ICTs may directly link into the pursuit of public and company policy.[41] Further, as Manuel Castells argues:

> These ... movements spreading throughout the world, are ending the neo-liberal fantasy of creating a new global economy independent of society by using computer architecture. The grand exclusionary scheme (explicit or implicit) of concentrating information, production and markets in a valuable segment of population, disposing of the rest in different forms, more or less humane according to each society's temper, is triggering, in Touraine's expression, a '*grand refus*'. But the transformation of this rejection into the reconstruction of new forms of social control over new forms of capitalism, globalized and informationalized, requires the processing of social movements' demands by the political system and the institutions of the state. The ability, or inability, of the state to cope with the conflicting logics of global capitalism, identity-based social movements, and the defensive movements from workers and consumers, will largely condition the future of society in the twenty-first century.[42]

Consequently, within this dialectic of collective mobilization and technological adaptation, it remains to be seen how public policy can contribute. Presently, the American government and, to a lesser extent, the EC have advocated the private expansion of the market through deregulation and minimalistic state intervention. In the summer of 1997, President Clinton, after attempting interventionist policies through decency amendments and 'no-export' rules, has turned *volte-face* by announcing a hands-off role for the state concerning the internet. The US policy document 'A Framework for Global Economic Commerce' proposes no more than a basic 'legal environment' allowing for blanket deregulation, corporate cooperation and the establishment of the internet as a tariff-free zone. In such a manner, Clinton hopes to place America at the centre of the global virtual economy and redefine the role of governments in world affairs. This initiative has been welcomed by anti-statist libertarians such as Douglas Rushkoff:

> Clinton understands that for the internet to become a level playing field cyberspace must be deregulated and demystified. Fewer laws, open standards and the promotion of literacy are crucial components. … The Clinton administration has taken its first baby steps towards relinquishing control of the future because it sees that no individual person, company, or government is capable of commandeering the human mission.[43]

Alternatively, in France, the Balladur and Juppe governments have pursued an interventionist *grand programme* which reflects the French state's original motivating role in developing high technologies such as Minitel.[44] French governments have developed strategies through which *inforoutes* may be employed to encourage economic growth and further the citizen's democratic rights. In particular, there has been an emphasis on the facilitation of 'quality of life', in which new working patterns will allow for greater efficiency in the distribution of national employment, and the increased 'equality of access' enables a broader distribution of information and knowledge.[45]

Currently, the British Labour Party's ICT policy proposals are characterized by an uneasy compromise between state provision and market-led economics. For example, British Telecom (BT) has agreed to establish fixed rate usage for schools, after the prompting of the regulator OfTel and competition from cable companies. Therefore, in light of the American and French models, questions need to be asked about how the British government can provide an appropriate policy framework through which public initiatives, encouraging the collective usage of ICTs, can be delivered. It is our belief that the state should have a significant role in creating and sustaining a level playing field through public investment to allow popular usage of information services and, by extension, the protection of citizens' knowledge rights. What follows is an outline for consideration.

A Public Service Model of Information and Communication Technologies

The final section offers a public service model for the economic and political organization of ICTs founded on collective principles.[46] In order to establish a popular and adaptable 'bottom-up' model, it will be necessary to establish an appropriate framework through which public intervention can be made. At its core, a new information communications infrastucture must provide universality of access across urban and rural communities. Ideally, this should be independent of income and could be developed through a public national communications grid.[47]

We should recognize that there will be significant difficulties in creating and sustaining a public communication network. In current circumstances, it would be financially prohibitive for any government to fully or partially re-nationalize BT due to the loss in corporation tax. Further, such a policy would mean that BT's ability to raise cash for future investment would be harmed. This means that the telecommunications hardware corporation will have to remain a private monopoly. A more achievable goal will be to enhance the public regulation and taxation of the social communications market-place.

To this end, detailed licensing may be used to control prices, profitability and services. For instance, there should be a continuation of fixed rate prices for internet users, graduated in accordance with income, and at cheaper rates for public institutions such as schools, colleges and libraries. It will also be necessary to bring in more effective regulations over BT to produce substantial cuts in current line rentals. Moreover, regulators must ensure that there will be a wide variety of producers, providing a plurality of diverse opinions. Therefore, significant cross-media and multi-media ownership rules will be required. In addition, national competition policies would have to be tightened to ensure anti-trust regulations. With regard to software, private service providers will be required to keep charges down to a negotiable minimum. They may continue to maintain profitability through selling advertising space and charging competitive rates for business usage. The regulator, however, will have minimal content objectives, beyond standards of taste and decency (which, in themselves, will be difficult enough to pursue).

It will be necessary for national regulatory bodies to form strategic alliances with each other and be governed under a general European Union-wide supra-national organization. Thus, local, national and regional regulation must be employed to ensure equality of access in the distribution of information and knowledge across societies. This proposal could be made workable by following Richard Collins and Cristina Murroni's advocacy of a single communications regulator for all services – OfCom. – This body would be responsible for licensing services, for positively ensuring the democratic distribution of communication and would be open and accountable to the public: '[it will)] be informed by the principle of encouraging and ensuring that UK citizens and consumers have ready access to a choice of authoritative and impartial sources and to investigative, iconoclastic and innovative material, even if this will inevitably offend some people.'[48]

Alongside regulation, monies could be raised through increased taxation on the media and computer corporations who want to exploit the communications market-place. Previously, these companies have circumvented taxes by claiming their transnational status. To close such a loop-hole, it will be necessary to redefine the national status of these organizations and enter into agreements with other states and supra-national bodies such as the European Commission. Further, additional revenues could be raised through a virtual tax on websites and service providers. This would mean a substantive rise in entry costs, so tax rebates would become available to individual knowledge producers and smaller service providers.

The virtual taxation system could also provide the foundation for a knowledge economy which is built on, and will sustain, collective working practices. First, if ICTs are to encourage greater growth and create new employment opportunities, it will be necessary to establish a skilled workforce. Therefore, the state taxation could fund public training schemes in educational institutions. Secondly, once the jobs have been established, the need to maintain labour protection rights through collective mobilization and unionization is vital. The dangers of creating private rights and undermining labour power, in the name of globalization, have become apparent. Thus, information technology workers should sustain proper working rights and cannot be perceived as a 'flexible' labour force who may be moved and downsized at will. Thirdly, through training and labour protection, an appropriate craft-base will be established which will encourage further initiatives, new forms of instruction and different cognitive approaches to the available technology.

Conclusion

It has been predicted that significant reforms may accompany the widespread application of ICTs into the third millenium. They have the potential to open up new areas for information distribution; they may decentralize the dissemination of communications; they allow for new opportunities for economic growth and can remove the apparent democratic deficit between governors and governed in advanced societies.

Within think tanks and amongst legislators in the US and Britain, many of the principal arguments and policy initatives concerning the Information Superhighway have been founded on an individualistic or libertarian justification of a free communications market-place (akin to the eighteenth-century conception of a free press market). It is suggested that these new technologies will be a panacea for economic development and political reform. In America, these ideologies have been sustained amongst the Silicon Valley technocratic elites, by futurists and, most especially, by President Bill Clinton's adminstration. His announcement of only minimalistic state intervention regarding the development of the internet has been hailed by the techno-populist libertarians as a victory and an admission that the state will have a limited, indeed marginal, role in establishing the future direction of the communications industry.

There are significant problems with these prognostications. Not least is that they ignore the centres of economic, social and political power in national, regional and global economies. The libertarian responses are fuelled by the belief that technology is an agency which will inevitably produce societal change. Several criticisms can be made. First, the notion that self-regulating networks of companies will equitably share information and knowledge rights is built on a misplaced faith in the freedom of the communications market – the belief that this market is established by freely associating individuals who can directly produce and consume information. However, the ICT market-place is being built on closure and the political economy of the multi-media is being characterized by corporate synergy between the media, telecommunications and computer organizations.

Secondly, this leads into a misguided view that the individual 'knowledge entrepreneur' will become the central unit for economic productivity and will allow for growth in the virtual economy. Ironically, despite the rhetoric which suggests we are moving from an industrial to information economy, this return to *individualism* refers to a pre-industrial conception of the polity. It ignores the networks of integrated power which exist between the political, economic and social elites Moreover, it fails to address the oligopolistic and monopolistic patterns of multi-media ownership and control which are being established.

Thirdly, technology has been used to justify the replacement of individual citizens' rights with their ability to consume information. In effect, the public nature of information will be privatized, thereby removing universality of access as a principle and suggesting that income alone should determine the dissemination of communication resources in the twenty-first century. This perspective reflects a specific view of the interrelations between information, communication, knowledge and power. In effect, it is claimed that political participation is guaranteed through the purchasing and selling of information. In such a manner, new forms of political association may emerge which defy the previous institutional constraints. Individuals will be confident to exercise their franchise in the future form of electronic democracy, in which referenda may replace representative assemblies and collective political practices will wane. However, we would contend that such an individualistic and decentralized form of information limits the distribution of knowledge and participatory rights. Instead of there being an equitable distribution of information, these arguments are pitched on the desirability of audience fragmentation. Therefore, individual liberation masks a true picture of limited choice in the consumption of information services.

In the light of these criticisms, it is apparent that collective responses to the Information Technologies are required, to enable people to enjoy their cultural rights in a social communications market-place. These comprise entitlements in four main areas: information; knowledge; representation; and communication. Information rights enable people to determine personal and political judgements effectively, and to analyse the actions of public and private agencies with significant power over their lives. As information is of only limited use in its raw state, it needs to be contextualized so that its connotations are understood and contested. In turn, knowledge rights 'promote these processes by underwriting the public's access to the widest possible range of interpretation, debate and explanation.'[49] This will encourage greater analysis of the issues within public forums, meaning that citizens can directly enter into meaningful transactions of information and effect the policy process. Such a development has already occurred in embryonic forms in city and communal based web-sites. For example, there have been successful locally-based initiatives in Amsterdam and Santa Monica. These projects have aimed to close the gap between politicians and the populace by expanding the amount of available information, promoting greater access, encouraging participation, allowing for more transparency in policy-making and pursuing shared forms of decision-making.[50] To establish such a social market-place, Andrew Calabrese and Mark Borchert are right to say:

> The global neoliberal tendency to conceive of communicative rights as negative rights is powerful, but we conclude that any meaningful affirmation of democratic principles demands a state committed to revisable consensus on how to promote civic competence in a world of rapid technological change in the means of communication.[51]

Therefore, a state-directed public service model for ICTs may allow for increased participation and more effective forms of democratic transparency. It would maintain universality, equitably distribute information and be regulated to maintain political independence. The system should be orchestrated to enforce appropriate labour rights to encourage new working practices. Concurrently, there should be the incorporation of ICTs into both the established and alternative mechanisms of political participation, organization and assembly. The technologies can be employed positively to reform the opaque nature of decision-making and may stem many of the abuses inherent in the structure of the British government.

Thus, there should be real openness in our response to the challenges of the technology. The need to activate ICTs for social welfare stands at the core of many of the current debates concerning globalization, the public sphere and the role of the state in the next century. It is vital that we remain vigilant in our anticipation of how democratic principles can be established through the multi-media. These rights have to be fought for and cannot be perceived as a given. Otherwise, the current media, telecommunication and computer 'knowledge entrepreneurs' will assume them. At the moment, the development of ICTs presents national and international governments with significant challenges. Consequently, it is our responsibility, as citizens, to ensure that current and future generations may use these electronic communication technologies to enhance, rather than diminish, societal rights.

NOTES

1. John Frow, 'Information Bought and Sold', *New Left Review,* No.219 (Sept.–Oct. 1996), p.89.
2. This essay focuses on economic governance and political participation. However, the impact of ICTs on democratic practices is a potentially limitless subject, much in the same way as the internet provides an infinite resource for information and communication. For a useful introduction to the many issues surrounding the Information Superhighway, see Brian D. Loader (ed.), *The Governance of Cyberspace: Politics, Technology and Global Restructuring* (London and New York; Routledge, 1997).
3. Charles Leadbetter, 'A slice of the Silicon pie: Californina's success into a knowledge based economy has important lessons for new Labour', *New Statesman* (23 May 1997), pp.28–9.
4. S. Flowers, 'Want it ? Well Gopher it?', *The Guardian* (5 Aug. 1993).
5. K. Laudon, *Communication Technology and Democratic Participation* (New York: Praeger Publishers, 1977).
6. Ivan Horrocks and Lawrence Pratchett, 'Electronic Democracy: Central Themes and Issues', in Joni Lovenduski and Jeffrey Stanyer (eds.), *Contemporary Political Studies*, Volume 3 (PSA, University of York: 18–20 April 1995), p.1219.
7. John Street, 'Remote Control: Politics, Technology and Culture', in Ian Hampsher-Monk and Jeffrey Stanyer (eds.), *Contemporary Political Studies*, Vol.1 (PSA, University of Glasgow, 10–12 April 1996), p.505.
8. Nicholas Negroponte, *Being Digital* (London: Hodder & Stoughton, Coronet Books, 1995).
9. Nick Stevenson, *Understanding Media Cultures: Social Theory and Mass Communication* (London: Sage Publishers, 1995), p.119.
10. Marshall McLuhan quoted in Christopher Reed, 'Inter Next World', *The Guardian,* (20 March 1995) (Section 2), p.15.

11. John Street, 'Remote Control? Politics, Technology and "Electronic Democracy"', *European Journal of Communication*, Sage Publications, Vol.12, No.1 (1997), p.30.
12. Ibid., p.30.
13. Carl Steadman, 'Netizen Caned: Carl Steadman on the Failings of "Way New" Journalism', 6 March 1996 (down-loaded from the Internet website 'Netizen Caned').
14. Alvin Toffler, *The Third Wave* (London: Pan Books, 1980), pp.291–2.
15. Leadbetter, *New Statesman*, p.29.
16. Ibid., pp.28–9.
17. Ibid. p.29.
18. Marcus Pollett, 'Challenging Martin Bangemann', *Electronic Government International*, GP Magazines & Exhibitions Ltd., Dec. 1996, p.32.
19. Tony Blair, 'Help Speed Britain Down the Superhighway', *The Evening Standard*, (17 July 1995), p.9.
20. Jon Katz,'Guilty', *Wired* (Sept. 1995), p.100.
21. Andrew Chadwick, 'Ideologies, Communication and Public Discourse', in Jeffrey Stanyer and Gerry Stoker (eds.), *Contemporary Political Studies 1997*, Volume One (PSA, Blackwell, 1997), p.72.
22. Noam Chomsky, (interviews with David Barsamian), *Keeping the Rabble in Line*, (Edinburgh: AK Press, 1994), p.148.
23. Street, *Contemporary Political Studies 1996* (Volume One), p.505.
24. Howard Rheingold, *The Virtual Community: Finding Connection in a Computerized World*, (London: Secker & Warburg, 1994), p.268.
25. For a detailed consideration of direct democracy, see Ian Budge, *The New Challenge of Direct Democracy* (Cambridge: Polity, 1996).
26. Andrew Adonis and Geoff Mulgan, 'Back to Greece: The Scope for Direct Democracy', *Demos*, Issue 3 (1994), p.7.
27. Ibid., p.7.
28. Graham Allen, '"Come the Revolution", Idées Fortes', *Wired* (Sept. 1995), 1.05, pp.46–8.
29. Geoff Mulgan, 'Party-Free Politics', *New Statesman and Society* (15 April 1994), p.18.
30. 'Lean Democracy', *Demos*, Issue 3 (1994), p.1.
31. Arthur Lipow and Patrick Seyd, 'The Politics of Anti-Partyism', *Parliamentary Affairs*, Vol.49, No.2 (April 1996), pp.273–4.
32. Street, *European Journal of Communication*, p.34.
33. Ibid., p 34.
34. John Gray, 'The Sad Side of Cyberspace', *The Guardian* (10 April 1995), p.18. Similar views are expressed by David Lyon, *The Electronic Eye* (Cambridge: Polity Press, 1994). Clifford Stoll has provided a critical account of the nature of the information on the internet in Stoll, *Silicon Snake Oil; Second Thoughts on the Information Superhighway* (London: Macmillan, 1995). Further, dystopian critiques have led to technophobic responses being advocated as the only acceptable form of resistance. For further details, see Kirkpatrick Sale's neo-Luddite arguments in Sale, *Rebels Against the Future; The Luddites and their War on Industrial Revolution* (London: Quartet Books, 1995).
35. Robert W. McChesney, 'Public Broadcasting in the Age of Communication Revolution', *Monthly Review*, Vol.47, No.7 (Dec. 1995), p.9.
36. Graham Murdock, 'Citizens, consumers and public culture', in Micheal Skovmand and Kim Christian Schroder (eds.), *Media Cultures: Reappraising Transnational Media* (London and New York, Routledge, 1992), p.19.
37. M.G. Dietz, 'Context is All. Feminism and Theories of Citizenship', *Daedalus*, Fall 1987, p.5.
38. Bob Mack, 'Inside Bill Gates's Media Empire', *The Guardian* (Media Guardian), (9 June 1997), p.2.
39. Lipow and Seyd, *Parliamentary Affairs*, p.281–2.
40. Street, *European Journal of Communications*, p.35
41. Anne-Marie Gingras, 'Internet and Democracy: What Impact Does the Internet Have on Collective Action?', paper presented to the European Consortium for Political Research Workshop on New Media and Political Communcation, 27 Feb. to 4 March 1997, pp.7–8.

42. Manuel Castells, *The Power of Identity: The Information Age: Economy, Society and Culture Volume II* (Oxford: Blackwell Publishers, 1997), p.109.

43. Douglas Rushkoff, 'Cyberlife: Collective Acts', *The Guardian* (OnLine), (9 July 1997), p.7. For further details see Victor Keegan, 'Economic Notebook: Lords of the Net Will Inherit Earth', *The Guardian* (7 July 1997).

44. For further details on France, see Hugh Dauncey, 'France and the Information Superhighway', *Politics,* Vol.16, No.2 (May 1996), pp.87–94.

45 Ibid., pp.90–1.

46. See Mark Wheeler, *Politics and the Mass Media* (Oxford: Blackwell, 1997), pp.103–5.

47. At the time of writing, the Labour government has produced a White Paper entitled *Excellence in Schools* proposing a 'National Grid for Learning' to wire all schools and libraries onto the Internet. For further details see Martin Bright, 'IT Revolution in the Classroom: But Will "National Grid" Produce a Generation of Young Cyber-Potatoes?', *The Observer* (13 July 1997).

48. Richard Collins and Cristina Murroni, *New Media, New Policies: Media and Communciations Strategies for the Future* (Cambridge: Polity Press, 1996), p.181.

49. Graham Murdock, 'Money Talks', in Stuart Hood (ed.), *Behind the Screens: The Structure of British Television in the Nineties* (London: Lawrence & Wishart, 1994), p.158.

50. For further details, see Kees Brants, Martine Huizenga and Reineke van Meerten, 'The New Canals of Amsterdam: An Exercise in Local Electronic Democracy', and William H. Dutton, 'Network Rules of Order: Regulating Speech in Public Electronic Fora', in *Media, Culture and Society*, Vol.18 (1996), pp.233–47 and 269–90.

51. Andrew Calabrese and Mark Borchert, 'Prospects for Electronic Democracy in the USA: Rethinking Communication and Social Policy', ibid., p.265.

Concluding Comments

VICKY RANDALL

These concluding comments return to the central issue raised in the Introduction, the interrelationship of democracy, the democratizing process and the media. As we have seen, this is a huge and complex subject, made the more so by the intrinsic open-endedness of one of its central terms, democracy. Each one of the studies approaches this issue in its own way, whether in terms of geographical focus, the forms of media selected for consideration or the conception of democracy that informs the analysis. As such, each sheds its own particular light. But it may also be possible to discern some more general themes of relevance to our introductory questions.

The essays in this volume span the whole spectrum from established democracies to societies where demands for democratization still run the risk of fierce reprisals. They also span societies very differently endowed in terms of the range and distribution of communications media. At one extreme is Mali, with an average literacy rate of 29 per cent, where the radio has only very recently become the key medium of communication. At the other, in the United States, already by 1960 there were televisions in nine out of ten households. Such heterogeneity is not only an opportunity to make comparisons but a reason to proceed with caution.

The Media's Contribution to Democracy

None the less we find a striking tendency for the authors' assessments of both the actual and the potential contribution of the media to democracy to be most positive in relation to societies where democratization is least advanced. It seems that the further democratization has proceeded, the more negative, or at least sceptical, the evaluation. Mervin's account of the American media is particularly pessimistic. Here, while newspapers potentially could provide in-depth news coverage, they have been influenced by television which in any case has long displaced newspapers as the main source of political information. Viewing rates are high, averaging seven hours a day since the early 1980s. The weakness of political parties, exacerbated by the proliferation of presidential primaries from the 1970s, makes the media's contribution to democracy potentially crucial. There is no question that the media are powerful and in some cases their intervention may be decisive, but the 'televization' of American politics has in many respects been harmful to the democratic process. Through trivializing and oversimplifying politics, treating elections like horse-races, exaggerating the power of the President as an individual and obscuring the functioning of Congress, television has helped to debase the process of public deliberation and has fostered public cynicism.

This negative picture is curiously echoed in Kuhn's account of the media's role in the Fifth French Republic. His central argument is that the ability of the French media to function effectively as a 'public sphere' in the Habermasian sense has been undermined over this period. This is despite the ending of the state's television monopoly in 1981. As in the United States, television has become the French public's single most important source of political information, but like Mervin, Kuhn judges its effect on political communication to have been largely harmful, with its tendency to personalize politics, reduce political discourse to 'soundbites', and replace old-style debates with more or less entertaining spectacle. However, while Mervin tends to explain television's effect on political communication largely by reference to its character as a medium, Kuhn puts more emphasis on the consequences of economic liberalization, 'the commodification of much media product in an increasingly commercialized sector of economic activity' – a point that will be returned to later.

In Kuhn's account also the direction of influence is not all one way. Whereas Mervin maintains that American television has further undermined the cohesion of the national political parties, in France political elites have to a degree shown themselves adept in handling the new media. This is reminiscent of the observation by Gurevitch and Blumler on the frequently all too cosy 'symbiosis' of politicians and journalists, where politicians need access to the media but journalists also need access to politicians for news and comment :

> For their part, politicians start to think, speak and behave like journalists – a tendency epitomised by presidential statements couched in one-liners designed to guide and ease the work of newspaper headline writers and to give television reporters pithy ten-second soundbites. For their part, journalists, despite their professional values, may be reduced to virtual channels of propaganda.[1]

In France, political elites have managed, most of the time, to remain key definers of the political agenda. One corollary has been the rise of communications consultants, like Jacques Séguéla, corresponding to Gurevitch and Blumler's concept of 'source professionalization' or the 'ever deeper and more extensive involvement in political message making of publicity advisers, public relations experts, campaign management consultants …'.[2]

There is an interesting parallel here with Dominic Wring's analysis of the way that in Britain the 'New Labour' party leadership have made use of the media – though in this case the focus is primarily on the broadly Labour-supporting national press and how the party leadership has used it in order to establish its own agenda within the party. Specifically, instead of the traditional recourse to movement papers like *Tribune*, party leaders used papers such *The Guardian, The Independent, The Observer* and *Daily Mirror* which together are read by more Labour party members than all party publications combined, to win acceptance for their 'modernizing' agenda. But this is in the broader context of an increasingly media-conscious leadership, amongst whom 'spin doctors' like Peter Mandelson have exerted a growing influence.

The democratic potential of the new Information Communication Technologies (ICTs) and in particular the internet is considered by Mark Wheeler, in an analysis that is placed towards the end by virtue of its glimpse into the future. He points first to the tremendously contrasting evaluations of their actual and potential contribution to democratic reform, ranging from the optimism of the free market 'techno-populists' to gloomy predictions that such technologies will simply become new tools for the most powerful business interests. He rightly argues that we should avoid excessive determinism; the contribution of ICTs depends on what societies decide to use them for. However, we are left with a distinct and depressing sense that in prevailing political circumstances the ICTs are most unlikely to be the bearers of a new democratic order.

Such generally sombre analyses in the context of advanced democracies, with their emphasis on the different ways in which the communications media serve to reinforce dominant political and commercial interests, is in considerable contrast with the 'upbeat' tone of assessments where democracy is fragile or yet to emerge. Thus in Mali a few local radio stations contributed crucially to the process of transition between the fall of Traoré and the 1992 general election; more generally the radio stations that have proliferated since 1991 when a multi-party democracy was officially established, have consciously seen themselves as agents of democratization.

In urban areas the radios tend to understand democracy in terms of party competition and in some cases are themselves vehicles of opposition to the ruling party. In rural areas, where radios tend to be run by local community organizations, democracy is understood in a more developmental sense to be about 'empowering' and giving a voice to the 'little person' in the face of the corrupt official, and to women and the young in the face of gerontocracy. Nor do these remain pious intentions on the part of broadcasters; the radios inspire 'wild enthusiasm'. Even in rural areas, where inevitably it takes time to overcome inequality of access to radio and people's deep mistrust and fear of officialdom, Mary Myers cites the findings of a (rare instance of) an impact study, which suggested that the radio in question had greatly increased local understanding of a government programme for decentralization. Also it emboldened such groups as women and youths to stand up for their rights.

In the Middle East both the numbers of television viewers and the channels for viewers to choose between have increased dramatically over the last seven years, spurred on by international news coverage of the Gulf War. Annabelle Sreberny-Mohammadi clearly recognizes the need for caution in any attempt to evaluate the democratic implications of this 'changing televisual landscape'. She stresses the internal heterogeneity of the region and is also sensitive to the dangers of imposing western-determined criteria of what democracy is or how it should be attained. None the less, there are increasing pressures upon state authorities coming both from outside the region and up from within to widen political participation and extend political freedom and democracy. Amongst these the media are likely to play a major role. Although many state authorities continue to seek to control the dissemination of any news that could be politically subversive, and to regulate transmission of culturally sensitive material, such regulation becomes increasingly difficult.

Moreover, Sreberny-Mohammadi suggests ways in which television as a whole not simply news coverage may be contributing to the emergence of a more democratic 'culture'. First, like Myers, she focuses on media impact on gender relations, pointing out that in the Middle East, where traditionally women have been largely excluded from public space, the penetration of television into the home already constitutes a significant subversion of this public–private divide. Secondly, although recognizing the extent to which television is a vehicle of (western) materialist and commercial values and has been identified as a threat to democratic processes in western industrial societies, she points out that such values are not in any case new to the Middle East. She suggests that these commercial media 'might bring more news, information and debate than many state systems had previously allowed' and that moreover there might be limits to the extent to which a population can be addressed solely as consumers without encouraging any other forms of participation in public life or decision-making.

In a different way, Richard Cullen and Hua Ling Fu are also optimistic about the media's role in expanding the rights which are a forerunner and aspect of democracy in mainland China. They conclude that 'perhaps the most important new factor in effecting positive change' has been the growth in communications technology. However this change is in the context of the accelerating drive for economic liberalization since 1979. It is this process which has reduced the state's ability to control media coverage of all but the most politically sensitive issues, as the government's resource-base dwindles and as established media lose government subsidies and face increasing competition from the rapidly expanding range of commercial media outlets. We shall return to the question of economic liberalization in due course. But note here that such a conclusion seems to contrast significantly with Garry Rodan's analysis, which implies that the commercial media, including, most depressingly, the international media, have been prepared to acquiesce in the relatively repressive media policies associated with the governments in Singapore and Malaysia. However, we might also suggest that to the extent Cullen and Fu equate increasing press freedom with unrestricted advertising and the publication of pornographic and violent material, the potential contradictions within the concept of democracy and specifically the issue of whose voices are freely expressed, are underlined. Is freedom to publish pornographic material such an unqualified advance?

Assessments of the media's contribution in the latter stages of democratic transformation in Taiwan and in Poland, could be described as cautiously optimistic.

Gary and Ming-Yeh Rawnsley contend that the relative smoothness and lack of violent conflict in Taiwan's transition process have owed much to the part played by its highly developed mass media, together with high literacy levels. Even before the lifting of martial law in 1987, 'illegal' media were important in sustaining both a tradition of criticizing government policy and the existence, albeit severely circumscribed, of local electoral opposition. Subsequently the liberalized media helped publicize political reforms, gave a powerful voice to the political opposition and exposed electoral malpractice and corruption. The media themselves have become a political issue around which opposition groups have campaigned. Though recognizing that it needs to be complemented by vigorous national, and mainstream broadcasting, the Rawnsleys are especially positive about the contribution of local cable television, in strengthening the growth of Taiwan's civil society and democratic culture. They note the scepticism frequently expressed about the proliferation of phone-ins and chat shows on American television but maintain that it is difficult to be equally sceptical of Taiwan's experience with call-in programmes. Here, listeners are eager to express their views about national developments and question officials over the air.

Frances Millard similarly describes how from the early 1970s a growing underground press, together with easier access to western newspapers and independent Catholic publications all helped to undermine the authority of the communist government in Poland.

However, both accounts also identify areas of concern. While relaxation of government censorship has encouraged a proliferation of newspapers, these have been increasingly subject to the forces of market competition. In Taiwan, the Rawnsleys suggest this has made it more difficult for radical publications to survive. In Poland, Millard notes increasing concentration of ownership in a few hands, including incidentally those of the French press magnate Robert Hersant, although she argues that the diversity of publications has persisted. In more complex ways, political elites have also sought to maintain their dominance over the media. In Taiwan, the pattern of ownership has ensured the ruling Kuomintang retains its influence in three of the four main television channels and in the country's leading newspapers. Millard describes graphically how attempts to transform state television into a public service broadcasting agency foundered on the rock of political infighting, especially between Solidarity and its former leader Walesa.

Such contrasting stories of the media's contribution to democracy might seem to lend support to a 'stage-ist' thesis that the media tend to be most supportive of democracy at a particular political conjuncture, when they are themselves emerging from political control, are strongly identified with the process of democratization and, moreover, benefit from the public's enormous hunger for news and for political change. At an earlier 'stage', their contribution will inevitably be more restricted but to the extent that they offer alternative accounts of social and political reality and even that they draw people into a sense of shared public space, they can be seen as helping to pave the way for democratization. As the process of transition approaches the consolidation stage, the media's contribution becomes more equivocal. When deprived of state financial support and facing a public whose news appetite has been blunted by growing cynicism, they increasingly become prey to the pressures of commercial survival.

However, such a model risks portraying the process of democratization as unilinear and irreversible, and underestimates the impact of local traditions and contingencies. For instance, Kuhn refers to the strong historical roots, especially the Gaullist origins, of the tendency for the French government to seek to control the news agenda. Secondly, it fails to take account of the widely varying notions of democracy involved. The kinds of democratizing cultural media effects which Myers and Sreberny-Mohammadi emphasize in their discussion of Mali and the Middle East may, to an extent, be taken for granted by those analysing the media's contribution in more advanced democracies.

But the model also needs to be integrated with an alternative dynamic concerning the global development of the communications media. For implicit in any question about the relationship between the media and democracy is a further question about whether the global expansion and technological evolution of the media have in themselves been a force for democracy. Although the cases reviewed in these studies cover countries and regions with very different media endowments, all have been affected by the comparatively recent development of the electronic media and by the growing internationalization of media communication. But the democratic contribution made by these developments in the media appear to be much more significant, positive and visible in the case of authoritarian regimes than where some ostensibly democratic (or even liberal democratic) institutions are already established. Indeed, in the United States, France and Britain these developments may be viewed as actually detrimental to the democratic process.

The contribution which constitutes the strongest warning against too reductionist or determinist an understanding either of the dynamic of democratization or of the role played in it by technologically advanced, international media, is Garry Rodan's discussion of media freedom in Singapore. Singapore remains a one-party city-state. Not only has its government successfully muzzled the indigenous media, it has largely persuaded the international press to exercise self-censorship in reporting politically sensitive issues. This is because of the government's ability to manipulate the attractions of Singapore as an English-language market and a base for reporting Asian news. Rodan contends that this pattern is not confined to Singapore; more erratically it is apparent in Malaysia and there are indications of similar developments in Hong Kong. While Rodan's analysis in some ways therefore runs counter to 'stage-ist' approaches, its central thrust is to sustain a theme taken up in other contributions and which we have already touched on: the potentially negative implications for the media and their role in democracy of commercialization and market competitition. For the media as businesses, commercial motives will be paramount, overriding any commitment to democratic principles and specifically freedom of the press.

Democracy and Media Policy

This brings us to our second and subsidiary question, the policies democracies or democratizing regimes adopt and should adopt towards the communications media.

Three particular issues have been highlighted in this volume: what direct role the state should have in the ownership and management of the media, how the state should regulate patterns of private media ownership and whether and how the state should regulate media content, that is, what the media say. Although all of the analyses endorse the need to end a virtual state monopoly of the national media, given what has already been said about the possible harmful effects of commercialisation and unrestrained competition, they do not generally subscribe to the view that the free market, on its own, is the best guarantee of democratic media.

In this context it is interesting to note that despite all the criticisms that have been made of the avuncular, socially conservative character of the British Broadcasting Corporation, it remains a continuing inspiration for media reformers in other parts of the world. It offers a way of combining independence from direct state control with an ethos of impartial public service, which increasingly has included the commitment to represent the full range of voices in British society. Millard describes how in the post-Soviet era not only Poland, but Hungary, the Czech Republic and Slovakia have all sought to emulate the British model. More speculatively, the Rawnsleys contemplate the benefits of such an institutional departure in Taiwan, while Wheeler advocates a public service model to ensure that the democratic potentialities of the new ICTs are realized. On the other hand, Kuhn suggests that a different form of direct state intervention, state subsidy of the press in France, which might have been expected to increase editorial autonomy and adventurousness, in practice has encouraged complacency and further weakened the press in relation to television.

Alternatively, the state can seek to counteract the tendency for market pressures and the economics of production to generate increasing concentration of ownership both within and across specific media forms by, for instance, applying anti-monopolistic measures. However, in practice such attempts to regulate media ownership are rarely reported; certainly they do not feature in the cases described here. Kuhn suggests one reason for the state's readiness to tolerate high concentration of media ownership in France, which might have wider relevance: the French state recognizes that only large media conglomerates will be able effectively to compete internationally. (This incidentally reinforces Rodan's argument that the increasing globalization of the media is not necessarily conducive to democracy.)

Beyond questions of ownership and overall control is that of regulating media output. Although freedom of the press is regularly cited as a criterion of democracy, in practice it must be weighed against other considerations. For instance, as Cullen and Fu point out, freedom of the press may clash with freedom of expression, when a newspaper denies coverage to a particular group's views, or obstructs the right to reply to criticism. In both Millard's discussion of the media in Poland and Myers' account of radio in Mali the possibility is raised that allowing different parties or religious or ethnic communities freedom of expression through their own media outlets could foster political division and instability. For instance, in Mali a number of radios called for a boycott of the recent elections. Myers suggests this shows that a free press has the potential to promote dangerous divisions and violence, raising the need for some form of politically independent regulatory body. Clearly such an argument needs to be treated with caution, however, since it has too often provided authoritarian leaders with the pretext for censorship and repression.

Cloonan examines the specific issue of the relative claims, within a democracy, of freedom of the press and the right to privacy. The Calcutt reports were about striking the right balance. By the 1980s the British tabloid press seemed to be setting new records of intrusiveness into people's private lives. Echoing a persistent theme in this volume, Cloonan partially attributes this to the pressures of circulation wars between the tabloids, as well as competition with television, and notes that in time its effects were also felt in the more reputable broadsheets. As Cloonan demonstrates, knowing where and how to draw the line between press freedom and privacy was by no means easy for Calcutt, although it is suggested that he weakened his case by paying too much attention to privacy rights of celebrities, as opposed to ordinary citizens. But finally, Calcutt's recommendations were rejected, and Parliament determined that the press should continue to regulate itself, possibly afraid to antagonize the press in the run-up to the 1997 general election.

The studies brought together in this volume have then demonstrated the present complexity of the relationship between the media, democracy and democratization. It is a relationship difficult to disentangle, in which the media are implicated in the very way that democracy is defined and the media's contribution to democracy is constrained by the power alignments of which they are to an extent an expression. The increasing salience of the media, and especially the electronic media, in all aspects of our lives none the less requires that we recognize the crucial part they have to play in the making or unmaking of contemporary democracy.

NOTES

1. Michael Gurevitch and Jay G. Blumler, 'Political Communication Systems and Democratic Values', in Judith Lichtenberg (ed.) *Democracy and the Mass Media* (Cambridge: Cambridge University Press, 1991), pp.269–89, 279.
2. Ibid.

Notes on Contributors

Martin Cloonan is Research Fellow in Lifelong Learning at the Institute of Education, University of Stirling. He is the author of *Banned* (1996).

Richard Cullen is Associate Professor in the School of Law, Deakin University, Australia and Visiting Fellow in the Faculty of Law, City University of Hong Kong. He is co-author of *Media Law in the People's Republic of China* (1996).

Raymond Kuhn is Senior Lecturer in Politics at Queen Mary and Westfield College, University of London and author of *The Media in France*.

Hua Ling Fu is Research Fellow, Faculty of Law, University of Hong Kong and co-author of *Media Law in the People's Republic of China* (1996).

David Mervin is Reader in Politics at the University of Warwick and is the author of *Ronald Reagan and the American Presidency*, of *The President of the United States*, and *George Bush and the Guardianship Presidency*.

Frances Millard is Senior Lecturer in the Politics of the Visegrad states in the Department of Government, University of Essex. She is the author of *The Anatomy of the New Poland* (1994) and *Polish Politics and Society* (forthcoming).

Mary Myers is a freelance development communications consultant, based in London.

Vicky Randall is Reader in Government at the University of Essex. She is the author, with Robin Theobald, of *Political Change and Underdevelopment* (revised edition forthcoming 1998) and of articles and chapters on democratization, the media and politics in the Third World.

Gary Rawnsley is Lecturer in Politics at the University of Nottingham. His research interests lie in the field of political communication and the politics of Taiwan, and he is the author of *Radio Diplomacy and*

Propaganda: the BBC and VOA in International Politics, 1954–64 (1996).

Ming-Yeh Rawnsley has just completed a Ph.D. on Public Service Television in Taiwan. She is the author of many Chinese-language articles on the media, and is a former producer for the Chinese Television Network.

Garry Rodan is Associate Professor and Chair of Politics and member of the Asia Research Centre at Murdoch University in Perth, Western Australia. His authored and edited books include *The Political Economy of Singapore's Industrialization* (1986); *Singapore Changes Guard* (1993); *Southeast Asia in the 1990s:Authoritarianism, Democracy and Capitalism* (1993); *Political Oppositions in Industrialising Asia* (1996) and *The Political Economy of South-East Asia* (1997).

Annabelle Sreberny-Mohammadi is Professor and Director of the Centrre for Mass Communication Research at the University of Leicester and is co-author of *Small Media, Big Revolution: Communication, Culture and the Iranian Revolution.*

Mark Wheeler lectures in the Politics and Modern History department at London Guildhall University.

Dominic Wring is Lecturer in Communications and Media Studies and a member of the Communication Research Centre, Loughborough University. He is currently preparing a book on *Marketing the Labour Party*, to be published by Macmillan.

Index